The Unknown 1930s

CINEMA AND SOCIETY SERIES
GENERAL EDITOR: JEFFREY RICHARDS

published and forthcoming:

*The Crowded Prairie: American national identity in the Hollywood Western*
Michael Coyne

*The Unknown 1930s: An alternative history of the British cinema, 1929–1939*
Edited by Jeffrey Richards

*Film Propaganda: Soviet Russia and Nazi Germany*
Richard Taylor (new edition)

*The British at War: Cinema, state and propaganda, 1939–1945*
James Chapman

*Distorted Images: Film and national identity in Britain, 1919–1939*
Kenton Bamford

*Spaghetti Westerns: From Karl May to Sergio Leone*
Christopher Frayling (revised edition)

*Somewhere in England: British cinema and exile*
Kevin Gough-Yates

*Harmless Entertainment: Hollywood cinema and consensus*
Richard Maltby (revised edition)

# THE UNKNOWN 1930s:
## An alternative history of the British cinema 1929–39

*edited by*
### JEFFREY RICHARDS

I.B. Tauris Publishers
LONDON · NEW YORK

Published in 1998 by I.B. Tauris & Co Ltd
Victoria House, Bloomsbury Square, London WC1B 4DZ

In the United States and Canada distributed by
St Martin's Press, 175 Fifth Avenue, New York NY 10010

A full CIP record for this book is available from the British
Library

A full CIP record for this book is available from the Library of
Congress

Set in Berthold Baskerville by Ewan Smith, London
Printed and bound in Great Britain by WBC Ltd, Bridgend,
Mid Glamorgan

ISBN 1 86064 303 5

# Contents

# Introduction

THERE is a received and well-established view of British cinema in the 1930s. It consists of the expensively mounted productions of Alexander Korda's London Films aimed at the international market; the 'cheap and cheerful' regional comedies featuring music-hall stars such as Gracie Fields and George Formby and intended mainly for the domestic market; the polished thrillers of Alfred Hitchcock; and the British documentary movement, led by John Grierson and claiming to present the only authentic picture of contemporary life in Britain. All of these aspects of 1930s cinema have received extended and excellent coverage from film scholars and historians.

But there was far more to 1930s British cinema than these admittedly important areas. It was one of the most prolific periods of British film-making, a boom era stimulated by the Cinematograph Films Act of 1927 which required a quota of the films shown on British screens to be genuinely British. Many of the films produced in that period and many of the personnel involved – producers, directors and stars – have never been properly examined, leaving the map of British cinema in the 1930s studded with areas of darkness and ignorance. This collection of 11 essays by leading British film historians aims to dispel some of that darkness and chart a new map of British cinema in this key decade.

John Sedgwick's essay seeks for the first time to establish scientifically which British films British audiences went to see, what their favourite British films were and who were their favourite British stars. He argues convincingly that there was a viable British film industry in the 1930s and that Gaumont-British, under Michael Balcon, and British and Dominions, under Herbert Wilcox, produced a stream of hit films. He also comes up with conclusions about the top box-office stars that challenges the received wisdom.

The careers of Alexander Korda, Michael Balcon and Herbert Wilcox have been charted in a succession of biographies and autobiographies. Linda Wood, though, looks at the career of one of the lesser-known film tycoons, giving the first in-depth analysis of the regime of Julius Hagen at Twickenham Film Studios. She explores how he tried to transform his operation from producing 'quota quickies' for American companies to a regime of British quality films, falling foul of the perennial problems confronting the British film industry: under-financing, ruthless US competition and the relatively restricted nature of the British market.

H. Mark Glancy, utilising MGM's own records, gives a fresh assessment of how one of the Hollywood majors sought to fulfil its quota obligations under both the 1927 and 1938 Acts and how its strategy evolved to the point at which it was committed to a full programme of quality film-making in Britain.

Two of the most popular genres with 1930s' cinema-goers were musicals and crime thrillers. Stephen Guy and James Chapman examine how British cinema sought to fulfil this demand, creating distinctive bodies of work that drew on both specifically British traditions as well as on Hollywood models. One of the most critically neglected genres is that of society melodrama and Tony Aldgate breaks new ground in his reassessment of the role of society melodrama, particularly the work of actor-director Miles Mander, in providing searching discussions of sex, class, morals and the role of women in the interwar period.

Sue Harper and Jeffrey Richards take us beyond the world of Fields and Formby to examine the careers and to assess the appeal of two currently less fashionable but then popular stars, Conrad Veidt and Tod Slaughter, who represent two important areas of input into British cinema: the influx of continental émigrés and the continuing influence of the Victorian stage.

The talents of a number of British directors of the 1930s have been highlighted in recent years. Apart from Hitchcock, the work of Victor Saville, John Baxter and Walter Forde has received sympathetic critical consideration. In this collection, Brian McFarlane makes out the case for the versatile 'jack of all trades' Robert Stevenson. Geoff Brown canvasses the virtues of Bernard Vorhaus, and Kevin Gough-Yates rediscovers Berthold Viertel, two of many talented émigrés who enriched British cinema in this decade.

Three themes emerge from this collection which will add a new dimension to the consideration of 1930s British cinema. One is the revaluation of the much mocked 'quota quickies'. The essays of Glancy, Brown, Richards and Wood detect work of real quality in this area, which served as a training ground for new talents and functioned in many ways as the equivalent of the regime of the Hollywood 'B' picture which is recognised as having produced some memorable films. A second is the revaluation of melodrama as a legitimate and powerful mode of cinematic expression. It can function as a means of articulating subversive excess or exploring social problems, of highlighting issues of class and gender. It should be seen as a continuing and significant strand in the British film culture. The third structuring theme is the contextualisation of British films in the wider cultural scene, the exploring of its potent links with popular fiction, the music industry and the stage. Together these essays and the issues and themes they raise lead us to a fuller and richer consideration of 1930s British cinema.

*Jeffrey Richards*

# Contributors

*Tony Aldgate* is Senior Lecturer in History at the Open University and author of, among other works, *Cinema and History, Censorship and the Permissive Society* and *Britain Can Take It.*

*Geoff Brown* is film critic of *The Times* and the author of studies of film directors Walter Forde, John Baxter, Frank Launder and Sidney Gilliat.

*James Chapman* is Lecturer in Film and Television Studies at the Open University and author of *The British at War: Cinema, State and Propaganda 1939–1945.*

*H. Mark Glancy* lectures in history and film at Queen Mary College, London, and is the author of a forthcoming study of Hollywood's depictions of England.

*Kevin Gough-Yates* is the author of a study of the influence of German *émigrés* on British cinema and of many articles on British film.

*Stephen Guy* is completing a study of post-war British cinema and has written an article on the film *High Treason.*

*Sue Harper* teaches film and cultural history at the University of Portsmouth and is the author of *Picturing the Past: the Rise and Fall of the British Costume Film* and many articles on British cinema.

*Brian McFarlane* is an Associate Professor in the English department of Monash University, Melbourne. His most recent books are *Novel into Film: an Introduction to the Theory of Adaptation* and *An Autobiography of British Cinema.*

*Jeffrey Richards* is Professor of Cultural History at Lancaster University and author of several studies of the cinema, including *Visions of Yesterday, The Age of the Dream Palace* and *Films and British National Identity.*

*John Sedgwick* is Principal Lecturer in Business at the University of North London and the author of several articles on cinema-going in 1930s Britain.

*Linda Wood* is the author of a study of British film director Maurice Elvey and editor of *British Films 1927–39*.

1. Filming in 1930s Britain: *This Week of Grace* being shot at Ealing Studios

## CHAPTER I

# Cinema-going Preferences in Britain in the 1930s

## *John Sedgwick*

THE 1938 Cinematograph Films Act signalled the end of a decade of achievement for the British film industry. The legislation made it easier for American renters to meet their quota obligations, by reducing the number of domestic productions they were required to handle in order to balance the volume of Hollywood films imported into Britain. The subsequent reduction in production in 1938–39 came on the tail of a crisis in production during 1936–37 caused by a combination of speculative financing and substantial corporate losses. Domestic film output fell from a high of 228 films registered in 1937/38 to 103 and 108 in the following two years.[1] Ian Jarvie has portrayed these events as representing a victory for American strategy in a trade war which was not fully understood either by domestic players or the British government.[2] The corporate configuration which had emerged during the decade following the 1927 Cinematograph Films Act was left in tatters, its assets being steadily acquired by flour-milling millionaire J. Arthur Rank.

The outcome contrasts markedly with the atmosphere in the industry during the years leading up to 1936. The 1927 Cinematograph Films Act had given a measure of protection to British film-makers by imposing a sliding scale quota – rising to 20 per cent by 1936 – on domestic renters and exhibitors. At a stroke the risks associated with film production had been changed in favour of domestic producers. The moribund industry of the 1920s was transformed. Not only did the volume of domestic feature film production increase annually as a consequence – rising from 13 films shown in 1927 to 125 films registered with the Board of Trade in 1930–31 and then steadily to a peak of 228 films registered in 1937–38 – but much of it was demonstrably popular with domestic audiences. However, this up-beat assessment does not conform to the orthodox depiction of film-making in Britain during the 1930s, well expressed in Rachael Low's comment: 'The 1927 quota legislation intended to solve all the industry's problems was a failure. Film production doubled during the thirties, but the increase consisted almost entirely of cheap and inferior films, the famous quota quickies and others not much better, which took advantage of the protected market and went far to ruin the reputation of British production as a whole.'[3]

The implication of Low's statement is clear; the 1927 legislation made little if any difference to the qualitative output of British studios and served merely to increase the quantity of domestic film.[4] While paying tribute to Low's monumental seven-volume history of the domestic industry from its inception until the outbreak of the Second World War, this work challenges Low's hypothesis. To do so, given the general absence of corporate accounting records of feature film performance, it has been necessary to establish an index of film popularity (POPSTAT) based upon a sample of contemporary cinema exhibition records.[5] The results demonstrate that the orthodoxy outlined above, particularly when viewed in the context of a substantial growth in industry-specific human and fixed capital formation, is in need of substantial revision.

## The popularity of film in Britain during the 1930s

Although cinema was the dominant paid leisure activity in Britain during the 1930s, accounting for approximately two-thirds of all entertainment admissions and expenditure,[6] it did not feature very prominently in household budgets, absorbing only 1 per cent of consumers' expenditure in real terms during the period. As far as the national economy was concerned the film industry was small. Annual per capita cinema attendance grew from 19 to 20 visits, resulting in a per capita expenditure of 16–17 shillings between 1934 and 1938, equivalent to a little more than 4 (old) pence per week. The slow upward drift in annual attendances from 903 million in 1934 to 987 million in 1938 appears to have kept pace with the growth in population but, if anything, the proportion of real personal expenditure devoted to cinema-going fell, albeit marginally, while real incomes and expenditure rose.[7] For the greater part, audiences did not conceive of cinema as a luxury. Indeed, in keeping with George Orwell's observations concerning the cinema-going habits of unemployed men in Wigan, cinema may well have been consumed as a necessity among the poorest members of the community.[8]

## The pattern of film distribution

The system of film distribution in Britain was similar to that of the USA[9] and can be explained in terms of price discriminatory practices, whereby films were entered at the highest feasible point in an exhibition hierarchy and subsequently cascaded down, over time, through clearly demarcated cinema 'runs'. As a general rule, a pre-release cinema exhibited films at an earlier date than a general release first-run cinema, which in turn had the exhibition opportunity before second-run houses. The scale of prices dropped very rapidly as a film was distributed downwards and outwards through the various 'runs'. The critical factor in this system for the distributor was the rent earned from individual films at each point of exhibition.

The typical commercial life of a feature film during the 1930s was brief, usually less than 12 months even for the most popular films. Although re-releases became more common towards the end of the period under investigation, they were never an important element in pre-Second World War film-going and hence not a significant source of box-office receipts. (This brief product life-cycle was reflected in the amortisation schedules – between 12 and 15 months – adopted by the principal Hollywood studios in assessing the profitability of their outputs.)[10]

Between 1932 and 1939 nominal cinema prices were largely stable. They were also invariant between the respective programmes of individual cinemas. Whereas the renter was able to set premium rates for those films expected to be highly popular with audiences – charging a flat rate plus between 25 and 60 per cent[11] of box-office grosses for major features – exhibitors, mindful of the extent of local competition, maintained their price structure irrespective of the film being shown. The distributor and exhibitor appear to have been engaged in a zero-sum game where, for any given film, the relative gains of one party were at the expense of the other.[12] As a general rule it was in neither's interest to handle films of an inferior quality, given the existence of discriminating audiences, and the supply of alternative film programmes available within localities at similar prices.[13]

## The POPSTAT (popularity) index

The POPSTAT index is based upon the exhibition records of between 81 and 92 leading London and provincial cinemas, listed in the *Kine Weekly* for the period 1 January 1932 to 31 March 1938.[14] The changing sample numbers reflect the entry and exit of cinemas into and from the *Kine Weekly* lists and/or operation. Where the *Kine Weekly* records are incomplete, or questionable, London and provincial city newspapers have been used as an additional source of information. The cinemas in the sample were of unequal size, ranging from the 4,200-seater Green's Playhouse in Glasgow to the 587-seater Electra in Sheffield, with a mean size of just under 1,700 seats. Further, their commercial status, manifest in their ability to obtain films from the major distributors before, at, or after the date of general release, significantly affected the prices they could charge. It follows, then, that their gross and net box-office revenue capacities differed considerably. In order to represent these differences each cinema in the sample has been given a weighting based upon its potential gross revenue capacity obtained by multiplying its mid-range ticket price[15] by the number of seats and expressed as a proportion of the mean potential gross revenue of all cinemas in the sample. Hence the weights reflect the relative commercial status of sample cinemas: the revenue capacity of the Empire Leicester Square was, for example, approximately twice that of the Davis Cinema Croydon, four times that of the Piccadilly Manchester, and eight times that of the Regent Glasgow. As the sample varied slightly over the period, so the weights of each cinema are marginally affected.

The record of each film is given as:

$$POPSTAT_{it} = \sum_{j=1}^{n} a_{jt} \, {}^*b_{ijt} \, {}^*l_{ijt}$$

where POPSTAT = popularity statistic; t = exhibition period; i = ith film; j = jth cinema; n = number of cinemas in the sample set; a = the weighting of the cinema around a mean value of 1; b = the weighting of the exhibition status of a film where 0.5 represents a shared and 1.0 a single billing; l = the length of exhibition at each cinema in weeks and half-weeks.

Rowson calculated that there were 4,305 wired cinemas in operation in Britain in 1934, while returns from Western Electric suggest 4,205 in 1933, 4,383 in 1934, 4,471 in 1935 and 4,582 in 1936.[16] The sample size of between 81 and 92 cinemas, hence, represents a tiny proportion of the overall cinema population. As could be expected, they were almost twice as large as the mean size cinema: approximately 1,700 seats compared with 900.[17] They were also much more expensive with the sample mid-range price of approximately 2 shillings being over twice the mean cinema admission price for all cinemas, estimated by Rowson as 10.54 (old) pence.[18]

Although the proposed index of film popularity (POPSTAT) draws upon the programmes of a selected and unrepresentative sample of cinemas, it can be maintained, with some confidence, that the sample cinema set captures the exhibition characteristics of the market for films as a whole. From a study of the diffusion of 119 'hit' films (all of which had extended London West End runs) as they were exhibited outwards in time and space – first from within the sample cinema set and then beyond to the cinemas of Bolton, Dover, and the Chelsea, Kensington, Fulham and Hammersmith area of West London – it has been possible to confirm the underlying premise: that films which were popular within the sample cinema set continued to be popular as they cascaded down through the distinct tiers of the distribution system.[19]

It may be objected that the extent of the concentration of ownership among cinemas of the sample set, and thus the potential for monopoly practices, seriously questions the assumption concerning the efficiency of POPSTAT as a measure of relative popularity. Indeed, approximately half of the cinemas in the sample were owned or controlled by the two leading British combines: with Associated British Picture Corporation (ABPC)'s share of seating varying between 16 and 18 per cent and that of Gaumont-British between 33 and 36 per cent. (A similar set of proportions emerges from the calculation of gross revenue potential, with ABPC's share ranging from 12 to 15 per cent and that of Gaumont-British between 36 and 38 per cent.) These proportions are considerably in excess of the respective shares of the two vertically integrated organisations with respect to the total population of cinemas, of which ABPC had 225 and Gaumont-British 331 in 1935.[20] However, while the exhibition records certainly show that cinemas from each chain biased their exhibition programmes in favour of in-house films, this did not lead to the exclusion of films from rival producers which might have been expected to generate greater box-office receipts. In other words, there is no evidence that the chains operated uncommercially by consistently favouring unpopular in-house films where more popular alternatives were available.

## The results

The annual POPSTAT frequency distributions of films released for 1932–37 are presented in Table 1.1. If drawn each is C-shaped, sloping downwards from left to right indicating a distribution in which the modal value is either 0 or less than 1 for all years and thereafter falls away gradually leaving only a small proportion of films achieving high

**Table 1.1** Annual POPSTAT frequency distribution of films released in Britain between 1 January 1932 and 31 December 1937

| POPSTAT classification | Number of films | | | | | |
|---|---|---|---|---|---|---|
| | 1932 | 1933 | 1934 | 1935 | 1936 | 1937 |
| = 0 | 62 | 72 | 80 | 100 | 131 | 200 |
| > 0–1 | 68 | 89 | 69 | 61 | 74 | 104 |
| > 1–2 | 48 | 51 | 41 | 58 | 67 | 67 |
| > 2–3 | 56 | 55 | 50 | 55 | 34 | 65 |
| > 3–4 | 56 | 47 | 56 | 72 | 49 | 65 |
| > 4–5 | 67 | 53 | 59 | 49 | 64 | 34 |
| > 5–6 | 40 | 36 | 53 | 46 | 50 | 37 |
| > 6–7 | 52 | 36 | 46 | 35 | 42 | 39 |
| > 7–8 | 29 | 37 | 41 | 38 | 38 | 33 |
| > 8–9 | 26 | 29 | 26 | 21 | 27 | 21 |
| > 9–10 | 26 | 27 | 24 | 26 | 13 | 22 |
| >10–11 | 26 | 22 | 22 | 25 | 23 | 16 |
| >11–12 | 20 | 15 | 10 | 24 | 18 | 7 |
| >12–13 | 7 | 15 | 11 | 14 | 14 | 10 |
| >13–14 | 4 | 3 | 13 | 3 | 7 | 13 |
| >14–15 | 11 | 12 | 4 | 12 | 14 | 6 |
| >15–20 | 24 | 18 | 27 | 27 | 42 | 30 |
| >20–30 | 19 | 23 | 22 | 18 | 20 | 20 |
| >30–40 | 5 | 4 | 5 | 9 | 7 | 8 |
| >40–50 | 2 | 2 | 4 | 5 | 6 | 5 |
| >50–60 | 1 | 1 | 0 | 2 | 2 | 0 |
| >60–70 | 0 | 0 | 1 | 1 | 0 | 0 |
| >70–80 | 0 | 0 | 0 | 0 | 0 | 0 |
| >80–90 | 0 | 0 | 0 | 0 | 1 | 1 |
| >90–100 | 0 | 1 | 0 | 0 | 0 | 0 |
| Total | 649 | 648 | 664 | 701 | 743 | 803 |

*Note*: Weighted mean POPSTAT for the period = 5.56.
*Source*: *Kine Weekly*, 1932–38.

POPSTAT scores: the most popular films of each year earned upwards of 60 times that of those films falling into the modal classification and 10 times that of those at the arithmetic mean.[21] It is clear that only a small number of films could expect to become 'hits', with approximately 65 per cent of films earning less than average box-office receipts. At the other end of the distribution only approximately 10 per cent of films earned more than twice the revenue of films at the arithmetic mean and only 2 per cent of films generated scores more than two standard deviations above the mean. The skewed nature of the distribution was important information to studio heads in devising, and allocating resources to, annual portfolios. 'Hit' production was an inherently risky activity, and clear evidence exists that the major Hollywood studios compensated for the variance in those rates of return associated with big-budget vehicles with the more reliable earning power of smaller-budget products.[22] Such strategic thinking contrasts with that adopted by studios such as Goldwyn in the United States and Korda's London Films in Britain, where production consisted of a small number of big-budget films. As Barry King writes:

> Looking at the global level of activity, we find that every season produces its hits, but that no particular producer can be absolutely certain of monopolising the 'hit' product. What this means is that any season of releases resembled, at first sight, a zero sum game with some producers having a time-dated monopoly of the total available market, theoretically speaking, since their film or films are the most popular.[23]

It has been argued earlier that even the presence of vertically integrated combines need not upset this view in that the popular success of Film $A$ produced by company $X$ will lead to a gain for company $Y$ where it is able to exhibit $A$ in its own cinemas. Thus, 'What the lucky producer has, therefore, is a monopoly (copy) right to a film which will give his company access to his competitor's screen time for a price.'[24]

*Market shares* Table 1.2 ranks American and British production companies according to market share, measured in terms of the POPSTAT index. It is clear that while the principal seven Hollywood producers (counting Fox and Twentieth Century-Fox as a single company) together took a dominant position in the British market, the dispersion of market shares between them and the major British production company – Gaumont-British – was such as to generate only a low measure of industrial concentration. Beyond these eight, and the dozen or so firms which achieved at least a 1 per cent share of demand, was a myriad of firms whose individual performance was negligible by industry standards, but which collectively contributed just under 30 per cent of market supply.

*Hollywood's 'major' studios* The seven high-volume Hollywood producers between them contributed almost a half of market supply for the period but achieved a market share of over 60 per cent. Furthermore, the POP:POP column shows that the films of Paramount, MGM, Warners and Fox/Twentieth Century-Fox achieved significantly higher mean POPSTAT scores than the population mean of 5.56. This evidence

is supported by Top 50 and Top 100 information contained in the last
two columns of Table 1.2 which sum to 163 and 366, respectively, for
the seven studios. If it is assumed that the Top 50 category consists of
the 'hit' productions for the years 1932–37 in which complete release
records have been collected, then between them the major Hollywood
studios accounted for 54 per cent of notable screen successes, with
Paramount and MGM producing 77 'hit' films – just under 30 per cent
of all 'hit' films. It would appear that the films of RKO, Columbia and
Universal were, in general, less popular with British audiences.

One of the most important aspects of any analysis of film consumption during the 1930s is not just the pre-eminence of the major
Hollywood studios, in terms of the volume of output and its general
quality, but also their apparent permanence. With the exception of
Universal, these studios generally made over 40 films each per annum.
Further, with the exception of Columbia's decision to distribute its own
films from 1933 and Universal's to disband its distribution operation in
1937 in favour of the newly formed British firm General Film Distributors (GFD), institutional arrangements remained unchanged during
the period. This stability is further emphasised in the annual pattern of
market shares for the years 1932–37, shown below.

| Paramount | 13–16% |
| MGM | 11–13% |
| Warners | 9–12% |
| RKO | 6–8% |
| Fox | 6–11% |
| Columbia | 5–7% |
| Universal | 4–5% |

A further measure of this is the number of films from these producers
achieving Top 100 status, the details of which are as follows:

|  | 1932 | 1933 | 1934 | 1935 | 1936 | 1937 |
|---|---|---|---|---|---|---|
| Top 50 | 30 | 29 | 24 | 21 | 30 | 29 |
| Top 100 | 63 | 64 | 59 | 58 | 62 | 60 |

*British volume producers* Perhaps the most remarkable results to emerge
from Table 1.2 are those generated by Gaumont-British. Although it
produced between approximately a quarter and a third of the feature
film output of major Hollywood producers over the duration, its record
of Top 50 hit production was second only to that of MGM.

**Table 1.2** Summary popularity statistics of films shown in Britain, 1 January 1932 to 31 March 1938

| Production company | Films released | Agg. POPSTAT | Supply share (%) | Market share (%) | Mean POPSTAT | POP:POP[a] | Top 50 films | Top 100 films |
|---|---|---|---|---|---|---|---|---|
| *Principal US Studios* | | | | | | | | |
| Paramount | 414 | 3731.77 | 8.71 | 14.14 | 9.01 | 1.62 | 33 | 103 |
| MGM | 291 | 3189.50 | 6.13 | 12.09 | 10.96 | 1.97 | 55 | 97 |
| WB-FNP | 380 | 2687.32 | 8.00 | 10.18 | 7.07 | 1.27 | 18 | 53 |
| RKO | 304 | 1907.50 | 6.40 | 7.23 | 6.27 | 1.13 | 16 | 33 |
| Fox[b] | 216 | 1561.02 | 4.55 | 5.92 | 7.23 | 1.30 | 13 | 28 |
| Columbia | 302 | 1558.21 | 6.36 | 5.91 | 5.16 | 0.93 | 12 | 19 |
| Universal | 243 | 1101.82 | 5.11 | 4.18 | 4.53 | 0.82 | 8 | 12 |
| 20 Cent-Fox[c] | 103 | 783.78 | 2.17 | 2.97 | 7.61 | 1.37 | 8 | 21 |
| Goldwyn | 27 | 588.03 | 0.57 | 2.23 | 21.78 | 3.92 | 13 | 20 |
| 20 Century[d] | 17 | 387.47 | 0.36 | 1.47 | 22.79 | 4.10 | 9 | 15 |
| Monogram[e] | 120 | 199.09 | 2.53 | 0.75 | 1.66 | 0.30 | 0 | 0 |
| Republic[f] | 91 | 171.76 | 1.92 | 0.65 | 1.89 | 0.34 | 0 | 0 |
| Selznick[g] | 5 | 148.55 | 0.11 | 0.56 | 29.71 | 5.35 | 4 | 4 |
| Reliance[h] | 7 | 112.60 | 0.15 | 0.43 | 16.09 | 2.90 | 3 | 7 |
| Wanger[i] | 6 | 73.27 | 0.13 | 0.28 | 12.21 | 2.20 | 2 | 3 |
| Chesterfield[j] | 24 | 68.81 | 0.51 | 0.26 | 2.87 | 0.52 | 0 | 0 |
| Mascot[k] | 15 | 56.72 | 0.32 | 0.21 | 3.78 | 0.68 | 0 | 0 |
| Invincible[l] | 23 | 55.44 | 0.48 | 0.21 | 2.41 | 0.43 | 0 | 0 |
| Majestic[m] | 23 | 53.33 | 0.48 | 0.20 | 2.32 | 0.42 | 0 | 0 |
| World Wide[n] | 17 | 34.71 | 0.36 | 0.13 | 2.04 | 0.37 | 0 | 0 |
| Total | 2628 | 18470.70 | 55.35 | 70.00 | 7.03 | 1.27 | 194 | 415 |

**Table 1.2** continued

| Production company | Films released | Agg. POPSTAT | Supply share (%) | Market share (%) | Mean POPSTAT | POP:POP[a] | Top 50 films | Top 100 films |
|---|---|---|---|---|---|---|---|---|
| *Principal British Studios* | | | | | | | | |
| G-B/Gains | 121 | 1843.04 | 2.55 | 6.98 | 15.23 | 2.74 | 48 | 77 |
| BIP/ABPC | 131 | 750.10 | 2.76 | 2.84 | 5.73 | 1.03 | 4 | 13 |
| B & D[o] | 106 | 695.05 | 2.23 | 2.63 | 6.56 | 1.18 | 16 | 22 |
| London Films[p] | 32 | 608.31 | 0.67 | 2.31 | 19.01 | 3.42 | 14 | 20 |
| Twickenham[q] | 48 | 250.36 | 1.01 | 0.95 | 5.22 | 0.94 | 1 | 3 |
| WBBR[r] | 102 | 225.78 | 2.15 | 0.86 | 2.21 | 0.40 | 0 | 0 |
| ATP | 28 | 207.45 | 0.59 | 0.79 | 7.41 | 1.33 | 2 | 5 |
| British Lion | 40 | 206.30 | 0.84 | 0.78 | 5.16 | 0.93 | 0 | 1 |
| Wilcox[s] | 15 | 157.31 | 0.32 | 0.60 | 10.49 | 1.89 | 1 | 5 |
| Capitol[t] | 12 | 138.88 | 0.25 | 0.53 | 11.57 | 2.08 | 3 | 4 |
| Real Art[u] | 45 | 131.30 | 0.95 | 0.50 | 2.92 | 0.53 | 1 | 1 |
| ParamountBr[v] | 10 | 69.42 | 0.21 | 0.26 | 6.94 | 1.25 | 1 | 1 |
| Criterion[w] | 4 | 58.35 | 0.08 | 0.22 | 14.59 | 2.63 | 1 | 3 |
| FoxBr[x] | 52 | 52.23 | 1.09 | 0.20 | 1.00 | 0.18 | 0 | 0 |
| New World[y] | 3 | 38.23 | 0.06 | 0.14 | 12.74 | 2.63 | 1 | 2 |
| Total | 749 | 5432.11 | 15.76 | 20.59 | 7.25 | 1.31 | 93 | 157 |
| *Films* | | | | | | | | |
| Total US | 3230 | 19562.14 | 68.03 | 74.14 | 6.06 | 1.09 | 200 | 427 |
| Total UK | 1296 | 6489.87 | 27.30 | 24.60 | 5.01 | 0.90 | 96 | 167 |
| US + UK | 4526 | 26052.01 | 95.32 | 98.73 | – | – | 296 | 594 |
| All films[z] | 4748 | 26386.30 | 100.00 | 100.00 | – | – | 300 | 600 |
| Other films[aa] | 222 | 334.30 | 4.67 | 1.27 | – | – | 4 | 6 |

Notes: [a] Measures the mean POPSTAT generated by each studio for the period of operation expressed as a proportion of the weighted mean (5.56) of all studios for that period [b] Films released up to and including 1936 [c] Films released from 1935 [d] Films released 1932–35 [e] Films released 1932–35 and during 1937 [f] Films released from 1935 [g] Films released from 1936 [h] Films released 1934–36 [i] Films from 1937 [j] Films released 1933–37 [k] Films released 1935–36 [l] Films released 1933–37 [m] Films released 1933–37 [n] Films released during 1933 [o] Films released up to and including 1937 [p] Films released from 1932. Includes Denham Films, Pendennis Films and Saville Productions [q] Films released 1932–37. Includes J. H. Productions and St Margaret's Films [r] Films released from 1932 [s] Films released from 1936. Includes Imperator Films [t] Films released 1936–37. Includes Cecil Films, Grafton Films and Trafalgar Films [u] Films released 1932–35 [v] Films released 1931–32 [w] Films released 1936–37 [x] Films released 1934–37 [y] Films released during 1937 [z] There is a disparity between the listed years and those recorded in Table 1.1 counts films released during the listed years and thus does not count films shown in 1932 but released in 1931 and films released during the first three months of 1938. [aa] Films which made the Top 100 POPSTAT category of their year but were produced by production companies other than those listed above were: *Congress Dances* (UFA, Germany), *Age of Love* (Caddo, USA), *Movie Crazy* (Lloyd, USA), *Tell Me Tonight* (F & S, Germany), *Sky Devils* (Caddo), *Blue Light* (Sokal, Germany), *Scarface* (Caddo), *Mr Robinson Crusoe* (Elton, USA), *A Nous la Liberté* (Tobis, France), *Congorilla* (Johnsons, USA), *Rain* (Feature, USA), *Corsair* (Art Cinema, USA), *Baroud* (Ingram), *FP1* (UFA), *Dick Turpin* (John Stafford Productions, UK), *Prince of Arcadia* (Nettlefold-Fogwell, UK), *Battle* (Liono, Anglo-French), *Cats Paw* (Lloyd), *18 Minutes* (Allied, UK), *Love Affair of the Dictator* (Toeplitz, UK), *Becky Sharp* (Pioneer), *Song of Freedom* (Hammer, UK), *As You Like It* (Inter-allied, UK), *Modern Times* (Chaplin, USA), *Gay Desperado* (Pickford, USA), *Sky's the Limit* (Buchanan, UK), and *Thunder in the City* (Atlantic, UK).

*Sources: Kine Weekly*, 1932–38; *Kine Year Books*, 1932–39.

Table 1.3 reveals a pattern of growth in production up to 1935 which falls back in 1936 and 1937. Of the volume producers marketing films in Britain during the 1930s, including the Hollywood majors, those features released from the Gaumont-British stable were, on average, the most popular for each of the years 1932–37 with an annual mean POPSTAT two to three times that of the population mean.

The contrast with films made by the ABPC organisation is marked. Although it produced a similar volume of films over the period, the company's commitment to film-making on the kind of scale sufficient to furnish its own cinemas with a significant number of programme features had ended by 1936. What is most striking about these results is that, given the size of its cinema chain, films from the studio did so poorly in terms of distribution. Not only were British International Pictures (BIP) films not widely shown in independent cinemas, they were not necessarily shown in ABPC-owned cinemas either. The POPSTAT results seem to confirm the studio as one producing support features as a deliberate strategy.

British and Dominions was a major domestic player between 1932 and 1935. Its output of films was divided between cheap quota productions made for Paramount which did very poorly in the sample cinema set and bigger-budget productions distributed by United Artists, which conversely did very well, securing 16 Top 50 'hits' over the four-year period. The performance of the films released in 1936 differs dramatically from the preceding years, and release levels in 1937 are less than half those of the peak years, as the company slipped into quota productions for Paramount at the new Pinewood Studios.

During the period 1932–35 these three studios dominated domestic production, with Gaumont-British/Gainsborough and British and Dominions supplying upward of 75 per cent of all domestic Top 50 productions. However, it is apparent from the lower release levels and market shares recorded during the 1936–37 seasons, that they were in decline: Gaumont-British's hold on the domestic market slipped back from the 9 per cent peak achieved with its 1934 and 1935 releases, while British and Dominions' last Top 50 films were released in 1935.[25]

***Smaller scale British 'hit' producers*** A number of studios operated a commercial strategy based upon the production of a small number of big-budget films, intended as principal screen attractions and for widespread distribution. Goldwyn, Selznick, Twentieth Century (before it merged with Fox in 1935 to become Twentieth Century-Fox), Reliance and Wanger in the United States and London Films (including

**Table 1.3** Annual market performance of the principal British film producers, 1932–37

|                  | 1932   | 1933   | 1934   | 1935   | 1936   | 1937   |
|------------------|--------|--------|--------|--------|--------|--------|
| *Gaumont-British/Gainsborough* | | | | | | |
| Films            | 12     | 19     | 21     | 22     | 19     | 15     |
| POPSTAT          | 237.55 | 312.43 | 375.86 | 391.02 | 276.86 | 192.00 |
| Mkt share        | 0.06   | 0.08   | 0.09   | 0.09   | 0.06   | 0.05   |
| AVEPOP           | 19.80  | 16.44  | 17.90  | 17.77  | 14.57  | 12.80  |
| POP:POP          | 3.22   | 2.74   | 2.88   | 2.80   | 2.32   | 2.59   |
| Top 50           | 6      | 9      | 13     | 10     | 4      | 6      |
| Top 100          | 9      | 14     | 16     | 15     | 13     | 10     |
| *ABPC (British International Pictures)* | | | | | | |
| Films            | 33[a]  | 18     | 28     | 14     | 6      | 9      |
| POPSTAT          | 145.93 | 102.35 | 198.94 | 128.73 | 41.58  | 80.66  |
| Mkt share        | 0.04   | 0.03   | 0.05   | 0.03   | 0.01   | 0.02   |
| AVEPOP           | 4.42   | 5.69   | 7.11   | 9.20   | 6.93   | 8.96   |
| POP:POP          | 0.72   | 0.95   | 1.14   | 1.45   | 1.10   | 1.82   |
| Top 50           | 0      | 0      | 2      | 2      | 0      | 0      |
| Top 100          | 3      | 1      | 4      | 3      | 0      | 2      |
| *British and Dominions (B & D)* | | | | | | |
| Films            | 14     | 22     | 21     | 17     | 16     | 9      |
| POPSTAT          | 198.95 | 196.88 | 82.57  | 139.11 | 34.24  | 12.51  |
| Mkt share        | 0.05   | 0.05   | 0.02   | 0.03   | 0.01   | 0.00[b] |
| AVEPOP           | 14.21  | 8.95   | 3.93   | 8.18   | 2.14   | 1.39   |
| POP:POP          | 2.31   | 1.49   | 0.63   | 1.29   | 0.34   | 0.28   |
| Top 50           | 7      | 4      | 1      | 4      | 0      | 0      |
| Top 100          | 8      | 8      | 2      | 4      | 0      | 0      |
| *London Films, Denham, Saville and Pendennis* | | | | | | |
| Films            | 3      | 5      | 2      | 3      | 7      | 10     |
| POPSTAT          | 17.57  | 76.21  | 59.22  | 109.15 | 159.96 | 170.85 |
| Mkt share        | 0.00   | 0.02   | 0.01   | 0.02   | 0.03   | 0.04   |
| AVEPOP           | 5.86   | 15.24  | 29.61  | 36.38  | 22.85  | 17.08  |
| POP:POP          | 0.95   | 2.54   | 4.76   | 5.74   | 3.63   | 3.46   |
| Top 50           | 0      | 1      | 1      | 2      | 4      | 6      |
| Top 100          | 1      | 1      | 2      | 3      | 5      | 8      |

*Notes*: [a] The high production number for 1932 including films from both British Instructional Films and Pathé Pictures, the latter being newly established at the Welwyn studio.   [b] Implies less than 1/2% share of the domestic market.

*Source*: *Kine Weekly*, 1932–38.

productions marketed under the Denham, Pendennis and Saville labels), Wilcox (including the Imperator label), Capitol (including Cecil, Grafton and Trafalgar labels), Criterion and New World in Britain, between them produced only 128 films – less than 3 per cent of releases – but accounted for nearly 9 per cent of demand as measured by the POPSTAT statistic, and, significantly, secured over one-sixth of Top 50 places (51) over the period. All achieved mean POPSTAT scores greater than ten with the principal studios in this category – Goldwyn, Twentieth Century and London Films – achieving twice that and more.

The opening of the Denham Studios in May 1936 caused Alexander Korda to expand his producing activities beyond London Films in order to spread the overhead costs. Those films made in 1936 and 1937 under the production labels of Denham, Pendennis and Saville were closely associated with the Korda organisation in terms of sharing key production staff on top of the more routine studio facilities and services. As such it seems sensible to group them together as a body of work. The success of *The Private Life of Henry VIII* is commonly used to explain Korda's subsequent success in raising the substantial capital to finance his production ambitions, including the building of Denham.[26] Certainly, POPSTAT and Top 50/100 information presented in Table 1.3 suggest that from the outset of 1934 the studio's films were very popular with domestic audiences, with annual mean POPSTAT scores comparable to those of the Goldwyn studio.

In Britain the lacuna left by the decline of BIP/ABPC and British and Dominions was partly filled by the emergence of many new smaller companies, established to raise short-term capital to finance small-scale but expensive production plans. Undoubtedly the emergence in 1936 of new first-rate production facilities at Denham and Pinewood stimulated the growth in what Low has termed 'tenant producers'. The production companies associated with Max Schach (Capitol, Cecil, Grafton and Trafalgar) and Herbert Wilcox (Wilcox and Imperator), as well as those previously discussed under London Films, fit this category as does the attempt by the Fairbanks to establish themselves in production in Britain by forming Criterion Films. New World Pictures represents the first example of one of the major Hollywood studios, Twentieth Century-Fox, producing at the quality end of the domestic industry with MGM and Columbia soon to follow.

The films of Associated Talking Pictures (ATP), Twickenham (including later variants in the form of J. H. Productions and St Margaret's Films) and British Lion form a residual category in that while they can hardly be described as 'hit' producers, they nevertheless made films which often achieved a respectable distribution within the sample set. As with B & D, a clear distinction can be made between those films made for principal Hollywood renters for quota purposes and more serious productions distributed by their respective in-house rental arms. In the case of ATP, several Top 50 hits were recorded and the releases of 1934, 1936 and 1937 generated a mean annual POPSTAT score above 10. The other two companies in general fared less well; not owning the contracts of performers as popular as ATP stars Gracie Fields and George Formby, they produced films with mean annual POPSTAT scores a little below that of the population mean.

The remaining British producers listed in Table 1.2, as well as those not listed, made films which received only a partial distribution, if any at all, in the sample cinema set. Their films were generally handled by the major Hollywood distributors and made for quota purposes.

The final row in Table 1.2 indicates that less than 5 per cent of the supply share and only a little over 1 per cent of the market share can be attributed to films not of an Anglo-American origin. Most of these films were made in either France or Germany/Austria, supplemented with a small number of Soviet and Australian imports. After 1932, with few exceptions, they were not distributed within the sample cinema set and found their outlets in the specialist 'art house' cinemas found in the large metropolitan conurbations and in the local film societies in smaller towns.

## Discussion

One interesting result which emerges from the rows at the bottom of Table 1.2 is that the films of those domestic companies listed under *Principal British Studios* account for less than 60 per cent of domestic supply, although some 84 per cent of registered demand for domestic productions. This implies that approximately 40 per cent of indigenous film production was made by short-lived, small-scale companies. The proportion of American films not accounted for by firms in the list in Table 1.2 is much smaller, at less than 20 per cent, taking up only 6 per cent of demand registered for films of American origin in the sample cinema set.

The films of the principal US and British studios generate almost identical mean POPSTAT results. This leads to the conclusion that British films made by the major producers were, on average, as popular as their American counterparts with domestic audiences. The results also imply that most of the 40 per cent or so of domestic output not represented by firms listed in Table 1.2 was very poorly received since its inclusion lowers the mean POPSTAT of British producers from 7.25 to 5.01. The principal US producers held around 70 per cent of the domestic market for all years other than 1932, with all American films holding approximately 75 per cent share between them.[27] On the British side, the listed domestic studios held a 22 per cent market share in 1934, 1935 and 1936, while overall British producers held around 25 per cent share; always in excess of quota requirements. The Top 50 category suggests even greater penetration for British films with British studios taking up to 36 per cent share of hit films in the 1934 and 1935 seasons. These results lend support to Marcia Landy's claim: 'My examination of British genres suggests that whether the British critics wished to acknowledge it or not, Britain did in fact have a viable national cinema.'[28] They are also broadly confirmed by qualitative information based upon trade journal film reviews presented to the Board of Trade Committee of Inquiry in 1936.[29] This source was analysed by Rowson who maintained that for the year 1934 he had demonstrated '[q]uite conclusively, the superior general average attractiveness of British films to British exhibitors, and presumably British audiences'.[30]

***British stardom*** A consequence of the ability of the POPSTAT index to indicate relative levels of film popularity in Britain is the light thrown on the 'stars' people paid to watch. With the emergence of a significant film production industry in Britain, in the decade following the 1927 Cinematograph Films Act, came the first serious efforts by domestic studio heads to develop indigenous stars. Stardom had been a central feature of the Hollywood mode of production since the early 1920s as the lesson that stars sold films, independently of other filmic qualities, became incorporated in studios' business strategies. In a volatile product environment stars served to attenuate the risk associated with film popularity. By tying stars to term contracts, studios sought to control the dynamic and unpredictable phenomenon of stardom. It also probably enabled them to pay less for star quality in the form of an economic rent than the additional sums that the star might have generated through the box office.

British studio heads, in adopting the Hollywood production model, were concerned to create their own phalanx of stars as an aspect of a broader strategy for competing with the ubiquitous Hollywood product in Britain. British stars were required to convince domestic audiences that home-produced films could be as entertaining as those emanating from the United States. Although it is well known that Alexander Korda took star-building activities very seriously, it is less well known that this activity was a critical element in Michael Balcon's strategy for Gaumont-British/Gainsborough to become a major player in the American market during the mid-1930s. Basil Dean's autobiography testifies to the sums necessary to keep Gracie Fields under contract.[31]

Table 1.4 lists a bank of stars derived from the POPSTAT scores of annual Top 100 domestic productions for the period 1932–37. A distinction has been made between first-billed and second-billed artistes by giving a weight of 1 to the former and 0.5 to the latter. Accordingly, the POPSTAT result per 'star' refers to the measure of popularity associated with the films in which he or she appears. The ranking order adopted in Table 1.4 is based upon the aggregate POPSTAT scores for the star and is clearly biased in favour of those stars appearing most frequently; i.e. a different order will result if the mean POPSTAT scores of the stars are used as the instrument of discrimination.

It is interesting to compare these findings with the lists of the most popular stars among British audiences found in the *International Motion Picture Almanac* from the 1937–38 edition (for the year 1936) onwards. These were compiled from a poll of domestic exhibitors. Jeffrey Richards has written in detail about the lists and used them as evidence of the degree of popularity enjoyed by Gracie Fields and George Formby in particular.[32] While for the greater part the two lists are comparable, Gracie Fields features much less prominently in the POPSTAT-generated lists and George Formby not at all. Indeed, since by the end of 1936 Formby's only releases for ATP were the moderately successful *No Limit* (1935) and *Keep Your Seats Please* (1936) – neither of which made the POPSTAT Top 50 for its respective year – it is difficult to conceive, as suggested by the *Motion Picture* poll, that Formby was more popular with audiences than Robert Donat, Jack Buchanan, Tom Walls, Ralph Lynn or George Arliss as a consequence of these two productions. Other points of contrast are the relatively high positions taken by Conrad Veidt and Raymond Massey in the POPSTAT lists, whereas Veidt is ranked by the Motion Picture poll as lying in the 11–25th band for 1936 (even lower for 1937), while Massey would appear to be even less popular.

A number of factors may explain these disparities. It may be that in adopting a sample of cinemas which drew their audiences primarily from the middle class, the POPSTAT index fails to discriminate between quite distinct social class patterns of film consumption in Britain. Drawing upon contemporary social survey material, the *World Film News* surveys of exhibitors[33] and the Mass Observation study at Worktown

**Table 14** The most popular stars appearing in British films, 1932–37

| POPSTAT rank | Motion picture rank 1936 | Motion picture rank 1937 | Star | Films in POPSTAT Top 10 | Leading credits | Aggregate POPSTAT of films | Mean POPSTAT |
|---|---|---|---|---|---|---|---|
| 1 | 7 | 7 | Tom Walls | 13 | 12 | 227.3 | 17.5 |
| 2 | 3 | 9 | Jack Hulbert | 8 | 8 | 218.4 | 27.3 |
| 3 | 2 | 3 | Jessie Matthews | 11 | 10 | 205.8 | 18.7 |
| 4 | 11–25 | 26–55 | Conrad Veidt | 8 | 7 | 193.7 | 24.2 |
| 5 | 6 | 5 | Jack Buchanan | 8 | 8 | 176.9 | 22.1 |
| 6 | 11–25 | 8 | Anna Neagle | 8 | 6 | 172.3 | 21.5 |
| 7 | 7 | 11–25 | Ralph Lynn | 4 | 3 | 135.5 | 12.3 |
| 8 | 5 | 11–25 | Robert Donat | 4 | 3 | 134.1 | 33.5 |
| 9 | 8 | 4 | Will Hay | 6 | 6 | 120.7 | 20.1 |
| 10 | 11–25 | 26–55 | Elisabeth Bergner | 4 | 4 | 119.8 | 30.0 |
| 11 | - | >86 | Raymond Massey | 4 | 2 | 113.2 | 28.3 |
| 12 | 26–55 | 26–55 | Leslie Banks | 6 | 2 | 108.9 | 18.1 |
| 13 | 11–25 | 26–55 | Madeleine Carroll | 4 | 2 | 96.5 | 24.1 |
| 14 | 1 | 1 | Gracie Fields | 6 | 6 | 92.5 | 15.4 |
| 15 | 9 | 6 | George Arliss | 4 | 4 | 91.2 | 22.8 |
| 16 | 56–85 | 56–85 | Douglas Fairbanks Jr | 4 | 3 | 87.3 | 21.8 |
| 17 | 11–25 | 11–25 | Cicely Courtneidge | 5 | 2 | 81.0 | 16.2 |
| 18 | 11–25 | 7 | Charles Laughton | 2 | 2 | 79.3 | 39.6 |
| 19 | 11–25 | 26–55 | Richard Tauber | 3 | 3 | 74.1 | 24.7 |
| 20 | 11–25 | 10 | Paul Robeson | 3 | 2 | 71.3 | 23.8 |
| 21 | 11–25 | 11–25 | Leslie Howard | 2 | 2 | 69.8 | 34.9 |

*Sources:* POPSTAT index of film popularity; *International Motion Picture Almanac,* 1937–38 and 1938–39.

(Bolton),[34] Jeffrey Richards has argued strongly that middle-class audiences were more favourably disposed towards British films than working-class audiences. Accordingly, the popularity of Fields and Formby with working-class audiences might explain their poor respective POPSTAT showing, while the dramatic vehicles in which Veidt and Massey appeared may have been of greater appeal to the middle class. Such reasoning provides, perhaps, an intuitively attractive solution to the Fields/Formby and Veidt/Massey dichotomies, although, as previously mentioned, my investigation of the diffusion of 119 London West End 'hits' through the lower order cinemas of Bolton, Dover and West London provides no evidence for Richards's hypothesis. There is a clear need for more focused research into distinct patterns of cinema-going preferences in Britain at the time.

Given the prominence of Gaumont-British in the Top 50 'hit' lists of the period, it is not surprising that its stars should feature so prominently in Table 1.4. Walls, Lynn, Hulbert, Matthews, Veidt, Hay, Carroll, Arliss and Courtneidge were all contract players at times or throughout the period and, of course, Donat was the male lead in Hitchcock's *The 39 Steps* (1935). Predictably, the poor showing of ABPC (British International Pictures) is reflected in the fact that, of those listed, only Hay and Tauber made appearances in the studios' films. Jack Buchanan and Anna Neagle were instrumental in maintaining the popularity of British and Dominions' major budget productions until 1936, with Neagle continuing to work with her husband Herbert Wilcox and starring in his 'hit' production of *Victoria the Great* (1937). Donat, Bergner, Leslie Banks, Laughton, Robeson and Howard all starred in Alexander Korda's productions for London Films.

From Table 1.4 it is clear that the Top 10 listing in the Appendix is dominated by stars renowned for their comic and/or light musical qualities. Of the 124 appearances of British stars in indigenous films which were counted in the Top 100 films for the years 1932–37, Walls, Hulbert, Matthews, Buchanan, Lynn and Hay featured in 57 between them. If we were to add to these the films of Fields and Courtneidge, the number would rise to well over half and indicates the importance and perhaps the strength of these genres to the British cinema of the period.

*The crisis of production in the late 1930s* Although British film-makers were able to produce films which were popular with domestic audiences, they were less successful in developing business forms and converting this success into profits. As Jarvie has observed: 'In the UK there was a protracted struggle that at one point seemed to be pushing back, but over confidence led to over extension.'[35]

'Over extension' manifested itself in a speculative bubble of independent film finance which peaked and then burst in 1936.[36] This coincided with the decision of the three domestic volume producers to cut back on production, which they increasingly viewed as loss-making. The expansion of studio floor space, and hence output capacity, peaked precisely at this time with the opening of both Denham and Pinewood studios. This left film-makers with plenty of studio capacity but for the first time since 1927 a shortage of operational finance. In the case of Korda's principal backer, Prudential Assurance, its attempt to gain control of London Films' costs failed and by 1937 it was looking to loosen its ties.[37] Unlike the American experience at this time, the British banking sector never became intimately involved with corporate strategy formulation in the industry, preferring to extend overdrafts and re-schedule loans to existing producers. It appears that the clearing banks were also an important source of the start-up finance for the plethora of film production companies set up through the Aldgate Trust; by arranging for those loans to be underwritten by Lloyds insurers, the Trust in effect removed the risks associated with film production and finance.[38]

In contrast to Hollywood,[39] the configuration of British production which had emerged by 1935 proved unstable. Although there is some evidence to suggest that some British producers were less efficient[40] and that the Hollywood studios enjoyed significant economies of scale advantages, ultimately the size and rate of growth of the domestic market may have been insufficient to allow the principal British producers to obtain positive rates of return from big-budget films.[41] The conundrum which manifested itself to ambitious domestic producers was that access to the American market was deemed possible only at the quality end of the market. Accordingly, the risks associated with 'hit' production were great, given that widespread distribution within the American market was not guaranteed. The failure of Gaumont-British to sustain a presence in this market, despite its corporate links with Fox and its effort in establishing an American distribution organisation in 1935, followed by the corporate losses in 1936, forced Britain's premier producer to rethink its strategy.[42] ABPC and British and Dominions had already done so. The government's decision to bow to the interests of the American renters and allow double and triple quota films[43] under the 1938 Films Act, encouraged MGM, Columbia, and Twentieth Century-Fox to make big-budget films in Britain and, as a consequence, reduce their need to distribute the products of indigenous companies. This feature of the legislation may well have killed off the 'quota quickie' but, more importantly, it strengthened the hold of American interests in the domestic 'quality' sector of the British market. As Jarvie has commented, these events represent the success of US commercial strategy in an environment in which British producers and government had lost their way: '(the British) appreciation of their situation was faulty. The fundamental secrets of the success of the Americans were opaque to them. They put it down to chicanery rather than strategy.'[44]

Nevertheless, the corporate and financial difficulties experienced towards the end of the decade should not deflect attention from the considerable achievements of the industry under quota protection. The heterogeneous nature of film as a commodity implies, even under quota regulations, an element of choice on the part of the distributors and exhibitors. The fact that the latter were compelled to take increasing proportions of domestic footage does not mean that they were indifferent to them. As argued earlier, distributors and renters preferred to handle films which were popular, given an environment in which the opportunities for consuming alternative programmes were readily available to urban communities. The quota legislation, hence, provided domestic producers who wished to operate at the quality end of the market the incentive of a protected market segment to make films which people wanted to see. The POPSTAT results indicate that such films were made in large numbers during the 1930s. Our understanding of the British film industry during this decade ought to be based upon these films and the fact that they were made, together with the corporate forms and configurations, human and physical capital formation which made them possible. From the viewpoint of the moribund state of the industry in the mid-1920s these developments appear nothing short of remarkable.

# APPENDIX

## Top 50 British Films, 1932–37

Key to the *Genre* column in the following tables:

a.  adventure
c.  comedy
d.  drama
f.  fantasy
h.  historical
m.  musical
r.  romantic
s.  with songs
t.  thriller

## Films released in 1932

| Rank | Title | Genre | Prod. | Dist. | POPSTAT | Producer | Director | Stars |
|---|---|---|---|---|---|---|---|---|
| 1 | *Jack's the Boy* | cs | GAINS | W&F | 50.120 | Michael Balcon | Walter Forde | Jack Hulbert, Cicely Courtneidge |
| 4 | *Rome Express* | d | GAU | GAU | 36.328 | Michael Balcon | Walter Forde | Esther Ralston, Conrad Veidt |
| 6 | *Goodnight Vienna* | cs | B&D | W&F | 34.190 | Herbert Wilcox | Herbert Wilcox | Jack Buchanan, Anna Neagle |
| 9 | *Love on Wheels* | cs | GAINS | W&F | 29.660 | Michael Balcon | Victor Saville | Jack Hulbert, Edmund Gwenn |
| 10 | *Night Like This* | cs | B&D | W&F | 27.985 | Herbert Wilcox | Tom Walls | Ralph Lynn, Tom Walls |
| 13 | *Thark* | c | B&D | W&F | 27.192 | Herbert Wilcox | Tom Walls | Tom Walls, Ralph Lynn |
| 31 | *Midshipmaid* | cs | GAU | W&F | 18.915 | Michael Balcon | A. de Courville | Jessie Matthews, Fred Kerr |
| 32 | *It's a King* | c | B&D | W&F | 18.760 | Herbert Wilcox | Jack Raymond | Sydney Howard, Joan Maude |
| 33 | *Service for Ladies* | c | PARBR | PAR | 18.598 | Alexander Korda | Alexander Korda | Leslie Howard, George Grossmith |
| 38 | *Faithful Heart* | rd | GAINS | IDEAL | 17.662 | Michael Balcon | Victor Saville | Herbert Marshall, Edna Best |
| 40 | *Flag Lieutenant* | d | B&D | W&F | 17.183 | Herbert Wilcox | Henry Edwards | Henry Edwards, Anna Neagle |
| 41 | *Say It with Music* | m | B&D | W&F | 16.765 | Herbert Wilcox | Jack Raymond | Jack Payne, Percy Marmont |

| Rank | Title | Genre | Prod. | Dist. | POPSTAT | Producer | Director | Stars |
|---|---|---|---|---|---|---|---|---|
| 42 | *Frightened Lady* | t | GAINS | IDEAL | 16.736 | Michael Balcon | T.Hayes Hunter | Norman McKinnell, Cathleen Nesbitt |
| 50 | *Leap Year* | c | B&D | W&F | 15.413 | Herbert Wilcox | Tom Walls | Tom Walls, Anne Grey |

**Films released in 1933**

| Rank | Title | Genre | Prod. | Dist. | POPSTAT | Producer | Director | Stars |
|---|---|---|---|---|---|---|---|---|
| 2 | Private Life of Henry VIII | hd | LFP | UA | 55.133 | Alexander Korda[a] | Alexander Korda | Charles Laughton, Robert Donat |
| 6 | I Was a Spy | d | GAU | W&F | 36.460 | Michael Balcon | Victor Saville | Madeleine Carroll, Conrad Veidt |
| 8 | Good Companions | ds | GAU | IDEAL | 31.730 | T.A. Welsh[b] | Victor Saville | Jessie Matthews, Edmund Gwenn |
| 11 | Falling for You | c | GAINS | W&F | 27.847 | Michael Balcon | Jack Hulbert[c] | Jack Hulbert, Cicely Courtneidge |
| 14 | Waltz Time | m | GAU | W&F | 24.441 | Herman Fellner | William Thiele | Evelyn Laye, Fritz Schultz |
| 16 | Bitter Sweet | m | B&D | UA | 24.237 | Herbert Wilcox | Herbert Wilcox | Anna Neagle, Fernand Gravet |
| 19 | Cuckoo in the Nest | c | GAU | W&F | 23.493 | Angus MacPhail[d] | Tom Walls | Tom Walls, Ralph Lynn |
| 21 | Yes, Mr Brown | cs | B&D | W&F | 23.179 | Herbert Wilcox | Herbert Wilcox[e] | Jack Buchanan, Elsie Randolph |
| 26 | Wandering Jew | hd | TWICK | GAU | 22.025 | Julius Hagen | Maurice Elvey | Conrad Veidt, Anne Grey |
| 28 | That's a Good Girl | cs | B&D | UA | 21.832 | Herbert Wilcox | Jack Buchanan | Jack Buchanan, Elsie Randolph |
| 33 | Soldiers of the King | cs | GAINS | W&F | 19.951 | Michael Balcon | Maurice Elvey | Cicely Courtneidge, E. Everett Horton |
| 35 | Friday the Thirteenth | d | GAINS | GAU | 18.607 | Michael Balcon | Victor Saville | Jessie Matthews, Ralph Richardson |

| Rank | Title | Genre | Prod. | Dist. | POPSTAT | Producer | Director | Stars |
|---|---|---|---|---|---|---|---|---|
| 37 | *Blarney Stone* | c | B&D | W&F | 17,648 | Herbert Wilcox | Tom Walls | Tom Walls, Anne Grey |
| 39 | *It's a Boy* | c | GAINS | W&F | 17,065 | Michael Balcon | Tim Whelan | Leslie Henson, E. Everett Horton |
| 41 | *Orders is Orders* | c | GAU | GAU | 16,766 | Michael Balcon | Walter Forde | Charlotte Greenwood, James Gleason |
| 43 | *Just My Luck* | c | B&D | W&F | 16,423 | Herbert Wilcox | Jack Raymond | Ralph Lynn, Winifred Shotter |
| 48 | *This Week of Grace* | cs | REAL ART | RADIO | 15,239 | Julius Hagen | Maurice Elvey | Gracie Fields, Henry Kendall |

*Notes:*
[a] Ludovico Toeplitz was credited as co-producer.
[b] George Pearson was credited as co-producer.
[c] Robert Stevenson was credited as co-producer.
[d] Ian Dalrymple was credited as co-producer.
[e] Jack Buchanan was credited as co-producer.

## Films released in 1934

| Rank | Title | Genre | Prod. | Dist. | POPSTAT | Producer | Director | Stars |
|---|---|---|---|---|---|---|---|---|
| 4 | Catherine the Great | hd | LFP | UA | 43.614 | Alexander Korda[a] | Paul Czinner | Elisabeth Bergner, D. Fairbanks Jr |
| 5 | Jew Süss | hd | GAU | GAU | 41.159 | Michael Balcon | Lothar Mendes | Conrad Veidt, Benita Hume |
| 6 | Blossom Time | m | BIP | Ward | 36.965 | Walter Mycroft | Paul Stein | Richard Tauber, Jane Baxter |
| 10 | Nell Gwynn | hds | B&D | UA | 30.806 | Herbert Wilcox | Herbert Wilcox | Anna Neagle, Cedric Hardwicke |
| 13 | Chu Chin Chow | m | GAINS | GAU | 27.447 | Michael Balcon | Walter Forde | George Robey, Fritz Kortner |
| 14 | Evergreen | m | GAU | GAU | 27.351 | Michael Balcon | Victor Saville | Jessie Matthews, Sonnie Hale |
| 16 | Jack Ahoy | cs | GAU | GAU | 26.872 | Michael Balcon | Walter Forde | Jack Hulbert, Nancy O'Neil |
| 20 | Camels are Coming | cs | GAINS | GAU | 24.537 | Michael Balcon | Tim Whelan | Jack Hulbert, Anna Lee |
| 28 | Evensong | m | GAU | GAU | 21.879 | Michael Balcon | Victor Saville | Evelyn Laye, Fritz Kortner |
| 29 | My Song for You | m | GAU/CINE | GAU | 21.659 | Jerome Jackson | Maurice Elvey | Jan Kiepura, Sonnie Hale |
| 30 | Cup of Kindness | c | GAU | GAU | 21.251 | Michael Balcon | Tom Walls | Tom Walls, Ralph Lynn |
| 31 | Man of Aran | d | GAINS | GAU | 21.08 | Michael Balcon | Robert Flaherty | Coleman King, Maggie Dirrane |

| Rank | Title | Genre | Prod. | Dist. | POPSTAT | Producer | Director | Stars |
|---|---|---|---|---|---|---|---|---|
| 32 | *Red Wagon* | rd | BIP | WARD | 20.68 | Walter Mycroft | Paul Stein | Charles Bickford, Raquel Torres |
| 37 | *Sing as We Go* | m | ATP | ABFD | 18.052 | Basil Dean | Basil Dean | Gracie Fields, John Loder |
| 41 | *Princess Charming* | m | GAINS | GAU | 17.288 | Michael Balcon | Maurice Elvey | Evelyn Laye, Yvonne Arnaud |
| 42 | *The Man Who Knew Too Much* | t | GAU | GAU | 17.181 | Ivor Montagu[b] | Alfred Hitchcock | Leslie Banks, Edna Best |
| 45 | *Little Friend* | d | GAU | GAU | 16.777 | Robert Stevenson | Berthold Viertel | Matheson Lang, Nova Pilbeam |
| 49 | *Unfinished Symphony* | hm | GAU/CINE | GAU | 15.958 | A. Pressburger | Willi Forst[c] | Marta Eggerth, Hans Yaray |

*Notes:*

[a] Ludovico Toeplitz was credited as co-producer.
[b] During this period Gaumont British introduced their Associate Producer (AP) system. Ivor Montagu and, for next listed film, Robert Stevenson with *Little Friend*, were credited as APs.
[c] Anthony Asquith was credited as co-producer.

## Films released in 1935

| Rank | Title | Genre | Prod. | Dist. | POPSTAT | Producer | Director | Stars |
|---|---|---|---|---|---|---|---|---|
| 3 | *Scarlet Pimpernel* | hd | LFP | UA | 51.202 | Alexander Korda | Harold Young | Leslie Howard, Merle Oberon |
| 4 | *Iron Duke* | hd | GAU | GAU | 45.675 | Michael Balcon | Victor Saville | George Arliss, Gladys Cooper |
| 6 | *Sanders of the River* | d | LFP | UA | 43.834 | Alexander Korda | Zoltan Korda | Paul Robeson, Leslie Banks |
| 8 | *The 39 Steps* | t | GAU | GAU | 40.198 | Ivor Montagu | Alfred Hitchcock | Robert Donat, Madeleine Carroll |
| 10 | *Escape Me Never* | rd | B&D | UA | 39.008 | Herbert Wilcox | Paul Czinner | Elisabeth Bergner, Hugh Sinclair |
| 15 | *Tunnel* | d | GAU | GAU | 32.632 | Michael Balcon | Maurice Elvey | Richard Dix, Leslie Banks |
| 17 | *Brewster's Millions* | c | B&D | UA | 30.209 | Herbert Wilcox | Thornton Freeland | Jack Buchanan, Lili Damita |
| 21 | *Bulldog Jack* | ct | GAU | GAU | 27.559 | Michael Balcon | Walter Forde | Jack Hulbert, Fay Wray |
| 26 | *Heart's Desire* | m | BIP | WARD | 23.879 | Walter Mycroft | Paul Stein | Richard Tauber, Leonora Corbett |
| 27 | *First a Girl* | m | GAU | GAU | 23.797 | Michael Balcon | Victor Saville | Jessie Matthews, Sonnie Hale |
| 32 | *The Love Affair of the Dictator* | rd | TOEP-LITZ | GAU | 22.824 | L. Toeplitz | Victor Saville[a] | Clive Brook, Madeleine Carroll |
| 33 | *Boys Will be Boys* | c | GAINS | GAU | 20.657 | Michael Balcon | William Beaudine | Will Hay, Gordon Harker |

| Rank | Title | Genre | Prod. | Dist. | POPSTAT | Producer | Director | Stars |
|---|---|---|---|---|---|---|---|---|
| 35 | Clairvoyant | df | GAINS | GAU | 19.964 | Michael Balcon | Maurice Elvey | Claude Rains, Fay Wray |
| 37 | Come Out of the Pantry | cs | B&D | UA | 19.649 | Herbert Wilcox | Jack Raymond | Jack Buchanan, Fay Wray |
| 39 | Abdul the Damned | rd | BIP/CAP | WARD | 19.28 | Max Schach | Karl Grune | Fritz Kortner, Nils Asther |
| 40 | Foreign Affaires | c | GAIN | GAU. | 19.249 | Michael Balcon | Tom Walls | Tom Walls, Ralph Lynn |
| 45 | Stormy Weather | c | GAINS | GAU | 17.481 | Michael Balcon | Tom Walls | Tom Walls, Ralph Lynn |
| 47 | Gwmor | c | GAU | GAU | 17.184 | Michael Balcon | Milton Rosmer | George Arliss, Gene Gerrard |

*Note:* [a] Alfred Santell was credited as co-producer.

## Films released in 1936

| Rank | Title | Genre | Prod. | Dist. | POPSTAT | Producer | Director | Stars |
|---|---|---|---|---|---|---|---|---|
| 6 | *Ghost Goes West* | c | LFP | UA | 41.062 | Alexander Korda | René Clair | Robert Donat, Jean Parker |
| 9 | *Things to Come* | fd | LFP | UA | 40.651 | Alexander Korda | W. Cameron Menzies | Raymond Massey, Cedric Hardwicke |
| 17 | *Secret Agent* | t | GAU | GAU | 28.532 | Ivor Montagu | Alfred Hitchcock | Madeleine Carroll, Peter Lorre |
| 29 | *Rembrandt* | hd | LFP | UA | 24.122 | Alexander Korda | Alexander Korda | Charles Laughton, Gertrude Lawrence |
| 32 | *It's Love Again* | m | GAU | GAU | 22.844 | Michael Balcon | Victor Saville | Jessie Matthews, Robert Young |
| 37 | *Amateur Gentleman* | a | CRITERION | UA | 19.927 | Marcel Hellman[a] | Thornton Freeland | D. Fairbanks Jr, Elissa Landi |
| 38 | *As You Like It* | c | INTER-ALLIED | FOX | 19.857 | J.M. Schenk[b] | Paul Czinner | Elisabeth Bergner, Laurence Olivier |
| 40 | *Rhodes of Africa* | hd | GAU | GAU | 19.213 | Geoffrey Barkas | Berthold Viertel | Walter Huston, Oscar Homolka |
| 41 | *When Knights were Bold* | cs | CAP | GFD | 19.19 | Max Schach | Jack Raymond | Jack Buchanan, Fay Wray |
| 43 | *Song of Freedom* | ds | HAMMER | BL | 19.025 | H.Fraser Passmore | J.Elder Wills | Paul Robeson, Elisabeth Welch, |
| 44 | *Queen of Hearts* | ds | ATP | ABFD | 18.923 | Basil Dean | Monty Banks | Gracie Fields, John Loder |

| Rank | Title | Genre | Prod. | Dist. | POPSTAT | Producer | Director | Stars |
|---|---|---|---|---|---|---|---|---|
| 45 | Jack of All Trades | cs | GAINS | GB | 18.44 | Michael Balcon | Jack Hulbert[c] | Jack Hulbert, Gina Halo |
| 46 | The Man Who Could Work Miracles | fc | LFP | UA | 18.236 | Alexander Korda | Lothar Mendes | Roland Young, Ralph Richardson |

*Notes:*

[a] Douglas Fairbanks Jr was credited as co-producer.
[b] Paul Czinner was credited as co-producer.
[c] Robert Stevenson was credited as co-director.

# Films released in 1937

| Rank | Title | Genre | Prod. | Dist. | POPSTAT | Producer | Director | Stars |
|---|---|---|---|---|---|---|---|---|
| 4 | *Victoria the Great* | hd | IMPERATOR | RADIO | 45.846 | Herbert Wilcox | Herbert Wilcox | Anna Neagle, Anton Walbrook |
| 18 | *Fire Over England* | hd | PENDENNIS | UA | 25.223 | Erich Pommer | William K. Howard | Raymond Massey, Laurence Olivier |
| 19 | *Knight without Armour* | ad | LFP | UA | 24.714 | Alexander Korda | Jacques Feyder | Robert Donat, Marlene Dietrich |
| 26 | *Farewell Again* | d | PENDENNIS | UA | 20.802 | Erich Pommer | Tim Whelan | Leslie Banks, Flora Robson |
| 27 | *Elephant Boy* | ad | LFP | UA | 20.751 | Alexander Korda | Robert Flaherty[a] | Sabu, Walter Hudd |
| 28 | *Good Morning Boys* | c | GAINS | UA | 20.631 | Edward Black | Marcel Varnel | Will Hay, Graham Moffatt |
| 32 | *Love from a Stranger* | t | TRAFALGAR | UA | 20.206 | Max Schach | Roland V. Lee | Ann Harding, Basil Rathbone |
| 34 | *Great Barrier* | a | GAU | GAU | 20.187 | G. Stapenhorst | Milton Rosmer[b] | Richard Arlen, Lilli Palmer |
| 35 | *Storm in a Teacup* | c | SAVILLE | UA | 19.579 | Victor Saville | Victor Saville[c] | Vivien Leigh, Rex Harrison |
| 36 | *OHMS* | d | GAU | GAU | 19.543 | Geoffrey Barkas | Raoul Walsh | Anna Lee, John Mills |
| 37 | *Wings of the Morning* | rd | NWP | FOX | 19.045 | Robert T. Kane | Harold Schuster | Annabella, Leslie Banks |
| 41 | *Dreaming Lips* | rd | TRAFALGAR | UA | 17.358 | Max Schach[d] | Paul Czinner[e] | Elisabeth Bergner, Raymond Massey |

| Rank | Title | Genre | Prod. | Dist. | POPSTAT | Producer | Director | Stars |
|---|---|---|---|---|---|---|---|---|
| 44 | Oh Mr Porter | c | GAINS | GFD | 17.171 | Edward Black | Marcel Varnel | Will Hay, Moore Marriott |
| 45 | King Solomon's Mines | ad | GAU | GFD | 16.946 | Geoffrey Barkas | Robert Stevenson | Roland Young, Paul Robeson |
| 46 | Okay for Sound | cs | GAINS | GFD | 16.891 | Edward Black | Marcel Varnel | Bud Flanagan, Chesney Allen |
| 47 | Dark Journey | rd | SAV-ILLE | UA | 16.838 | Alexander Korda | Victor Saville | Conrad Veidt, Vivien Leigh |

*Notes:*

[a] Zoltan Korda was credited as co-director.
[b] Geoffrey Barkas was credited as co-director.
[c] Ian Dalrymple was credited as co-director.
[d] Paul Czinner was credited as co-producer.
[e] Lee Garmes was credited as co-director.

2. Ivor Novello and Ida Lupino in *I Lived With You*

CHAPTER 2

# Julius Hagen and Twickenham Film Studios

## *Linda Wood*

I N *The Age of the Dream Palace*, Jeffrey Richards states that films are
entertainment produced by a conveyor-belt mass production process
and 'often represent considered decisions made by men not actually
involved in translating the script into visual images but who nevertheless
retain the final say in the production [i.e. producers].'[1] He points out
how, for instance, at London Films, producer Alexander Korda provided
the 'unifying intelligence'.

Yet the pivotal role played by the producer is largely overlooked,
most probably because it is difficult to specify precisely where his
influence operates and how it takes effect, given the absence of any
direct input into a film. It is fairly easy to connect other contributors to
particular facets of a film: the cameraman and the art director are
responsible for the look, the writer provides the story, the editor controls
a film's pace. For most people, 'the unifying intelligence' is provided by
the director. Yet without the producer the film would not be made, for
it is he who provides and sustains the environment necessary for making
the product. He raises the finance, chooses the directors, finds and
approves projects. He oversees those non-film activities associated with
businesses in general, such as marketing and administration. He also
acts as a link between the film studio and those other industry branches
– distribution and exhibition – responsible for getting the completed
film to its audience. In a way which is difficult to define, the producer
sets the tone of the studio he runs.

Producers in the 1930s fell largely into two categories. There were
the businessmen who had made their money in other areas but who
saw film-making as a potentially lucrative field into which they could
extend their activities. These, as personified by John Maxwell, tended

to stay away from the studio but, while leaving the day-to-day running to others, still set the parameters. Then there were the wheeler-dealers who started off with very little except a certain flair, a talent for selling and enormous ambition and drive. They got caught up in film-making in its early days and did whatever came their way: they sold films, handled publicity, and acted as general managers before setting up on their own. These tended to be more flamboyant and colourful characters, whose whole life revolved round film-making and who in the end overshot their mark. This group included Alexander Korda, Herbert Wilcox and Julius Hagen.

Hagen was born Julius Jacob Kleimenhagen in Hamburg in 1884 and came to Great Britain as a child. He started out on the stage and was an actor with the Fred Terry and Julia Neilson London-based company which put on lightweight popular plays such as *The Scarlet Pimpernel*. First entering the film trade in 1913 as a film salesman for Ruffels Pictures, by 1917 he had become a partner with H. F. Double in his own company. Although this started out as a distribution company, an early indication that Hagen was really interested in production came when he started making *Kinekature Komedies*, a series of shorts starring top music-hall artist Lupino Lane at Eel Pie Island. In 1919, like many other companies around this time, it went into bankruptcy but Hagen was in no way discouraged.

There followed a couple of difficult years when Hagen and his wife lived in one room in Clapham. He did odd jobs and travelled through Britain hawking films which nobody else wanted to handle. Hilda Hagen later recalled that cinema-owners would tell her: 'He's a nice man but I wish you would try to keep him away. He is always selling me films I don't want.'[2] He was a natural salesman, flamboyant and gregarious, and willing to take chances. From the beginning he loved show business and the film industry. Lacking any technical skills which would have allowed him to become a film practitioner, he nevertheless possessed considerable flair and a relish for making deals, qualities vital for a producer. He also possessed stamina, determination and the ability to pursue relentlessly whatever he wanted, oblivious to any setbacks and at times flying in the face of common sense. Once he set his mind on something, he usually got it.

In the early 1920s Hagen was taken on as a production manager at Stoll Studios, a big new production outfit operating from a converted aircraft hangar in Cricklewood. This was Hagen's first experience of large-scale film production run on factory lines and it was here he really learned his trade as producer.

In 1926 another film industry depression led to major cutbacks at Stolls and once more Hagen found himself looking for work. However, his luck held and he was taken on as a general manager by Astra National for whom he co-produced with Henry Edwards *The Flag Lieutenant* (1926). Thanks in no small part to Hagen's skilful exploitation, this film starring Edwards, then Britain's most popular screen actor, was one of the box-office hits of the year; this at a time when British screens were saturated with American films and British film production was verging on extinction.

So serious was the situation that, in 1927, in response to vociferous demands from production interests and, more importantly, the powerful Empire lobby, the government passed the Cinematograph Films Act (1927) which made it compulsory for cinemas to show a proportion of British films. Once a market had been guaranteed for British films, the theory was that finance would follow. If distributors were going to continue to earn the very substantial profits previously made largely from handling American films, then they had to establish a supply of British films.

Always quick to recognise an opportunity when one presented itself, and with the right experience behind him to capitalise on the new legislation, in April 1927 Hagen formed Neo Art Productions with Henry Edwards. After a gap of ten years Hagen was back running his own company. There was little agonising over what their first film should be; they quickly concocted *The Further Adventures of the Flag Lieutenant* (1927), blatantly capitalising on their previous hit. Although a competently made film which had a reasonably successful release, the most significant thing about *The Further Adventures of the Flag Lieutenant* was that it took Hagen to Alliance Studios, Twickenham, which for ten years became his home.

Over the next 18 months Hagen was involved in a series of complex deals while he struggled to establish himself as a major player in the British film industry. During this time he issued a series of press releases which tended to be vague about what he had definitely agreed, and, probably deliberately, gave a false impression of the progress of various negotiations. In January 1928, the trade press announced that Hagen was the prime mover in the formation of a '£250,000 company', as yet unnamed, which in the near future would make a public share issue.[3] It would appear that at this point he was negotiating for the acquisition of Twickenham Studios, realising that if he was to be anything more than one of a plethora of independent production companies scrambling for contracts on the strength of quota legislation, then he had to gain control of the studio.

The hyperbole accompanying the introduction of a quota requirement had led to the wildly unrealistic expectation that British films would be able to earn the kind of profits made by their Hollywood counterparts. During the early period of euphoria a spate of independent production companies had floated themselves on the Stock Exchange and found their share issues being massively over-subscribed. However, investors soon discovered that not only did British films make much smaller amounts than anticipated, but also the costs of what amounted to establishing a new industry from scratch had been woefully under-estimated. Within months these companies were making huge losses, the bottom dropped out of the market and, as a consequence, Hagen's proposed flotation was unable to go ahead.

With City finance no longer forthcoming, Hagen recognised that his best, indeed only, course of action was to try to woo those distributors who suddenly found themselves encumbered with the legal obligation to handle a proportion of British films but had no production facilities of their own. At the beginning of May, he was able to announce that he had won a contract from Argosy Films, a small British distributor, to produce two films, the first – *The Passing of Mr. Quin*, an adaptation of an Agatha Christie story – going into production immediately. From then on other contracts began slowly to trickle in.

Hagen worked indefatigably to establish his new company and came up with a variety of ingenious solutions for keeping his venture afloat. For instance, in that pre-talkie era, through the relatively cheap process of inserting foreign-language intertitles, the potential audience could be widened from a domestic to an international one, thus introducing the possibility of attracting overseas finance. At the end of November, shortly before *Ringing the Changes* went into production, Hagen returned from Berlin where he had sold the German rights. Consequently, Henry Edwards, who had been lined up to star in the film, found himself with a German leading lady, Margot Landa. To win the contract, he must have committed himself to a quick delivery of a completed film because *Bioscope* reported: 'Some hustler this man Hagen! Had his company out at St. Margaret's at 10 o'clock last Saturday morning and they kept at it till 5 a.m. on Monday.'[4]

If necessary, Hagen was prepared to work through the night and over the weekend, and expected his staff to do likewise. While there was little other activity on the production side, with just three films being made by Hagen's company that year, there had undoubtedly been a lot of hard bargaining going on behind the scenes. In December 1928 Hagen was finally able to announce he had secured the lease of Twicken-ham Film Studios.

Hagen scarcely had the opportunity to congratulate himself on pulling off this impressive coup before he was confronted by a major new challenge: 1929 saw the arrival of 'talkies' in Britain. The popularity of the new medium was such that he realised that his newly acquired studio had to be converted for sound production if it was to remain viable. On 22 April 1929, therefore, Julius Hagen signed a contract with Radio Corporation of America for the immediate equipping of Twickenham Studios with RCA Photophone apparatus. According to the critic A. Jympson Harman, Hagen later confessed that 'he was in the middle of a silent film *To What Red Hell* starring Sybil Thorndike, when he saw *Sonny Boy* one night. The next day he had a headache. The world was breaking up for him. So he went out and brought up the second talkie-making machine. The deposit was £1,000. He hadn't got it. But just in the nick of time he found the money.'[5]

Needing to generate income quickly and with sound facilities still in short supply, he made certain that any producer looking for a studio floor knew that space was available at Twickenham. Although in the long term Hagen wanted to keep the Twickenham stage busy with Twickenham productions, letting out floor space in the interim helped to cover immediate debts and expenses. As pointed out in the *Daily Telegraph*: 'His capital was tiny. To equip a new studio, or even to rent one on ordinary terms, was out of the question. He solved the problem by hiring the Twickenham studios by night while others used them, by day.'[6]

From Hagen's standpoint, the quota film was the only effective means of building up his company and it was a device he was not ashamed to use. Given the fact that City money had completely dried up, independent producers had no alternative but to turn to the US distributors who were prepared to make only minimal finance available – average budgets appear to have been around £6,000. Films of this era were often disparagingly referred to as 'quota quickies'. Whereas a handful of producers were interested only in their fees and put no effort into making their films, the majority, like Hagen, put everything they had into making decent films despite the limited resources at their disposal.

This did not mean that Hagen refrained from pursuing any other potential source of finance. During 1929, with talkie fever at its height, there was much wishful talk of Britain becoming the co-production capital of Europe. Hagen, as was so often to be the case, could be found in the forefront of exploiting a newly perceived opportunity. In October, *At the Villa Rose* was made at Twickenham in English and

French, and proclaimed as the very first bilingual film to be made in England.

The practicalities involved in making multi-lingual films turned out to be more problematic than envisaged – the costs were high, the end product inferior – so after that one experiment Hagen dropped the policy. His lack of capital meant that he could not proceed with any venture which did not deliver an immediate profit, unlike the British major, BIP, which spent large sums on making a series of high-cost, multi-language films despite initially discouraging results, in the hope that, over the long term, profit levels would improve.

Any disappointment Hagen might have felt over this hiccup would soon have been forgotten when, at the end of 1929, he won his first big contract with an American distributor: he was to make six films for Warner Brothers. This was to mark a turning point in his career: Hagen had finally managed to put Twickenham on a solid footing. Although progress up to then had been painfully slow, the early 1930s witnessed a phenomenal expansion in his level of operation, and 1930 was the last year he needed to take in a substantial number of outside lets to cover overheads. Other US renters had obviously been impressed by the way Hagen fulfilled his contracts for Warners because between 1931 and 1933 he won contracts with MGM, Radio, Fox, United Artists and Universal. He made 12, 15 and 20 films respectively in those years. In its review of 1931, *Kine Weekly* reported: 'Not only has the consistently high standard of its product been maintained, there have been produced at Twickenham the second largest number of films from any British studio this year. Julius Hagen stands out among independent British producers as the man who has achieved more than any other unaffiliated to the renter–exhibitor section of the industry, to forward British films at the box office.'[7]

By 1932 Twickenham was so busy that the practice of late-night shooting became formalised and the studio employed both a day and a night shift.[8] Ray Elton, a camera assistant, recalled that when he arrived in the morning the camera would still be hot from being used all night.[9]

Hagen established a reputation for making films on time and within budget. Equally, his films were popular with the public. As A. Jympson Harman observed five years later: 'Since he has been an independent producer he has concentrated on making films that the masses want. He has no time for us critics and our highbrow ideas. We laughed at his *In a Monastery Garden*, *The Rosary*, *The Lost Chord* and such-like simple sentimental dramas. But millions about this country of ours loved them.'[10]

The ability to turn out so many popular and entertaining films while operating under the most daunting circumstances can be attributed to the quality and cohesiveness of the Twickenham team which Hagen had put together very early on. Its principal members were James Carter (art director), Sydney Blythe and Basil Emmott (cameramen), Cyril Stanborough (stills), Baynham Honri (sound), William Trytel (music), H. Fowler Mear (script) and Jack Harris (editor). Leslie Hiscott was a regular director; Maurice Elvey, Henry Edwards, George Cooper all did long stints at the studio. Hagen's technical team showed enormous loyalty in an industry where it was common practice to jump from company to company, and they stayed with him till the end.

Given that pressure of time often prevented technicians from referring to the director for specific instructions, teamwork was an essential factor in maintaining output levels. This was particularly important as Twickenham budgets allowed little scope for rehearsal and retakes. Familiarity with each other's working habits cut down the need for explanations both between fellow technicians and between the director and technicians. In addition Carter, Emmott, Stanborough and Harris were among the best technicians working in their field. Director Berhard Vorhaus described Cyril Stanborough as the best stills man in England and recalled

> the quite amazing art director Jimmy Carter, who managed to get an amazing quantity of sets overnight ... He had an amazing effective plaster department with a tremendous number of moulds. He would whip up scenes with elaborate plaster Tudor beams, trees, God knows what, which were quite out of proportion to the meagre resources in general. He was extremely adept as were the men who worked for him.[11]

Even those technicians who were competent but uninspired, such as Fowler Mear and Trytel, were perfectly tuned in to the demands of popular audiences and were good at churning out material non-stop.

Hagen fully realised that the quality of his films reflected the quality of his film-makers. Later, when Hagen went into higher-cost films, Ray Elton recalled that while he was a £4 a week camera assistant, his boss Curt Courant was earning £120 a week.[12] While wages generally at Twickenham were low, Hagen was always prepared to pay well for key staff, not just on the technical side; Vorhaus also recalled that Hagen would use expensive actors as long as it was for a limited period.[13]

Already by 1933 it was possible to observe that British producers, including Hagen, were beginning to make better films. British studios, which now had good quality equipment, and British film-makers, who now had acquired the neccessary technical skills, were eager to take on more ambitious projects than hitherto. Moreover, the American majors, badly hit by the depression, had cut back on their own production schedules with the result that some companies, such as United Artists, found themselves with insufficient films to fulfil their distribution obligations. Consequently they were prepared to pick up a small number of films from outside sources. The charming comedy *I Lived With You* (1933) provides a good instance of the different calibre of film beginning to be made at Twickenham. It starred and was written by Ivor Novello, one of the most important stars of the West End who would have commanded a princely salary. Hagen paid over £2,000 for the film rights alone. There was also *The Wandering Jew* (1933), with the charismatic German actor Conrad Veidt, described by *Kine Weekly* as 'the most ambitious and spectacular subject yet attempted at Twickenham'.[14] Both these films were made for distribution by W & F, a subsidiary of Gaumont; but it would seem that they were partly financed by Gaumont and Hagen himself. Also in 1933, after falling out with Basil Dean, who up to then had been making their quota films at Ealing, Radio asked Hagen to produce *This Week of Grace* (1933) with Gracie Fields, then the top-earning and most popular female British star who, as such, merited quality vehicles. Admittedly, the majority of the 20 films Twickenham turned out during 1933 were typical quota fare; nevertheless, it is possible to identify a handful of films that did not come into the 'churn them out quick and cheap' category.

Nineteen thirty-four was a landmark year not just for Hagen and Twickenham but for the entire British film industry. Up to then British films, with only a handful of exceptions, were made for domestic release, the majority being financed by American distributors who wanted to keep expenditure to a minimum. The hugely successful US release of Alexander Korda's *The Private Life of Henry VIII* in late 1933 was attributed to this film's unusually high production values and established a myth that if other British producers made high-cost, 'quality' films, they too could break into US markets. Throwing off its former wariness of the film industry, the City was persuaded that production could yield high returns with little risk. By the middle of the decade, City institutions, particularly insurance companies, were falling over themselves in the rush to tie up established producers, and the industry was deluged with money.

This was the opportunity Hagen had been waiting for. While prepared to grind out low-cost films for American producers to build up his operation, five years after setting up his own company he still had no real independence. Being totally reliant on the readiness of the US distributors to renew their contracts, Hagen had no bargaining power whatsoever – he either accepted the terms being offered or they went elsewhere. As these terms incorporated a flat fee rather than a percentage of box office, the opportunities for making a profit were very limited.

The alternative source of finance offered both independence from the Americans and the possibility of earning really big money. Hagen, like many producers, had a strong gambling streak. So far, following his instincts had served him well and here was his chance to step into big-time production of mainstream films. Furthermore, because his take would be based on a percentage of profits earned in what were perceived as the lucrative US markets, his potential earning capacity skyrocketed. Wealth and respectability beckoned. In January 1934, Hagen announced he was embarking on the production of films targeted at the international market.[15]

As yet Hagen was not able, nor altogether ready, to abandon the type of production on which he had so successfully built up his company. He still had a number of contracts negotiated during the previous year and it was not until the middle of 1934 that the finance was definitely in place. Initially he planned to raise finance through a public issue in May 1934, but in the end this proved unnecessary. As has been seen, around this time insurance companies were investing heavily in film production and Hagen was able to get the finance he needed from the insurance company C. T. Bowring (later absorbed by the Prudential).

By the beginning of 1934, Hagen found that his large production schedule could no longer be accommodated at Twickenham itself, and work began in February on building a new studio floor with extensive outbuildings. Concluding a report on the progress of construction, *Kine Weekly* commented: 'this remarkably active organisation becomes a formidable rival in output to Elstree and Shepherd's Bush.'[16] In fact, 1934 was to see production at Twickenham reach its peak with 21 films being made there (another three films were also made at Merton Park). The new studios, which Hagen claimed had cost £100,000, were officially opened on 17 September 1934.

Hagen excelled at publicity and maintained very cordial relations with the press, particularly the trade press. He would regularly supply stories for them to use and journalists were always made welcome. He was also generous with his hospitality and the announcement of any major new venture would be accompanied by a lavish dinner or party. At the opening of Twickenham Studios, *Kine Weekly* observed: 'Few people in the Trade throw a better party than the Twickenham people and Monday's celebration surpassed even the high standard set by Mr Hagen.'[17] This was not a trivial matter. For an independent producer who lacked the influence to demand and the budget to pay for good press coverage, a friendly and personal relationship with the press was essential. Equally, when trying to win financial backing, a portfolio of very positive write-ups about his dedication, business acumen, reliability, and so on proved very useful.

Early 1935 saw Hagen exuding optimism about the future of British films and stressing Twickenham Studios' total commitment to the production of 'quality' films. He asserted in *Kine Weekly*: 'Our pictures are no longer sneered at by foreign buyers or contemptuously spoken of by audiences. The way is now clear for British films of the future to enter the world's theatres, and it is up to every one of us to see that the films shown are of the type of which we can be proud.'[18] His plans for the year included the production of over 30 films, most of which would be 'on a larger scale', and the artists signed up for these films included Betty Balfour, Stanley Holloway, John Garrick, Jane Carr, Ian Hunter and Seymour Hicks. While none of these was a major cinema star, they were all first-rate artists. For instance, Seymour Hicks was one of the foremost names of British theatre, John Garrick was a hugely popular singer of the day and Ian Hunter was an urbane and polished player who was quickly snapped up by Hollywood.

Hagen's plans for expansion were not restricted to production; in May 1935 he set up his own renting organisation, Twickenham Film Distributors Ltd. In Britain, at any rate, the film industry was dominated by the distribution sector which provided the finance for production and then laid claim to the largest slice of box office. Hagen undoubtedly felt that if he was to become a major operator in his own right, he had to set up his own distribution arm. He saw this as something which would give him real autonomy:

> If I make pictures for other companies, as I have done for the past few years, it is inevitable that others should have a right to discuss the type of films to be produced. Now I am making films for myself and the company I control, I have complete ruling over the subjects chosen and also over the stars and directors employed. I can spend what money I think adequate on each picture.[19]

Furthermore, even if a major distributor could be persuaded to handle Hagen's films, it was unlikely they would promote them as vigorously as their own. Hagen was an excellent salesman and had previously worked in distribution. It was a logical stop for him to take over the selling of his own films.

Hagen put considerable effort into wooing his customers, the exhibitors. He placed great stress on personal contact and his staff toured
round the country canvassing individual cinema managers rather than
negotiating with the circuit head offices, though this would indicate he
was dealing to a larger extent with the independent cinemas rather than
the circuits. He saw publicity as an important weapon in the success of
his company. Twickenham Film Distributors produced press books
which, while failing to meet the standard of the full-colour booklets put
out by the American distributors, were lavish for an operation of its
size. He told the trade press: 'I have realised the full value of a forceful
publicity campaign in gaining the attention and appreciation of the
public and exhibitors.'[20] He held regular sales conferences at which he
both boosted the morale of his salesmen and exhorted them to do
better. If good marketing skills had been a factor in the company's
success, Twickenham Film Distributors would have done very well.

In October 1935, Hagen experienced his first major setback when a
fire completely destroyed the old studio building at Twickenham. The
fire was spotted by Jack Dexter, a night telephone operator, who saw
smoke coming from a camera room. Thirty men working in the studio
at the time escaped, but despite the fire brigade's efforts the flames
spread and gutted the entire building. The camera equipment and the
sound recording department were completely destroyed. Cyril Stanborough, the studio's stills cameraman, lost 15 years of work, but
fortunately no film negatives were destroyed. Although the labels on
some tins were burnt, the reels inside were unharmed. (During the
much later bankruptcy proceedings, it was revealed that the insurance
company paid out only £50,000, whereas Hagen himself put the
estimated loss at £100,000.)

This in no way slowed Hagen down. By the end of the month he
had acquired Whitehall Studios, Elstree, which provided him with
alternative floor space. A new company called J. H. Productions was
formed to make films in the newly acquired studio. Maurice Elvey, who
had directed for Hagen during the early 1930s and had a proven record
of turning out commercially successful films, was made head of production. All the films made under the J. H. label were intended to be
'quality' productions and were given appropriate budgets. At the end of
May, to crown all his other achievements, Hagen announced that the
legendary D. W. Griffith had been signed to remake his silent classic
*Broken Blossoms*. (Although Griffith was brought over to England, alcoholism had taken too strong a hold of him and Hagen had to find another
director to make the film.)

On the surface all seemed to be going well. At the first sales conference of Twickenham Film Distributors, its managing director, Arthur Clavering, made encouraging noises: 'I am pleased to say that since our incorporation which is less than five months ago we have reached a position ranking equal to any of the major renting companies.'[21] A number of its films had won enthusiastic reviews: *Scrooge*, a version of Dickens's *A Christmas Carol* with Seymour Hicks, whose performance as Ebenezer Scrooge has yet to be surpassed; *She Shall Have Music*, a pleasant piece which was really an excuse to feature one of Britain's top dance bands (Hagen paid Jack Hylton and his band over £1,000 a week and Hylton was to receive a percentage of the film's profits); *A Fire Has Been Arranged*, featuring a rich selection of Flanagan and Allen routines and songs; and *The Last Journey*, a portmanteau film set on a runaway train with director Bernard Vorhaus winning fine performances from a particularly good cast which included Hugh Williams and Godfrey Tearle.

In April 1935 with the handing over of *Inside the Room* to Universal, Twickenham made its final 'quota' film. While this could be interpreted as Hagen moving on and up as a producer, it nevertheless meant that from that point on his income now depended on his films getting cinema bookings. The following month he declared: 'I am being backed so confidently that I can make as many films as my studio floor space and shooting schedules allow.'[22] In fact, this was far from the case, and from around this time it is possible to detect a marked decline in output. Yet in public Hagen remained bullish. In December 1935, reporting a conversation with Hagen, journalist Jympson Harman wrote: 'His name is so good among his City colleagues and his plans are so inspiring that they have £500,000 ready for him to spend.'[23] Nevertheless, during 1936 the number of films produced by Hagen dropped to 11. To a certain extent the reduction in output can be attributed to the fact that Hagen had taken the decision to make fewer but better-quality films which required a longer shooting schedule. But in the past Hagen had always pushed his resources to the limit, so if he produced only 11 films, he had finance for only 11 films.

Though Hagen was now following a policy of 'quality' production aimed at a wider market, it needs to be pointed out that Hagen never indulged in the kind of extravagances associated with Korda's London Films or Max Schach's Capitol group of companies. According to Hagen, the six J. H. films cost around £200,000 while Gaumont's *The Tunnel* (1935) cost that alone.[24] In a *Kine Weekly* article entitled 'Pictures that Pay their Way – Quality but Not Extravagance', Hagen reasserted his commitment to making films aimed at the international market but not to unlimited expenditure. He declared:

> I feel strongly on the question of finance. I do not intend to spend fantastic sums in order to compete with film companies who do not consider a film worthwhile unless it costs anything up to £100,000. I shall spend freely, but not extravagantly, during 1936, as I believe it quite possible to make box-office winners without running up exorbitant and non-commercial production costs. In this way I am certain that I shall get my money back on each film.[25]

The J. H. films were staged and carefully scripted. Sufficient studio time was allocated to create a finely crafted film. In the first half of the decade, Twickenham technicians were almost exclusively British, as were the on-screen personnel, but from the middle of the decade there were an increasing number of European and American artists and technicians to be found at the studio. These included Edward Everett Horton, Richard Barthelmess, Lupe Velez, John Brahm, Curt Courant and the British-born but Hollywood-based Cedric Hardwicke and Boris Karloff. Hagen wrote: 'When I consider an American artiste or Continental technician can do a particular job of work better than anyone else. I shall not hesitate to employ him. In this way I hope that I shall make our product welcome in every country of the world.'[26]

Technically, the films were far superior to anything the company had made in the early 1930s. However, money still had to be spent carefully. Battle sequences, for instance, would be replaced by an intertitle announcing the result. It should have been possible to recover the cost of these films from a good British release, and even a modest level of overseas earnings should have yielded handsome profits.

The first indication to the outside world that all was not well came in February 1936 when Arthur Clavering resigned as joint managing director of Twickenham Film Distributors. His departure, however, was accompanied by a plausible explanation: he was leaving to manage a cinema group he had acquired. Any lingering unease would have been assuaged when Hagen revealed new plans for a major expansion of his operation.

In March 1936 Hagen announced that Twickenham Film Distributors had acquired the assets of Producers Distributing Corporation (PDC) which included Triumph Studios, Hammersmith. A new stage was being constructed at J. H. Studios, Elstree, which meant Hagen would soon have at his disposal five large shooting stages. As late as September 1936, at a Twickenham Film Distributors' sales conference, Hagen was optimistically forecasting that before long Twickenham would be in a position to supply exhibitors with one film every fortnight.

Yet just three months later, the week before Christmas, it was announced that in future Twickenham product would be released through Wardour, Twickenham Film Distributors would disappear as a separate renting entity and the sales force would be disbanded. Hagen stated: 'I am taking this step because although the bookings on my films have been so far quite satisfactory, I am of the opinion that the huge cost of a renting organisation cannot be justified with the limited number of pictures that are produced at my studios.'[27]

While undoubtedly a serious setback, it was not seen as one which would affect the core business. Hence the industry was totally unprepared for the announcement on 8 January 1937 in the *Daily Film Renter* of 'Receiverships For Three British Companies! – Twickenham Film Distribs., J.H. Productions and Twickenham Studios.' There was widespread shock that, after so many years of hard work building up the Twickenham operation into a really solid success, it should apparently crumble almost overnight. The trade paper *Kine Weekly* gave expression to the general dismay under the heading 'The Twickenham Tragedy'. It observed:

> It is a serious thing when a concern with such a fine steady production record over a long period comes to grief. The irony of it is that Hagen is the very last man who can be accused of that prodigal studio waste which has existed in one or two other enterprises. Twickenham has successfully followed a policy of well-organised expenditure on films planned and carried out with the minimum of delay. Hagen himself is a big-hearted, hard-working chief of real experience, and on that score I cannot re-call any personal failure in the Trade being received with more sympathetic regret.[28]

It was not immediately apparent that the Twickenham failure signalled the end of the film boom and the beginning of a general collapse of film production in Britain which lasted until the outbreak of the Second World War. The *Daily Telegraph*, for instance, sanguinely observed: 'it is not expected that the failure of the group of independent film companies will have any serious repercussions.'[29]

The receiver was appointed to Twickenham Film Studios on behalf of the Westminster Bank and to Twickenham Film Productions and J. H. Productions on behalf of the insurance companies which had been guaranteeing the finance for Hagen's various activities.

Initially Hagen showed his usual buoyancy. Within a few days the

*Evening News* reported that Hagen was about to form a new production company whose films would be released by John Maxwell of Associated British Pictures Ltd.[30] The new company was to be based at Twickenham Studios and the original Twickenham unit was to be re-employed. This scheme was largely dependent on Hagen's being able to go into voluntary bankruptcy and Hagen pledged a proportion of profits would be used to repay debtors over the next five years. Although the majority of debtors were in favour of accepting the scheme, including Bowring (the biggest debtor), a minority, headed by the Westminster Bank, insisted on proceeding with compulsory winding up. A petition was submitted in the Chancery division on 22 February 1937 by Betty Balfour who was owed £59.

The Official Receiver's report which finally appeared in September 1937 observed that the crisis was brought about by the sudden withdrawal of promised support by an insurance company before the director could obtain financial assistance from other sources. It revealed that, while to the outside world the end had appeared with brutal suddenness, in fact Hagen had been negotiating with creditors over a long period and the insurance companies had been seriously considering pulling out for some time.

Film companies have always tended to be rather circumspect about their finances, either because they want to hide the size of their profits, as in the case of the American distributors, or because they want to hide quite how shaky their position is, as in Hagen's case. The receiver's report revealed that Hagen's various companies had built up around £370,000 of debt (£269,409 relating to J. H. Productions). His financial affairs turned out to be extremely tortuous, with, for example, one of his companies lending money to another. Assets had been substantially over-valued. For instance, the sale of Twickenham Film Studio assets valued at £75,000 fetched only £36,369 16s. 2d.

The collapse of Hagen's business was attributed 'to heavy salaries paid to the directors, particularly Mr. Hagen, to the excessive optimism of Mr. Hagen regarding the value of film production and the omission of the directors to make proper provision for the capital necessary to finance the programme on which they embarked.'[31] The Official Receiver's report revealed that Hagen drew out between 10 and 20 per cent for studio rental on every picture the company produced, plus 25 per cent of the company's net profits. Rachael Low compares Hagen unfavourably to Michael Balcon at Gaumont Studios,[32] but it should be remembered that Balcon was simply an employee of Gaumont. The company's owners, the Ostrers, would have been taking far more out

of the company. Twickenham was Hagen's – without him there would
have been no company. During the bad times he had ploughed back the
profits to build up the company. During good times, it was quite
acceptable for him to earn a generous portion of profits. Moreover,
however generous the salary, this would not have been a major con-
tributory factor to the company's huge debts. The accusation of the
over-optimistic valuation on the earning power of his films was true, but
it was not a policy Hagen deliberately followed to defraud investors; he
was genuinely convinced that his films would make substantial profits.
The company's lack of capital, however, *was* an important factor, one
which has been responsible for driving many small producers into
bankruptcy. Hagen had always chosen to expand rather than accumulate
reserves. He saw his world as being made up of opportunities for him
to build a bigger and better company. No sooner had he achieved one
goal than he would set out in pursuit of another. Over-commitment of
finance was almost a way of life at Twickenham. With the arrival of
talkies in 1929, he had over-stretched himself to buy sound equipment;
but on this occasion the gamble paid off handsomely. In the mid-1930s,
he similarly stretched his resources to the limit, spending on films, a
distribution company and studios. However, this time the gamble went
badly wrong and he found his income dropping dramatically. The lack
of reserves meant that he had nothing to offer creditors which might
have bought him time to restructure his operation or ride out market
fluctuations. The receiver's report, however, was that of an accountant
looking at the immediate mechanics which led to the collapse of Hagen's
empire and it refrained from looking at the wider context within which
the failure occurred.

In the late 1920s/early 1930s, low-budget films made for quota
purposes provided the economic base upon which Twickenham, and a
substantial section of the British film production industry, was built.
Although today low budget is automatically associated with independent
and large budget with major, this was not then the case. The output of
most production companies in this period was predominantly made up
of low-budget films. These allowed an industry which was short of both
film-making facilities and trained personnel to make good this deficiency.
By the mid-1930s, things were moving on. An astute observer like Hagen
could deduce that the type of film on which he had concentrated had
had its day. Audiences were becoming more sophisticated. Britain had
built up a number of strong cinema circuits which had the bargaining
power to demand good supporting features. Other companies with which
Hagen had to compete were moving over to higher-cost production.

There was now a pool of skilled and experienced personnel along with first-class production facilities; so the excuses which were previously used by US distributors to justify the small sums made available for their British films were no longer valid and, given the pressures being put on the government, it seemed very likely that either a cost or a quality test would be added when the 1927 Films Act came up for renewal in 1938. Hagen had to change with the times if his company was to remain viable.

While it is possible to argue that Hagen's move into higher-cost film production was a logical step from the standpoint of operating in the British industry, he was not altogether motivated by logic, having been swept away by the euphoria then affecting the film industry. He was presented with an opportunity to transform his company into a large-scale operation and for the first time he had access to the kind of finance which would allow him to give full vent to his ambitions. After the collapse of Twickenham he openly admitted that on being told that *The Private Life of Henry VIII* had opened the American market to British pictures for ever, he had 'joined the gold rush'.[33] Ironically, the very ambition and drive which accounted for his success prior to 1935, now led Hagen to over-reach himself.

It did not take long for disillusionment to set in. Like Gaumont, Korda and Wilcox, Hagen discovered that the US film industry had successfully devised a means of sabotaging British films not sponsored by the Hollywood majors in the US market. He related, for instance, how the Americans had told him they wanted 140 prints of *Scrooge* and, when they arrived, he was informed they were too late for Christmas distribution.

As has been shown, Hagen always kept a strong rein on expenditure and although the films he made in 1935–36 were considerably more expensive than his earlier output, the average budget appears to have been around £31,000. Unlike Gaumont, Max Schach or Korda films, which cost four or five times as much as Hagen's and which were financed on the basis of earning sizeable revenues in overseas markets, the Twickenham films could have broken even if they had received a good UK release. Not being able to get a proper British release was as much responsible for Hagen's losses on the film-making side as not being able to break into the US market. Hagen revealed that the earnings of the first three J. H. films to be released came to the astonishingly low amount of £256, showing the extent to which Hagen's films, once he had lost his tie to the US distributors, had failed to get even a modest domestic release.[34]

In an interview with Seton Margrave following his bankruptcy, Hagen commented on how he had found it much harder to persuade exhibitors to take his films than had been the case when he had worked in distribution companies 20 years earlier.[35] This could be directly attributed to the decline of the independent exhibition sector and the growth of combines. Whereas even in the late 1920s there were a large number of small independent cinema circuits, by the mid-1930s exhibition was dominated by three major circuits which accounted for most premier sites. A successful release became dependent on being picked up by one of these, and a system of informal but ironcast 'understandings' resulted in practically all bookings being allocated to the British and American majors. There no longer existed a clear-cut correlation between the quality of an individual film and its ability to win bookings. In fact, the films Hagen made for American distributors had a better chance of being screened than did the generally better films made for his own distribution company.

The situation was exacerbated in the mid-1930s by a surfeit of good quality British films against which Hagen's films were having to compete. The problem of finding outlets for his films resulted in cash-flow difficulties and he lacked the capital which might have allowed him to sit out a period of losses. Hagen's failure can be compared with Rank's success. The major difference between the two was that Rank had a fairly large family fortune on which he could call to cover his early losses; once established, he then acquired his own circuit when he discovered, like Hagen, he could not get his films booked by existing ones.

Hagen had faced major problems in the past, including an earlier bankruptcy, and had overcome them, but not on this occasion. The last ten years had used up too much of his energy and the nature of the film industry had changed so it no longer offered a sympathetic environment for independent producers such as himself. By 1937 the British industry was already heading into a major slump and the situation was exacerbated by the Cinematograph Films Act of 1938. The possibility of Hagen returning to the production of low-cost films in order to rebuild his operation was no longer an option. Production never again returned to the volume levels of pre-1937 and independent producers found themselves scrambling for one-off commissions from American distributors. The mid-1930s assault on overseas markets was not simply motivated by the desire to make large sums of money. Had British producers been able to secure new markets the additional revenue could have been used to finance their production programmes and free them from being financially dependent on the US and British majors. This was seen as vital if Britain was to have a powerful independent production sector, since the experience of the early 1930s had demonstrated that the US companies were not interested in promoting good British films and the British majors lacked the resources to back more than their own production schedule. It had been a gamble with high stakes and one lost at a high cost, not only to Hagen personally but to the entire independent production sector; in the future, it was only through being sponsored either by US distributors or by one of the British majors that films made by independents could gain access to the cinemas. What happened to Hagen can be seen as reflecting the major weakening of the independent production sector then taking place. At the end of the 1930s, the monopoly control over the British film industry was far tighter than it had been in 1927.

Just how important Julius Hagen was to the production of films at Twickenham can be seen from the fact that once he lost heart and gave up the fight, there was no one else from within the company who could step forward and retrieve the situation. He had been the dynamo which gave the operation life and without him it could not survive. Julius Hagen had been Twickenham Films.

Although Hagen made several efforts to start up again, the odds against him were just too steep and years of overwork, stress and disappointment had taken their toll. On 8 February 1940, P. L. Mannock reported in *Kine Weekly* that Julius Hagen, who had been in poor health for some time, had died suddenly at his home from a stroke. Praising the 'sporting spirit' in which he took his reverses and 'his courageous attempts' to make a comeback, the tribute concluded: 'Hagen's record, over dozens of pictures, was one of real achievement, and his withdrawal from the field made a serious difference to British output.'

3. Robert Donat in the MGM-British production *Goodbye, Mr Chips*

CHAPTER 3

# Hollywood and Britain: MGM and the British 'Quota' Legislation

## H. Mark Glancy

B RITISH cinema of the 1930s was shaped by two Acts of Parliament, the 1927 Cinematograph Films Act and the 1938 Cinematograph Films Act. Both were designed to bolster the British film industry, which had almost ceased to exist in the mid-1920s. The primary problem for Britain's film-makers was that American films took the vast majority of Britain's box-office revenues, while the British industry was faced with a shortage of investment and a cinema-going public that seemed content with American films. The Cinematograph Films Acts sought to redress this by requiring that British film distributors and exhibitors handle a certain percentage, or 'quota', of British-made films. The Hollywood studios distributed their own films in Britain, and so these regulations led to large-scale American investment in the British film industry.

American films continued to dominate in Britain during the 1930s, but the British film industry became more active than ever before under the 1927 Films Act. Nevertheless, the first quota system has been perceived as a failure because it did not stipulate a minimum cost requirement for British films, and the films financed with American money are said to have been inexpensive and worthless 'quota quickies'. The 1938 Films Act did set a minimum cost test, and it gave incentives for the Hollywood studios to invest in more expensive British films, but its progress was interrupted by the war, and thus its success or failure has been difficult to gauge. The widespread conception of 1930s British cinema, however, is that it suffered under the flawed first quota, and the second quota was too late in arriving. Indeed, it seems to be taken for granted that Hollywood's powers of commerce and entertainment

57

completely overshadowed British films in the 1930s. Apart from the lavish productions of Alexander Korda, and the musicals and comedies of stars such as Gracie Fields and Jessie Matthews, the general conception is that British cinema of the 1930s consisted mainly of the terrible 'quota quickies', which lacked any artistic or technical merit.

Metro-Goldwyn-Mayer Studios (MGM) plays a uniquely villainous role in this sad story. Film historian Rachael Low has accused Hollywood's most powerful studio of being the worst exploiter of the 'quota quickies'. According to Low, MGM deliberately 'dredged' the British film industry to find 'conspicuously bad' films to use for quota purposes.[1] Film-maker Sidney Gilliat has also criticised MGM's role in the British film industry. When the 1938 Films Act spurred MGM to produce more expensive films in Britain, the newly created MGM-British production company made three of the most popular British films of the decade: *A Yank at Oxford* (1938), *The Citadel* (1938) and *Goodbye, Mr Chips* (1939). Yet Gilliat has said that these three films were made only to influence the revision of the quota laws. In his words, MGM-British was a 'window-dressing' exercise that was carried out to subvert the revision of the quota laws.[2]

These accusations fit well with notions of a beleaguered British film industry which was continually outmanoeuvred by its superior and more powerful rival, Hollywood. However, they do not fit well with what must have been MGM's primary purpose in Britain, to maximise the company's foreign earnings. It is not my intention here to seek redress on behalf of Hollywood or MGM. The Hollywood studios sought only to serve their own interests in Britain and had little to gain from promoting the growth of the British film industry. Rather, the issue at stake is the extent to which such accusations under-estimate the achievements made by British film-makers in the 1930s. Low's argument rests on the notion that the 1927 Films Act harmed the industry, and that many of the films made in Britain during this period were grossly inferior and worthless. Gilliat's claim, meanwhile, suggests that MGM's only purpose in becoming involved with British film-makers was a devious and underhanded one. My own contention is that Britain and the British film industry were of far more consequence to Hollywood than these accusations suggest. The British film industry made remarkable progress under the first quota system, and came to represent a significant threat to Hollywood in the 1930s.

## The 1927 Cinematograph Films Act

The British film industry was facing oblivion in the mid-1920s. In 1926, there were just 36 British films made, and these comprised only 5 per cent of all films released in British cinemas. By comparison, 620 American films were released in Britain that year, and these accounted for 84 per cent of releases.[3] The American distributors' practice of 'block-booking', a system in which an exhibitor agreed to release not just one film but the entire annual output of a studio, added to the British film industry's difficulties. Hundreds of American films had advance booking dates in Britain's cinemas, leaving little room for the few British films that were made. The British film industry could never hope to compete with Hollywood, even in its home market, so long as British cinemas and box-office earnings were being lost to its main competitor. British producers needed a source of financing, and they needed a measure of protection within Britain. The 1927 Cinematograph Films Act addressed these needs by attempting to place curbs on block-booking, and by requiring film distributors and exhibitors to offer a quota of British films to their customers.[4]

Such legislation was becoming increasingly common throughout Europe. In Germany, for example, from 1925 onwards film distributors were required to handle one German film for each foreign film that they imported.[5] The British quota was not so ambitious, and it was far less punishing for Hollywood. This was partly in deference to British exhibitors, who wanted to continue reaping the benefits of Hollywood's popular films, and partly in recognition of the limitations of the British film industry itself. A prolific industry could not be born overnight. In the first year of the British quota system, 1928, the regulations stipulated that only 7.5 per cent of the film footage offered by distributors and 5 per cent of the footage shown by exhibitors was required to be British-made films. The quota figures then rose each year until 1936 and 1937, when they reached a plateau of 20 per cent for both distributors and exhibitors.

British films were defined in the legislation as films that were made in a studio within the British Empire, with 75 per cent of the film's labour costs – apart from the salary of either an actor or a director – going to British citizens or citizens of the British Empire. The company making the film had to be British, but this did not mean that the company had to be controlled completely by British citizens. Rather, the majority of the company's directors had to be British citizens. This may seem a small detail, but it allowed the American film companies to set up British subsidiary companies, with British citizens on the board of directors, to make films for quota purposes. A majority of the board of directors may have been British, but they were likely to be employees of the larger American company, from which financing and control stemmed. This was not an unforeseen development. In fact, it was a straightforward option for a government that did not want to grant state support to its own film industry, but sought some means of ensuring that the industry received funding. Funding would come partly from British investors, but it also would come from the American film companies which were eager to maintain their control of the British film market.

Hollywood was dependent upon its foreign earnings. American films usually recouped their production costs in the United States, and then made their profits in the foreign markets. In the mid-1920s, Britain already supplied 35 per cent of Hollywood's foreign earnings, making it the most lucrative foreign market for American films.[6] Over the next decade, however, the advent of 'talking pictures' and the spread of more punitive quota systems in Europe made Hollywood increasingly dependent upon the British market. Earnings from other foreign markets were declining, while earnings from Britain were on an upward trend. It was crucial to the Hollywood studios that their British earnings were maintained; their profit margins depended on this.[7] Hence, they were willing to make British quota films, but sought to keep the costs of such films to a minimum. The 'quota quickie' was born. These low-budget British films were produced or financed by the British subsidiaries of the American companies at a low cost, and then distributed in Britain along with the parent company's American films.

## The 'quota quickie'

'Quota quickie' is, of course, a term of denigration, and it has become an all-inclusive means of referring to a wide variety of low-budget British films made between 1928 and 1938. According to many sources, 'quota quickies' were made in great haste and at very low costs, and British audiences loathed them. Stories abound of their low quality and poor reception. It has been said that the films drew hisses in the more up-market cinemas, while bottles were thrown at the screen elsewhere.[8] The most frequently recounted anecdote can be found in producer Michael Balcon's autobiography. Balcon recalled that the films were so unpopular that one major West End cinema showed its quota films in the mornings, when only the cleaning staff had to be subjected to them.[9]

Such stories may be true, but one must question whether they refer to all low-budget quota films, to most of the films, or simply to a minority that were truly awful. Director Michael Powell, who directed many 'quota quickies' between 1931 and 1936, offered a balanced view of his experiences. Powell clearly felt limited by the low budgets and the fast pace at which the films had to be made (four minutes of finished film each day was the standard), but he also recalled the 'miracles' he was able to perform despite these limitations.[10] Furthermore, he remembered that his first film as director, *Two Crowded Hours* (1931), 'dazzled' the audience at its premiere and became a 'surprise hit'.[11] Unfortunately, *Two Crowded Hours* is – like so many 'quota quickies' – a lost film. Film historians often have such anecdotes as their only evidence.

The most outspoken critic of the quota legislation, and of Hollywood's British business practices, is Rachael Low. Low's *Film Making in 1930s Britain* has many merits, and it is a valuable source of information and data on this period, but her view of the 1927 Films Act is unequivocally negative. The quota regulations are said to have had a 'profound and damaging effect' on the British film industry.[12] Moreover, a sense of great injustice permeates her discussion of the many American-financed British films.[13] The same studios that made such polished and high-quality films in Hollywood are accused of deliberately choosing the cheapest and worst British films for distribution. The latter are described as 'shelf-fillers'; films that the distributors realised had no box-office value.[14] Yet Low reports that each of the major Hollywood studios was spending between £100,000 and £150,000 annually on British production.[15] Given the importance Hollywood attached to its foreign earnings, it seems extraordinary that such sums could be wasted on films that were worthless. But Low insists that, when compared to the cost of top Hollywood films, these costs were insignificant to the studios.[16]

The contrast between Hollywood extravagance and British economy, however, is somewhat misguided. The leading Hollywood studios did produce polished and expensive films, but they also made films on low budgets. The annual production roster at a Hollywood studio would consist of a few 'super-specials', made at exceptionally high costs, many moderately expensive 'A' films, and often an equal number of inexpensive 'B' films. The 'B' films were more likely to be profitable than the 'super-specials'. They were a low-risk and low-return investment that balanced the far larger and riskier investment involved in more expensive productions.[17] 'B' films were also made at the smaller studios known as Hollywood's 'poverty row' studios. All of these 'B' films were made for an established audience. They either played in tandem with more expensive films, as a double feature, or they were shown in the smaller, neighbourhood theatres, where there was a market for certain types of 'specialty' films. Many of Hollywood's cheapest 'B' films, for example, were serial westerns aimed at a young audience.

To consider 'quota quickies' to be British 'B' films not only diminishes the contemptuous implications of the 'quota quickie' label, but also allows for the possibility that some of the films may have had admirable qualities and achieved a moderate popularity.[18] The films came from a wide array of producers and studios. Warner Brothers maintained its own production unit at Teddington for much of the 1930s, while most of the other American companies, including MGM, purchased or financed films from producers such as Sound City at Shepperton Studios, Real Art at Twickenham Studios and British Lion at Beaconsfield Studios. These film-makers shared a common ability: they were able to make films at the standard cost of £1 per foot of finished film. The concern for cost-per-foot of film arose from the way in which the quota was calculated. The American distributors knew how much British footage they needed to meet their quota, and arranged their contracts with British producers accordingly. The costs were low, but at a rate of £1 per foot, most of the films would have had costs in a range between £5,000 and £7,500. This was no less expensive than the cheapest 'B' films produced in Hollywood in the early 1930s, including those made at leading studios such as MGM, Radio-Keith-Orpheum (RKO) and Warner Brothers.[19]

The low-budget British films, like Hollywood's 'B' films, provided early opportunities for young or developing directors and actors. The film careers of directors such as John Baxter, Adrian Brunel, Michael Powell and Carol Reed began with 'quota quickies', as did the careers of actors Errol Flynn, Vivien Leigh, James Mason, John Mills and Laurence Olivier.[20] It is also noteworthy that 'quota quickies' provided film roles for British stage performers such as Max Miller and Tod Slaughter. The comical 'cheeky chappie' character Miller had established in music halls, and the Victorian thrillers with which Slaughter had toured the provinces, were already familiar to British audiences. Their popularity continued in films, but their appeal was peculiarly British and the films were unlikely to have any box-office value outside Britain. Thus, the strategy employed with these films appears to be the opposite of that pursued by prestige British producers such as Alexander Korda. Whereas Korda spent heavily in hopes of making films with an international appeal, the low budgets of the Miller and Slaughter vehicles allowed for films made specifically for a British audience.

## MGM's quota films

Questions of quality and popularity are the most difficult to assess. Many of the films no longer exist, and box-office records are rare. However, Rachael Low's accusation against MGM is clearly exaggerated. Low insists that 'no other company handled such a collection of mediocrities', and suggests that MGM made a 'total loss' on its quota films.[21] As noted previously, though, MGM handled the films of several different producers, whose films were also used by several other American film distributors. With so many sources, the quality of the films was bound to vary, and some received notably bad reviews. The worst films appear to be those that came from British Empire countries. Two Canadian films released by MGM, *The King's Plate* (1935) and *Under Cover* (1935), received openly contemptuous and hostile reviews.[22] Low indicates that MGM also released poor quality Indian films, but these appear to have been ignored by critics.[23]

The MGM quota films that were made in Britain, including those by prolific film-makers such as Julius Hagen, George King and James Fitzpatrick, drew mixed responses. Some were judged to be 'shoddy', 'slow', and 'unconvincing', and the cost limitations were at times obvious.[24] Fitzpatrick's *David Livingstone* (1936), a biopic of the African explorer, encountered a predictable problem for a low-budget film set in a faraway locale. In the exterior scenes, according to the *Monthly Film Bulletin*, 'trees appear which would seem more at home in Shepperton than in central Africa'.[25] Another notable failure was *The Invader* (1936), which starred Buster Keaton. Keaton had been one of MGM's top stars in the 1920s, but this film represented another step in his sad decline.[26]

There were also many MGM films of merit or interest. John Baxter's *Doss House* (1933), with its unusually downbeat setting and characters, foreshadowed the director's most noted and successful film, *Love on the Dole* (1941). The Abbey Theatre Players appeared in *Irish Hearts* (1934), a 'charming film' with 'beautiful photography' directed by Brian Desmond Hurst.[27] Will Hammer, later known for the Hammer horror films, made the flippantly titled *The Public Life of Henry the Ninth* (1935) for MGM. The story of a man determined to bring cheer to his fellow Londoners, it was described as being 'genuinely amusing' and 'good light entertainment'.[28] MGM also distributed two of Michael Powell's films, *Born Lucky* (1932) and *The Man Behind the Mask* (1936). The latter was said to have a 'melodramatic and absurd' story, but the direction, acting, photography, lighting and sound were praised.[29] Then there were the six Victorian melodramas that starred Tod Slaughter. Reviewers seem to have felt some hesitation in expressing their enjoyment of 'gruesome' films such as *The Crimes of Stephen Hawke* (1936), *Sweeney Todd* (1936) and *Sexton Blake and the Hooded Terror* (1938). While the stories were criticised for being improbable, the zest Slaughter brought to his maniacal roles was applauded.[30]

Clearly, MGM's quota films were a mixture of the good, the bad and the ugly. The managing director of MGM's British operations, Sam Eckman, said that MGM had spent between £7,000 and £10,000 to acquire each of its quota films, and claimed that there was little point in spending more. Eckman, speaking in 1936, pointed out that the American companies needed to produce 104 British films that year, and in his opinion the British industry simply was not capable of matching quality to that large quantity. The elite among British producers – British International Pictures, Gaumont-British and London Films – had their own distribution arrangements, and according to Eckman they would not deal with companies such as MGM.[31] Hence, MGM turned to the cheaper production units. Eckman's argument is undoubtedly self-serving. At this point, MGM had little incentive to spend more than necessary on its quota films. However, this does not mean that MGM wasted £100,000 each year on films that were worthless. In fact, MGM was operating according to established Hollywood practices. While American films and the more expensive British films supplied British cinemas with 'super-specials' and 'A' films, the 'quota quickies' filled the lower end of the double feature, or played to a speciality audience in smaller theatres, and they featured the work of young film-makers and actors. Many of these films may have been of a regrettably low standard, but the same could be said of some of Hollywood's own 'B' films.

## Revising the quota

When the quota laws were revised in 1938, a cost test was instituted for quota films and the 'quota quickie' was killed. This appears to suggest that the 1927 Films Act was fatally flawed and that this first quota had served little purpose. However, it is apparent that remarkable progress was made in the late 1920s and early 1930s. From the low point in 1926, when only 36 films had been made in Britain, production increased to 156 films in 1932. Whereas British films had comprised only 5 per cent of all releases in 1926, by 1932 the British share had grown to 24 per cent.[32] The latter figure was far greater than the 12 per cent required by the quota regulations, and indicates that British films had achieved considerable popularity within Britain itself. This had already been noted by *Film Weekly* in 1931, which reported that 'British films are doing a better business at the cinema, and are proving more popular with filmgoers than ever before in the history of the industry'.[33]

Production continued to expand until 1936, when 225 films were made in Britain. Of course, many of these films were made on low budgets. It has been estimated that one-half of the films made under the first quota were 'quickies'.[34] Much of Britain's film industry thus consisted of production units akin to Hollywood's 'poverty row'. While the 'quota quickies' may not have been worthless, they would have had limited box-office value in Britain and extremely limited value abroad.

If the 'poverty row' productions can be seen as a training ground for British film-makers, the 1938 Films Act put an end to the period of training and promoted investment in fewer and more expensive films. The quota numbers were kept relatively low – the distributors' quota was set to rise from 15 per cent in 1938 to 30 per cent in 1947 – but the regulations ensured that the films would be made at higher costs. Under the new legislation, the definition of a British film did not change, but the films had to have British labour costs of at least £7,500 in order to qualify for the quota. Labour costs were estimated to be one-half of a film's total costs, so these films would have total costs of approximately £15,000.[35] More importantly for the American companies, double quota credit was available to a single film with labour costs of £22,500 (or a total cost of £45,000), and triple credit would be awarded to a single film with labour costs of £37,500 (or a total cost of £75,000). There was also a 'reciprocity' clause that enabled producers to gain additional quota credit when they sold the foreign distribution rights for a double or triple quota film. These provisions were successful in concentrating investment into fewer and more expensive films. However, they also ensured that British films would be controlled increasingly by American companies. In 1938, British production dropped to 103 films, and 78 of these were made with American financing.[36]

For the Hollywood studios, the new regulations proved to be less cumbersome than those in the 1927 Films Act. Previously, each of the companies had been required to distribute approximately ten feature-length British films annually, and they complained that this exceeded the supply of good British films. Under the new regulations, though, one-half of their British footage could be derived from triple quota films and 'reciprocity' credits, while the remaining footage was required to come from either single or double quota films. In practice, this meant that an American film distributor could release the annual output of a Hollywood studio (approximately 45 feature films), while distributing only three or four British films in the same year. In 1938, for example, MGM released the two MGM-British films, *A Yank at Oxford* and *The Citadel*, which were triple-quota productions, and it purchased the distribution rights for two double-quota films made by Gaumont-British Studios (Alfred Hitchcock's *The Lady Vanishes* and Carol Reed's *Climbing High*).

In fact, MGM could have met its quota without producing its own films in Britain. It needed only to distribute films made in Britain, such as the Gaumont-British films. Yet MGM decided not only to produce its own films in Britain, but to spend far more than necessary to achieve triple-quota status. *A Yank At Oxford*, for example, had British labour costs of £112,000.[37] Sidney Gilliat's explanation for this was that MGM announced its lavish production policy, and set the first few productions in motion, while the new quota regulations were being drafted. This, he says, was done only to highlight the benefits of the multiple quota credit system, which Hollywood preferred. Then, once the preferred system was in place, MGM closed its British production unit as planned.[38]

There were, however, far greater reasons for establishing MGM-British in 1937. By the late 1930s, the Hollywood studios were encountering increasing problems in nearly every other major foreign market. As earnings from these other markets declined, the British market was given greater priority than ever before. Britain was the source of $35 million in revenues each year, and this comprised over 50 per cent of Hollywood's foreign earnings.[39] It was a relatively trouble-free and highly lucrative market, but there was one dark cloud on the horizon: British films and British stars were becoming increasingly popular. In 1936, a survey of British cinemas found that eight of the twenty most popular films of the year were British films, an accomplishment that would have been hard to imagine ten years earlier.[40] British film-makers and stars had achieved success and notoriety, and enjoyed a growing following. This was not in Hollywood's interests. A successful and independent British film industry could only diminish Hollywood's foreign earnings even further. The logical reaction, therefore, was to move into British production and to place Britain's own film-makers and stars under contract. The purpose of MGM-British was not 'window-dressing', but to colonise the British film industry.

## The MGM-British films

From the outset it was apparent that MGM-British would be one of Britain's leading production firms, and that the films would be made by Britain's leading film-makers. Studio space was rented at Denham Studios, the new state-of-the-art facility that had opened in 1936. Michael Balcon, one of Britain's most successful film producers, was hired as the head of production at MGM-British. Britain's best-known director, Alfred Hitchcock, was offered a contract for six films, but Hitchcock had his sights set on Hollywood and turned down the offer.[41] Victor Saville, the director of Jessie Matthews's musicals and many other leading British films, accepted an offer from MGM-British. So did Robert Donat, one of the few British stars to have achieved international fame in the 1930s. Donat's contract offered him £150,000 for six films.[42] Leading screen-writers such as Ian Dalrymple, Sidney Gilliat, Frank Launder, R. C. Sherriff and Emlyn Williams were also employed.

Michael Balcon spent the first six months of 1937 at MGM in California, where he planned the production roster for MGM-British with studio executives. His correspondence indicates that many scripts were being prepared, and several went into the initial stages of pre-production at this time. Both Balcon and MGM were enthusiastic about *Shadow of the Wing*, an 'aerial adventure' that was set to star Clark Gable. A script was completed, and some background footage was shot, but the flying scenes required the cooperation of the Air Ministry, which eventually refused MGM's requests.[43] Several treatments of James Hilton's *Rage in Heaven* were prepared, but Balcon disliked the story and convinced the studio that it was unlikely to be successful.[44] A succession of writers was assigned to adapt Rudyard Kipling's *Soldiers Three*, as well as a magazine story by Tennyson Jesse entitled *Finishing School*, but both were eventually abandoned.[45] An adaptation of *Silas Marner* was intended for Lionel Barrymore, but Barrymore became ill.[46] Two further scripts, *And So Victoria* and *The Wind and the Rain*, were also prepared and ultimately abandoned.[47]

At first, Balcon considered his new post to be a 'heaven sent opportunity' for a British film-maker. British writing and acting talent would be combined with Hollywood money, stars, distribution power and technical expertise.[48] It soon became apparent, however, that MGM intended to control all aspects of production, and to use as much American talent in the films as the quota rules allowed. Balcon became disillusioned, and so did his British screenwriter, Sidney Gilliat. Gilliat contributed to the scripts for *A Yank at Oxford*, *Shadow of the Wing*, *Soldiers*

*Three* and *Finishing School*, and he loathed MGM's factory-like approach to screenwriting.[49] The standard Hollywood procedure was to assign a script to many different writers in succession, in hopes that each would improve and refine the earlier work. Gilliat clearly resented this, and left MGM-British after one year. The fact that most of the films he worked on were cancelled or postponed may have convinced him that MGM did not intend to make more than three films in Britain, but this was not a remarkable fall-out rate for a studio that employed hundreds of writers. It is evident, too, that Gilliat resented the control exerted by the parent studio and was deeply frustrated by the time he left.

The MGM-British films were intended to be transatlantic rather than truly British, which would ensure that they had appeal in the United States as well as in Britain. Indeed, MGM-British was simply another production unit within MGM, like the many units that existed within the California studio. The stories were chosen and approved by MGM's own executives, and the initial treatments were written in California by MGM's own writers. Balcon began to lose his patience when one of these writers, Leon Gordon, arrived in Britain to oversee the British writers. The final straw, though, came when MGM's chief executive, Louis B. Mayer, also arrived at Denham to launch the first film, *A Yank at Oxford*. Mayer and Balcon got into argument about a casting decision. Balcon had cast Vivien Leigh, who was still unknown to American audiences, in a co-starring role and reacted angrily when this was questioned. The issue was not Leigh's suitability, but Mayer's authority. Mayer not only gave Balcon the 'ticking off of a lifetime', but opened one of the studio windows so that he could be overheard.[50] When *A Yank at Oxford* had been completed, Balcon resigned and Victor Saville took over as head of production.

Balcon claimed later that he had been promised 'autonomy' at MGM, but this promise could not have been made in sincerity.[51] Studio executives would not relinquish control over films involving such high costs and the studio's most valued stars and film-makers. Robert Taylor, then at the peak of his popularity, was sent over for *A Yank at Oxford*, along with one of MGM's leading directors (Jack Conway) and editors (Margaret Booth). *The Citadel* had a British star in Robert Donat, but MGM's Rosalind Russell was his co-star, and the director was the American King Vidor. *Goodbye, Mr Chips* appears to have more substantial British credits. Robert Donat starred with Greer Garson, who had been 'discovered' by Louis B. Mayer on his 1937 visit to London, and the producer was Victor Saville. However, the film was planned and controlled entirely from California. MGM's Sidney Franklin acted as the producer during the scripting process and, when the script was sent to Denham, Victor Saville was warned 'not to change a comma or a period'. Once filming was completed, the footage went back to California, where Franklin presided over the editing process. He was then bitterly disappointed that he lost the producer's credit to Saville.[52]

These were British films only by virtue of being filmed in Britain. They also bear striking similarities to Hollywood's own 'British' films; films that were made in Hollywood, but set in Britain and usually based on British literature or history. Many 'British' films featured the work of British writers, directors and actors, but there were often American stars in the cast to ensure box-office success. Such films were a key part of the studios' pursuit of the British market, and they consistently ranked among the most popular films of the year in Britain. Of course, the American market was always the primary consideration, and so only the most well-known and immediately recognisable British stories were filmed. Most of the Hollywood studios made 'British' films, but MGM was the undisputed leader in this field. Shortly before MGM-British got under way, *Treasure Island* (1933), *David Copperfield* (1934), *The Barretts of Wimpole Street* (1934), *Mutiny on the Bounty* (1935) and *A Tale of Two Cities* (1936) had been made by MGM in California. MGM-British offered the opportunity to make 'British' films in Britain, where they would benefit from location shooting and a greater variety of British talent.

Having temporarily exhausted famous British literature in the mid-1930s, MGM turned to famous British institutions in *A Yank at Oxford* and *Goodbye, Mr Chips*. The American perspective of *A Yank at Oxford* is built into the story, which is a comedy centred on a thoroughly modern American's experience of Oxford's ancient traditions and odd customs. Indeed, the students seem to spend most of their time carrying out time-honoured rituals and pranks, while the elderly dons are lost to absent-mindedness. The Anglo-American oppositions are broadly drawn and easily reconciled in the ending, but getting the right balance of characters and patriotic sentiments proved very difficult. An original treatment was written in 1934, when the film was to be made in California, but it took three years and 35 writers to complete a satisfactory script.[53] This prolonged effort did prove to be worthwhile for MGM, as *A Yank at Oxford* became a resounding success in the United Sates and in Britain.[54]

*Goodbye, Mr Chips*, which was based on a popular novella by the British writer James Hilton, is set in a similarly antiquated British institution. The public school has its own age-old traditions, and 'Chips', the beloved Latin master, upholds them all. They are portrayed with reverence rather than for comedy, though, and contribute to the sense of nostalgia that pervades the film. When the film was first intended for production at MGM in 1936, Irving Thalberg was planning a straight-forward adaptation of Hilton's story. Chips was to be a mediocre man whose life is given meaning by the love of his students and his adoring wife.[55] Then Sidney Franklin took over the project in 1938, and took a very different approach to the story. Chips became the embodiment of sacred English values, and his death gave the film a timely and bitter-sweet flavour. When it was released in the summer of 1939, *Goodbye, Mr Chips* seemed to be a sad farewell to all things English, and it became the most popular of the three MGM-British films.[56]

*The Citadel* has the transatlantic credits that are common for 'British' films, but the story strayed far from such ancient and lovingly portrayed English settings, and into an impoverished Welsh mining village. Indeed, dire poverty is at the very centre of the plot, as a young doctor's frustrated attempts to help the poor lead him to lose his medical ideals. When he then takes up an offer from a Harley Street practice, even London is portrayed with a stark contrast between rich and poor. The realism was tempered by an uplifting and romantic ending, and certainly went no further than Hollywood's other social conscience films. Never-theless, *The Citadel* represents a rare departure for 'British' films. The decision to make the film must have stemmed from the recent success of the novel by A. J. Cronin, and the fact that Victor Saville had purchased the screen rights shortly before he joined MGM-British.[57] It was another great success in Britain, and although it was less popular than *A Yank at Oxford* and *Goodbye, Mr Chips* in the United States, it still returned a substantial profit.[58]

By 1939, it was overwhelmingly apparent that MGM-British was a great success. The first three films ranked among the most popular films of the decade in Britain, and each had achieved that rare status for British films: box-office success in the United States. If the war had not intervened, MGM certainly would have wanted to continue along this path. Several films were being planned as upcoming productions when the third film, *Goodbye, Mr Chips*, was completed in April 1939. Most would continue with the practice of mixing American stars and directors with British writers and actors, as well as continuing to offer an American perspective on the British setting. *A Yank at Eton* would substitute a public school for the university setting of *A Yank at Oxford*. In *Death on the Table*, Wallace Beery was set to play an American gangster in London; and *National Velvet* was due to be made with Spencer Tracy starring, presumably as the father of the young female jockey, in an adaptation of Enid Bagnold's story.[59] The most immediate plans were for *A Yank at Eton*. A script had been completed, exterior shots were filmed in Windsor during the summer of 1939, and MGM director John Considine was due to arrive shortly with stars Mickey Rooney and Judy Garland.[60] When war was declared in September, though, the project was shelved until 1942, when it was made (without Garland) in California.

MGM was unlikely to send its stars and directors to Britain once war had been declared. In fact, Victor Saville and Greer Garson immediately left Britain and fulfilled their contracts in California. Robert Donat was asked to go, but Donat had become unhappy at MGM-British. He refused to go to California, and he also refused to appear in many of the films that MGM proposed for British production. He pulled out of *Busman's Honeymoon* (1940) at the last minute and was replaced by MGM's Robert Montgomery, who happened to be in Britain on other business. MGM also offered *Standby for Action* and *Beau Brummell* to Donat, but he refused these and they were ultimately made in California. Eventually, the matter went into litigation, and Donat appeared in the only other films made by MGM-British during the war, *The Adventures of Tartu* (1943) and *Perfect Strangers* (1945).[61] MGM continued to meet its quota by distributing films made at Gainsborough Studios until the quota itself was suspended in 1942. Maintaining the quota had become impossible due to the wartime difficulties that plagued British film-makers. Studio space had been requisitioned for war production, studio technicians were called up, and the materials for sets, costumes and props were rationed. Far fewer films were made and, of the American companies, only Warner Brothers remained active at Teddington. It, too, closed when Teddington was bombed in 1944.[62]

## Conclusion

*A Yank at Oxford* was the first film to be registered for triple-quota status, and officials at the Board of Trade noted its high cost with pleasure. The expense seemed to suggest that the 1938 Films Act would benefit the British film industry.[63] In purely commercial terms, this was true. The Hollywood studios were ready to invest their highest costs and to send their top stars to Britain, and they were adept at making films for an international audience. If the aim of the legislation was to create an independent British film industry and to enable the development of a unique British film culture, though, the MGM-British films could not be used as examples of its success. With such high costs at stake, MGM was not ready to relinquish control over the films, and Balcon, Gilliat and Donat were soon frustrated by the studio's methods. It is also apparent that the films were more 'British' than British, and that many similar films were planned. If the war had not intervened, such trans-atlantic and 'British' productions were likely to be the future of British cinema.

Sidney Gilliat's claim, that MGM-British was only window-dressing, under-estimates the importance Britain held for Hollywood, and the strides the British industry had taken over the previous ten years. The 1927 Films Act had brought about investment and a period of training for many British film-makers, several of whom went on to contribute to British cinema's 'golden age' in the 1940s. It is apparent that the first quota had a serious flaw, and that this was exploited by the American companies. But Rachael Low has over-stated this flaw. Many of the 'quota quickies' were perceived to be reasonably well-made films at the time of their release, and to suggest that all of MGM's quota films were worthless denigrates an entire decade of British cinema. Furthermore, by the mid-1930s British films had an established following and were proving to be more popular than ever before. The fact that this was troubling to Hollywood, and that its studios felt the need to move into British production, signifies that British cinema had come of age in the 1930s.

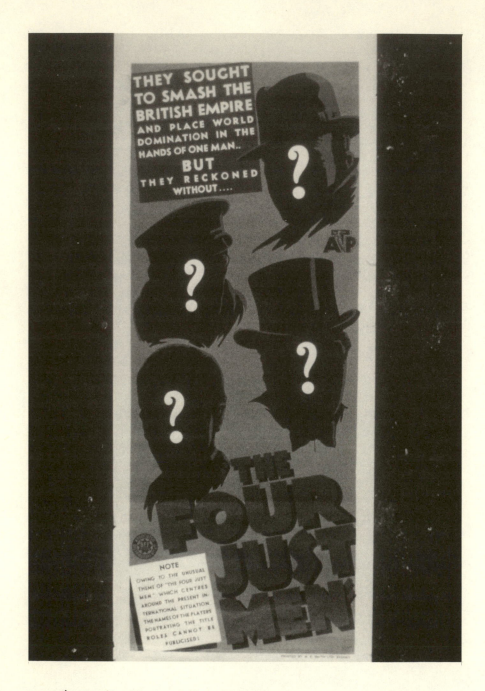

4. *The Four Just Men* (1939) illustrating the mystery and the patriotism at the heart of the spy shocker

CHAPTER 4

# Celluloid Shockers

*James Chapman*

*Shocker.* 1824. Something which shocks or excites; esp. a work of fiction of a sensational character. *Shorter Oxford English Dictionary*

THE aim of this chapter is to explore the forgotten history of the thriller genre, or shocker, in the British domestic cinema of the 1930s. It is indeed a forgotten history, for the thriller has been noticeably absent from the standard critical historiography of the British cinema. Yet the genre has been a prolific and highly popular one, and the 1930s in particular have an excellent claim to be regarded as the golden age of the British film thriller. Some 350 thrillers were produced in Britain between 1930 and 1939, a figure which approximates to about one-fifth of all feature films made in the country.[1] It is evident that the thriller was one of the staple genres of the British cinema during the decade (in sheer numbers it was surpassed only by the comedy), which suggests both a durability with the film industry and a popularity with cinema audiences. It is, after all, one of the commercial imperatives of the film industry that successful and proven narrative formulas are repeated and recycled through genres. However, one of the legacies of traditional film criticism in Britain has been to ignore or denigrate the 'popular' at the expense of a 'quality' cinema identified with art and culture (which in Britain has usually meant documentary-style realism or adaptations of classic literature). The thriller narrative, as an essentially low-brow form of popular entertainment, has been excluded from the canon of what is deemed critically respectable. Indeed, rarely has such a prolific genre been so neglected in film scholarship. This chapter seeks to redress that neglect by arguing that the celluloid shockers of the 1930s do deserve to be taken seriously. It will do this by locating them in the context of a British national cinema and film culture. First, it will be shown that the film shocker was the cinematic equivalent of a type of popular

75

fiction which had emerged in the late nineteenth and early twentieth centuries and which, despite its low-brow status and sensational nature, has nevertheless been taken seriously by literary critics as an important site for the construction of ideologies of national identity. In so far as the film shocker drew upon the same cultural tradition then it too deserves critical recognition on similar grounds. And second, the chapter will provide a contextual history of the shocker in the British cinema of the 1930s. An analysis of the trends within the genre and a discussion of some of the key films will show that, like much British cinema of the decade, the shocker narrative contained particular ideologies of class and nation.

It will be useful in the first instance to establish how the thriller can be defined. Given the dearth of critical writing on the film thriller, the main work on the genre is to be found in literary criticism.[2] However, most attempts to pin down the thriller to a fixed generic formula prove unsatisfactory because the precise boundaries of the genre are almost impossible to establish. The subject matter of the genre is usually crime and mystery, but does this mean that it should include the classic detective story? Given that most writers have argued that there is a fundamental difference between the thriller and the detective story, this is a good place to start. Dorothy L. Sayers, one of the two grand ladies of the classic English detective novel, once divided crime fiction into two categories, which she termed 'the purely Intellectual and the purely Sensational'.[3] This distinction could also be described in terms of the 'whodunit' on the one hand and the 'thriller' or 'shocker' on the other. In the whodunit the basis of the narrative is the rational solution of a crime puzzle. This was the type of fiction in which, between the wars, Sayers herself and Agatha Christie excelled. In such fiction the emphasis is on the construction of an intricate plot where a mystery is established and resolved through the deductive prowess of a central character. There is, as Tzvetan Todorov points out, a duality in the typical detective story in that it 'contains not one but two stories: the story of the crime and the story of the investigation'.[4] The narrative of the whodunit chronicles the process whereby the crime (usually a murder) is reconstructed from pieces of information (clues) which are discovered by the detective during the investigation. The crime is solved through the intellectual efforts of the detective: the exercise of the 'little grey cells', in the words of Christie's Hercule Poirot. The pleasure for the reader lies in the unravelling of the murder mystery leading towards the denouement where the detective reconstructs the crime (often in front of an audience) and reveals the identity of the murderer. The genre is governed by a fairly rigid set of conventions or rules which regulate the pleasure which the reader derives. In the words of W. H. Auden, the whodunit is distinct from 'thrillers, spy stories, stories of master crooks, etc., where the identification of the criminal is subordinate to the defeat of his criminal designs'.[5] This was the category which Sayers termed 'the purely Sensational'. The key difference is that whereas the whodunit works principally as an intellectual puzzle, the thriller narrative instead places its primary emphasis on action. The pleasure for the reader is generated not through the revelation of the criminal's identity (sometimes this may even be known from an early point in the narrative) but rather through the adventures which befall the hero as he fights to defeat the villain's criminal conspiracy. In the thriller it is the rapid succession of events, fights and chases which provide stimulation (thrills) for the reader. As David Glover observes: 'Where the classic mystery story sought genuinely to exercise the mind, patiently sifting through the clues and evidence in search of the sole correct solution, the thriller could offer only a hypertrophied emotionalism, a heady roller-coaster ride whose abrupt plunges and climbs gave one little time to think.'[6]

Furthermore, the thriller hero relies more on physical action than deductive prowess; characters such as Richard Hannay and Bulldog Drummond were more likely to overcome their opponents through violence rather than through the exercise of the 'little grey cells'. The common assumption, prevalent since the interwar years, is that whereas the whodunit appealed to a middle-class (and largely female) readership – the 'coffee break and commuter classes'[7] – the more low-brow thriller was read predominantly by working-class males. Whether this distinction is valid has been questioned by some literary critics and historians who suggest that reading habits were not necessarily so rigidly defined.[8]

In the historical genealogy of crime fiction the thriller can be seen to have emerged into its classic form earlier than the detective story, which really did not become prolific until the interwar period. By this time, however, the 'shockers' or 'penny dreadfuls' had enjoyed several decades as popular, escapist reading matter in Britain. Michael Denning places the emergence of the genre in its historical context:

The word 'thriller' came into use in the 1880s and 1890s together with 'shocker' as a designation for the proliferating cheap sensational fiction which emerged at the moment when a mass-produced culture started to come into being in Britain, a moment signalled by the Education Act of 1870 and by the creation of *Pearson's Weekly* (1890), Newnes' *Tit-bits* (1881), and Harmsworth's *Daily Mail* (1896), the first popular daily newspaper.

By the first decades of the twentieth century, the imperial adventure stories of H. Rider Haggard, Arthur Conan Doyle, and Robert Louis Stevenson, which were often aimed at schoolboys, were being supplanted by the first thrillers, the stories of William Le Queux (beginning in 1891), E. Phillips Oppenheim (beginning in 1887), and the king of them all, Edgar Wallace (beginning in 1905), which were aimed at an adult male audience.[9]

Denning therefore identified the thriller or shocker as emerging at a particular historical moment. The increase in working-class literacy, combined with developments in the publishing industry – including cheap editions and, particularly, serialisations in weekly magazines – provided the context for the emergence of a new type of fiction. Of course, the genre was not born in a vacuum; as Jerry Palmer points out, 'it was born out of the literary conventions of its time'.[10] To some extent the thriller was influenced by the heroic romance, which had a long tradition in English literature. A more direct influence was the Gothic literature of a century before, from which the thriller borrowed the characterisation of intrepid hero/imperilled heroine/wicked villain and such trappings as dark castles, secret passageways and sinister goings-on in the night. Furthermore, in Palmer's words, the Gothic 'offered to the thriller the sense of sheer malevolence, the sense of evil as a pathological manifestation'.[11] Both the Gothic novel and the thriller narrative were based on a sense of paranoia, where the ordered world could be disrupted at any moment by the machinations of the forces of evil and chaos. They created a world where chaos lay hidden just below the surface of society, ready to erupt at any time. For Palmer, the key figure in the development from the Gothic to the thriller was Edgar Allan Poe. *The Murders in the Rue Morgue* (1841) combined elements of both: the irrational murders are committed by an escaped orang-utan (Gothic malevolence) but are solved through the deductive prowess of Auguste Dupin. The figure of the investigator was to become a central one in the development of the late Victorian thriller story, immortalised in the Sherlock Holmes stories of Sir Arthur Conan Doyle. Although Holmes may have been the archetypal detective hero, he appeared well before the golden age of detective fiction and the stories are perhaps better located in the tradition of the thriller or shocker due to their fast-paced narratives and often sensational crimes. 'Shocker' was a more specifically British term which was most common between the 1880s and the Second World War, after which it was superseded by the more general label 'thriller'. It was used to describe a type of narrative characterised by its unlikely content and rapid pace. For example, John Buchan described his classic spy thriller *The Thirty-Nine Steps* (1915) as 'that elementary type of tale which Americans call the "dime novel" and which we know as the "shocker" – the romance where the incidents defy the probabilities and march just inside the borders of the possible'.[12]

The popularity of the shocker fictions of writers such as Edgar Wallace, John Buchan, Sax Rohmer, 'Sapper' (H. C. McNeile) and many others in the early twentieth century was one of the reasons why British film-makers turned to their work for source material. Shockers were easily adaptable for the cinema, where their fast-paced narratives provided ideal filmic material. This was understandably the case before the advent of sound when film was a purely visual medium, but it was also the case during the 1930s when talking pictures had replaced the silent cinema. One of the possible explanations for this is that cinema audiences simply preferred action and thrills to lengthy dialogue sequences and over-wordy exposition. As Jeffrey Richards has observed: 'It is very revealing of audience tastes and preferences that in the golden age of the detective story, it was not the clever intellectual puzzles of Dorothy L. Sayers or Agatha Christie that dominated the screen – there was only one Sayers film and four Christie films in the entire decade – but rather the less demanding thriller, full of fights, chases and mayhem.'[13]

Another explanation for the proliferation of the thriller during the 1930s can be found in the economics of the British film industry. By the end of the 1920s the conditions which enabled the thriller to become one of the staple British film genres had already emerged. A number of factors, including the arrival of the talkies and the rise of large film corporations such as British International Pictures and the Gaumont-British Picture Corporation, had brought about the standardisation of the feature film as the dominant mode of film practice. The most important factor, however, had been the introduction of the Cinematograph Films Act of 1927. More commonly known as the Quota Act, this was a piece of protective legislation which had been prompted by widespread concern over the economic and cultural hegemony of Hollywood. The intention was to assist the ailing British film production industry by establishing a minimum quota of British films which had to be shown by all exhibitors. Unfortunately, the Act's most obvious and immediate legacy was the proliferation of cheap and shoddy British films – the notorious 'quota quickies' – which exhibitors often had to take regardless of quality just in order to fulfil their British quota. Rachael Low estimates that 'approximately half the enormous number of films turned out by British studios up to 1937 were produced at minimum cost simply to exploit the projected market or, at worst, to comply with the law'.[14] The cheapest films to make were thrillers and comedies because they required relatively little expenditure on sets and costumes in comparison to more expensive genres such as the musical and the historical film. It is hardly surprising, therefore, that thrillers and comedies dominated the generic profile of the British cinema in the wake of the 1927 Act. It does not follow that all cheaply made British thrillers were poor films, of course, or that they were not appreciated by some cinema-goers. Leslie Halliwell, at the time a young film fan growing up in Bolton, recalled in his memoirs that although one of his local cinemas, the Capitol, showed mainly glossy MGM Hollywood productions, nevertheless 'it had to fulfil its British quota, and in doing so it usually turned up something fairly mouthwatering in the way of a thriller'.[15] Nor does it follow that all thrillers were 'quota quickies', for example, the series of celebrated spy films directed by Alfred Hitchcock – *The Man Who Knew Too Much* (1934), *The 39 Steps* (1935), *The Secret Agent* (1936), *Sabotage* (1936) and *The Lady Vanishes* (1938) – also attracted considerable critical acclaim abroad.[16] These Hitchcock films, however, represented the more prestigious end of a genre which varied considerably in terms of quality and ambition. Many thrillers were intended only for the domestic market to provide cheap quota pictures for exhibitors. But given that they were made for home consumption only, such films were able to draw upon the indigenous literary and cultural tradition of the shocker. Therefore it was the combination of film industry economics and the existence of a particular form of popular fiction which provided the context for the proliferation of celluloid shockers during the 1930s.

Perhaps it was the thriller's origins in a stream of low-brow popular culture which has caused its neglect by most film critics. This neglect is also a legacy of the high-brow film criticism of the day. There existed in Britain a minority film culture, represented by the burgeoning film society movement, by the film critics of the quality press, and by successive specialist film journals such as *Close Up, Cinema Quarterly* and *World Film News*. This film culture was characterised by a disavowal of the 'popular' (which included most genre films) and a championing of the 'art' or 'quality' aspects of the cinema (which usually meant European films). Critics such as John Grierson expounded the view that the natural vocation of the British cinema was a form of social realism, which meant the representation of the lives of ordinary people. Genre films such as thrillers were seen as the antithesis of this realism. In November 1931, for example, Grierson called for 'the breath of reality in our films' and complained: 'We need something better to build with than racing scandals or the campaigns of silly asses against impossible

Bolsheviks.'[17] The documentary school of critics complained that the picture of British life put on the screen by popular films was unrealistic and trivial. In August 1937, for example, Russell Ferguson made a scornful attack on British cinema in *World Film News*, a journal devoted to the documentary-realist aesthetic:

> Our national life, as reflected in British films, is full of interesting features. We are a nation of retired business men, millowners, radio singers, actors, detectives, newspapermen, leading ladies, soldiers, secret servicemen, crooks, smugglers, and international jewel thieves ... Our greatest trouble is spies and fanatics, who threaten from time to time to blow up London, or to bring down all the machines at Hendon with death rays ... What with armaments rings, assassins and political madmen, it is a mercy that a good proportion of our population are in the secret service.[18]

Ferguson ridiculed the British cinema for its concentration on these subjects rather than real problems such as 'unemployment, malnutrition, distressed areas, disease or poverty'. However, such criticisms missed the point in that the cinema was seen by audiences as a provider of escapist entertainment rather than social realism. As one of the respondents to a Mass-Observation survey into cinema-going habits and film preferences in Bolton in 1938 remarked:

> When I go to the pictures I go to be entertained. For this reason I don't like seeing what producers fondly imagine are true to life films, simply because they are not true to life. I know far more about my own problems than film producers do or ever will, so that when I go to the pictures I don't want to see these problems solved (to the satisfaction of the producers) in what are called true to life pictures ... I like Musical Comedies or a really good Detective Picture because they take my mind off everyday things, and going to the pictures is a change and a tonic if I can see the films that I have mentioned.[19]

As so often, the views of the high-brow critics were not in tune with popular taste.

The first critic to pay any serious attention to the 1930s British film thriller at all was Peter John Dyer in an article for *Sight and Sound* in 1961. Dyer argued that the genre flourished during the 1930s largely through the efforts of a handful of directors; Hitchcock was of course pre-eminent as the British cinema's 'one true "critics director"', but Dyer also identified 'adept disciples' in Walter Forde, Carol Reed, George King, Arthur Woods and David MacDonald. The success of Hitchcock's *The Man Who Knew Too Much* ('its very recklessness gave it an excitement hitherto unknown in the British cinema') was the catalyst for the others to follow in his footsteps: 'Kidnapping, hypnosis, codes inside shaving brushes, brilliantined sharpshooters, scarred and smiling anarchists, sun-worshippers and sieges in Wapping – these were among the outlandish elements that went to make up Hitchcock's declaration of independence; and since it paid off, and was good cinema, it was by way of being a starter's pistol for other film-makers.'[20]

For Dyer, the history of the thriller could therefore be seen in auteurist terms, and is attributable mainly to Hitchcock. More recent writers have turned to the idea of genre rather than the director-as-auteur and have placed the thriller in relation to its literary and cultural roots. As Tom Ryall has suggested: 'It can be argued that the most vigorous cinematic strands of the period were in those genres which were rooted firmly in British popular culture – the music hall comedy, the crime picture and the thriller – yet critical orthodoxy has often been dismissive of these genres.'[21] The literary origins of the genre are seen to be as important as the directors who made the films. As Jeffrey Richards points out, although 1930s British cinema was characterised by a large number of literary and dramatic adaptations, the most popular sources were those which were deemed low-brow in the cultural hierarchy, particularly the shocker from literature and the farce from the stage. He observes: 'if the literary Thirties were the age of Priestley and Cronin, the cinematic Thirties were pre-eminently the age of Edgar Wallace and Ben Travers.'[22]

Edgar Wallace is a key figure in the history of the shocker, not only for his prolific literary output (he wrote some 200 novels and plays in addition to countless pieces of miscellaneous journalism) but also for the way in which he provides a bridge between the literary and cinematic versions of the genre. If there is one writer who might be held as the exemplar of the shocker (just as Agatha Christie is often held in relation to the classic detective story) then it has to be Wallace. 'Edgar Wallace became a habit', declared a leader in *The Times* after his death in 1932: 'It was with some not a point of honour but a plain need to read every story that he wrote. They could not have enough of his criminals, firearms, poisons, jewels, warehouses by the river – all the wonderful outfit of crime, and the mysteries and dangers and horrors that he could spin out of it.'[23]

Wallace also proved to be highly popular with film-makers. Between 1925 and 1939 there were some 50 British films which were adapted from Wallace stories. A number of these were even produced or directed by Wallace who moved into film production for a short time at the end of the 1920s. Ever in need of immediate cash to fund his gambling and extravagant lifestyle, Wallace sold the film rights of his stories to the British Lion Film Corporation, one of the smaller production companies founded after the Films Act in order to make cheap films for the domestic market. Wallace was invited to become chairman of the board on the strength of the proven popular appeal of his plays such as *The Ringer* and *The Squeaker*, which he had produced successfully for the stage during the 1920s. British Lion was soon turning out Wallace film adaptations, including *The Ringer* (1928), *The Flying Squad* (1929) and *The Clue of the New Pin* (1929).[24] However, none of these films was particularly successful, being considered too theatrical by the critics. Herbert Thompson, the editor of *Film Weekly*, wrote of *The Flying Squad*:

> It is time that the British Lion Film Corporation realised that not all Edgar Wallace stories are suitable for filming.
> 'The Flying Squad', just privately shown, lacks coherence and plausibility. The direction of Arthur Maude is uninspired, and the acting on the whole no more than adequate, but obviously the principal fault lies with the producers who decided to produce a subject which gives no evidence of having been good film material.[25]

Wallace's response to the criticism was to take the director's chair himself for an adaptation of *Red Aces* (1929). *Film Weekly* suggested that Wallace took up directing because he was 'dissatisfied with the versions of his stories which his company has produced. I am not very surprised', the reporter added, somewhat mischievously, 'because some of them at least that I have seen are among the worst of recently produced films'.[26] Wallace's first attempt at direction was not any better received. His biographer Margaret Lane considers that he was 'an indifferent "silent" director. He was too thoroughly imbued with stage technique to adapt himself at short notice to the very different requirements of silent film'.[27] Wallace's great flair for showmanship was not always matched by sound business sense. Although he told journalists that 'Films are interesting to me from a business point of view only', and confidently predicted that 'I shall make my first picture a commercial triumph',[28] his association with British Lion did not bring him the riches which he had expected. After its first year the company was some £50, 000 in the red, and during the course of 1929 the studio at Beaconsfield had to be re-equipped for sound at considerable expense.

Following the conversion to sound, Wallace had another go at directing with *The Squeaker* (1930), starring Gordon Harker who had appeared in the original stage version. Margaret Lane describes Wallace's way of working thus:

It was work he loved, and he quickly showed that in talking pictures at least he had the makings of a director. His stage technique was now no hindrance, for the early talkies were nothing but filmed plays, and he was able to use his theatre experience with the added pleasure of discovering the possibilities of a new medium. As a film director he took himself very seriously indeed and demanded, as always, the maximum of hard work from everyone concerned ... The film studio was to him an exciting extension of the theatrical world, and he responded with gusto to its technical problems and its peculiar atmosphere of nerve-strain, excitement and exasperation. Heavily seated in his canvas chair, his hat tilted back from his brow and script in hand, he enjoyed his new role so much that he would accept no money from the company for playing it. It was pure pleasure, and he shrewdly took advantage of the excellent publicity which it afforded; it pleased and flattered him to appear before the public in this new character.[29]

However, Wallace was to direct no more films personally after *The Squeaker*. In 1931 a deal was struck between British Lion and Gainsborough Pictures whereby a series of joint productions would be made at Beaconsfield, produced by Michael Balcon and employing technicians from both studios. Walter Forde, a former silent film comedian who had turned his hand to directing rather more successfully than Wallace had done, directed another version of *The Ringer* (1931), starring Gordon Harker, which was more successful than any of the previous Wallace adaptations. 'It has taken a comedian, Walter Forde, to give us an English crime story that not only convinces, but is presented with all the efficiency, polish and slickness of the American product', said Lionel Collier, the reviewer of the fan magazine *Picturegoer*. 'Edgar Wallace has never been better served than he has been in this adaptation of his big stage success.'[30] The production policy at British Lion was to diversify in the 1930s as the company turned to films of music-hall turns and revue sketches. Wallace himself had by then left for Hollywood, where he died suddenly of pneumonia at the age of 58 while working on the script of *King Kong*.[31]

If Wallace's own involvement with the film industry was short-lived, however, his influence over the British cinema if anything became more pronounced after his death. 'His stories were rapidly to become one of the staples of the cinema, used by many different companies', writes Rachael Low.[32] Most of the films made from his stories were produced by the smaller production companies, but there were a few which benefited from the better facilities and bigger budgets available to the larger producers. Alexander Korda produced another version of *The Squeaker* (1937), directed by the American William K. Howard, while

Herbert Wilcox produced *The Frog* (1937) and *The Return of the Frog*
(1938). Yet these films have been overlooked by most historians who
have concentrated instead on their producers' more 'respectable' films:
Korda's historical and imperial epics and Wilcox's costume dramas
starring Anna Neagle. Furthermore, the first film which Michael Balcon
produced after taking over at Ealing Studios was *The Gaunt Stranger*
(1938), yet another adaptation of *The Ringer* which was again directed
by Walter Forde. This film was really more of a whodunit than a blood-
and-thunder shocker and scriptwriter Sidney Gilliat had misgivings about
the form: 'I think it's a purely mechanical convention. I don't like a
convention whereby absolutely any one of eight people, or whatever the
number is, might be responsible for the crime, which in any form of life
or characterisation is nonsense, really.'[33]

Nevertheless, the film is a polished and entertaining mystery story
with an attractive light-comedy performance from Sonnie Hale as the
crook-turned-hero and a sinister turn from Wilfrid Lawson as the
murderer. Lawson, a craggy-faced character actor now best remembered
for his role as Alfred Dolittle in *Pygmalion* (1938), was often cast in
menacing parts. Nowhere was his menace better exemplified than in
*The Terror* (1938), directed by Richard Bird for Associated British, another
one of the larger companies which occasionally turned its hand to
Wallace adaptations. The play was a crime melodrama with overtones
of horror which had already been filmed as an early talkie by Warner
Brothers in 1929. The British remake cast Lawson as The Terror, a
crime boss who exacts a terrible revenge on two crooks (one of them
played by Alastair Sim in an early film appearance) who had betrayed
him over a gold robbery. With its masked organ-playing villain and
creepy old priory – not to mention Sim's fate in being walled-up in the
crypt – the film has enough ingredients to qualify as an example of the
'horrific' trend in the shocker which was more usually associated with
the smaller production companies.

The fact that even the larger British studios sometimes turned to
Wallace's stories for subject matter proves just how popular his particular
style of thriller was during the 1930s. However, it was still the smaller
and cheaper producers who accounted for most of the films. While they
are far from being cinematic masterpieces, nevertheless some of the
films are interesting for the way in which they fit into the profile of
1930s British cinema. In one or two cases the shocker can be seen as
a site for the construction of themes and ideologies which go against
the grain. Historians have suggested that British films promoted consensus values which presented 'the vision of England as one happy,

close-knit community, a vision of domestic harmony and national integration to be found most often in British films of the 1930s'.[34] In particular, the class system is presented in a favourable light by stressing the importance of tradition and shared social values. However, in Wallace's play *The Case of the Frightened Lady* the social structure is shown to be unstable in that the aristocracy, the standard-bearers of tradition, turn out to be corrupt, selfish and ultimately insane. The play was filmed twice, once in 1932 as *The Frightened Lady* (one of the British Lion-Gainsborough co-productions), and again under the original title in 1940. The latter version, produced and directed by George King, is a splendidly macabre thriller with elements of the Gothic tradition. The setting is Mark's Priory, a creepy baronial hall which is the home of the Lebanon family. Lady Lebanon (Helen Haye), a snobbish and manipulative aristocrat of the old school, is anxious that her son and only heir Lord Lebanon (Marius Goring) should marry his cousin Isla (Penelope Dudley-Ward) in order to continue the family line ('Before there was a history of England there was a history of the Lebanons, and it must go on. It would be wicked if the line were to be broken'). However, the young lord does not want to marry just for the sake of 'siring children', and in the event his half-hearted proposal is turned down by Isla. Several murders are then committed at the Priory in the manner of the Indian Thuggee cult (strangulation by scarf) and Isla's own life is in jeopardy. Inspector Tanner (George Merritt) investigates the crimes and traps Lord Lebanon as he attempts to murder Isla, whereupon Lebanon shoots himself dead. The explanation for the crimes is that madness runs in the male Lebanons. The film hints strongly that Lady Lebanon was aware of her son's murderous insanity but concealed it for the selfish interests of the family. The film thus reveals the aristocracy as manipulative, weak and finally insane; they have lost the moral leadership of society. It ends with a quite remarkable shot where Lady Lebanon, walking directly towards the camera, declares: 'A thousand years of being great – gone out, like a candle in the wind.' Given the time of production, it is tempting to interpret this as a statement about the social changes and reconfiguration of the class system brought about by the Second World War. Such an interpretation should perhaps not be stretched too far, however, for there was nothing in the reactions of contemporary critics to suggest that it was seen in such a way. Indeed, *The Times* opined that it was essentially an old-fashioned film, describing it as 'Wallace in a retrospective mood, attempting a Victorian melodrama in the grand manner, wildly romantic about the last of the Lebanons and the sorrows of their line; here there are no painful intimations of the modern world.'[35] The interpretation of the film reflecting social change is one which is available with hindsight but which was not necessarily evident at the time. Nevertheless, the film is unusual in that it portrays the upper classes in a negative manner in an age when most films promoted traditional social values and the importance of consensus.

*The Case of the Frightened Lady* is an example of a particular trend which can be identified in British shockers of the 1930s towards the horrific or macabre. The exploration of madness and the identification of an exotic but sinister foreign influence which lurks below and disturbs the norms of British society (the Thuggee had been a real murder cult which existed in India in the nineteenth century) were both to become important themes of the British horror film. The most famous horror films of the 1930s, of course, were those made in Hollywood by Universal Studios, though they often used British actors and directors. In Britain the production of what were termed 'horrific' films was limited to a mere handful during the decade, largely because such films were frowned upon by the British Board of Film Censors. It was the increase in the number of American horror films which caused the BBFC to introduce the 'H' category into its censorship system, first as an advisory classification in 1933 and then as a formal certificate in 1937, which prohibited exhibition to anyone under 16.[36] Although a British 'horror cinema' did not really emerge until after the Second World War, nevertheless, as Peter Hutchings observes, 'while horror films as such were discouraged, other genres of the period were regularly incorporating the macabre and the morbid into their narratives'.[37] Both *The Terror* and *The Case of the Frightened Lady* can be identified as examples of this tendency. Two other examples of the 'horrific' shocker, both of which have been largely overlooked by film historians, are *The Ghoul* (1933) and *Dark Eyes of London* (1939) which provided roles for, respectively, Boris Karloff and Bela Lugosi. The employment of the two stars most associated with the Universal horror cycle of the 1930s could be seen as an attempt by British producers to cash in on the success of the Hollywood product, though both films are just as easily located in terms of their 'Britishness' than as imitations of American horror.

*The Ghoul* had impressive production credentials: it was made by the Gaumont-British Picture Corporation during the reign of Michael Balcon and employed a number of European *émigrés* who had worked in the German cinema during the 1920s, including art director Alfred Junge (who had worked for several years at UFA before embarking upon a career in Britain) and cameraman Günther Krampf (who had shot G. W. Pabst's *Pandora's Box*). It is not surprising, therefore, that the visual style of the film, with its low-key lighting and pronounced use of shadows for artistic effect, is strongly influenced by the cinema of German Expressionism. The film also has a very interesting cast: as well as Karloff it features such well-known British character actors as Ernest Thesiger and Cedric Hardwicke, as well as an early appearance by a young Ralph Richardson. Directed by T. Hayes Hunter, *The Ghoul* is an old dark house thriller in which Karloff plays an Egyptologist who apparently rises from the dead to terrorise the relatives gathered for the reading of his will. Denis Gifford describes it as 'the only British horror film in the true Hollywood tradition',[38] and certainly it bears comparison with Universal films such as Karl Freund's *The Mummy* (1932) – from which it borrowed Karloff and the Egyptian theme – and James Whale's *The Old Dark House* (1932). The latter film, although American, was nevertheless very 'English' in its cast (it had again featured both Karloff and Thesiger), in its director (Whale was an English *émigré* working in Hollywood), and in its source (it was based on a novel by J. B. Priestley). *The Ghoul* is at least the equal of Whale's more celebrated film in terms of its fluid camera-work and even surpasses it through its strongly expressionistic style where the angles and shadows serve to create a slightly disorienting effect which heightens the moments of suspense. As in the best horror films, *The Ghoul* works principally through the suggestion of horror rather than explicit shock moments. Karloff's emergence from his tomb and a scene where he breaks through a barred window to get at the characters hiding inside the house are both filmed with lines of shadow falling at angles across the frame: the 'unreal' lighting effects contribute to the atmosphere of menace and tension. There is a strong case to argue that *The Ghoul* can be placed within a movement in the British cinema of the time which sought to differentiate itself from Hollywood films by emphasising aspects of 'European' style. When Hitchcock employed expressionist motifs in *The Lodger* (1926), the film was seen as a conscious attempt to imitate the style of German cinema; there is no reason why a film by a lesser-known signatory should not also be seen in the same context. These 'German' influences are added to elements of the English Gothic tradition (a creepy old house, hidden treasure, and a sense of the irrationality of the unleashed forces of malevolence) which together make *The Ghoul* part of the early British 'horrific' cinema. It is an interesting film which deserves to be better known than it is.[39]

*Dark Eyes of London* has been hardly less neglected within British film historiography, usually earning no more than passing reference as the first British film to be given an 'H' certificate. Its production credentials were not as impressive as those of *The Ghoul*: produced by John Argyle at the small Welwyn Studios, with a star who was already in decline, it was very much a bargain-basement production. Yet, under the slick and capable direction of Walter Summers, this adaptation of Edgar Wallace's 1924 novel emerges as a superior thriller which illustrates perfectly the 'horrific' trend within 1930s British cinema. It is less obviously expressionistic than *The Ghoul*, but it is also faster paced; it works not so much on building and sustaining an atmosphere of menace throughout as it does on a number of memorable individual scenes and shock moments. Lugosi was imported to play Dr Orloff, a disgraced surgeon who, in the guise of a kindly philanthropist, runs an institute for the blind in Greenwich, where he conspires to have his patients murdered for their insurance money by drowning them in the River Thames. The film to which it bears most resemblance is *Murders in the Rue Morgue* (1932), a Universal film which had starred Lugosi as another mad surgeon whose victims are dumped into a river, though the opening shot, where a corpse is seen floating in the Thames, also anticipates Hitchcock's *Frenzy* (1972). Much of the narrative is taken up by the investigation into the crimes by Inspector Holt of Scotland Yard (Hugh Williams), but the film differs from other mystery stories in that it contains a number of genuinely horrific moments. There is one scene in particular, where Lugosi uses an electric shock to render one of his victims deaf as well as blind, which is notably callous and shocking. The characterisation of the killer Jake (Wilfred Walter) as a hulking monstrosity who terrorises the captive heroine (Greta Gynt) also located the film within the horror genre. It was the gruesome plot elements which most attracted the attention of the critics. The trade paper *The Cinema* declared:

> This adaptation of one of Edgar Wallace's best-known thrillers has an 'H' certificate and deserves it. The macabre nature of the story – an investiga-tion into a series of murders by drowning – is emphasised by its grisly concomitants. It is to some extent located in a home for the blind, and among its highlights are the murderous assaults of a blind and hideously deformed killer, and the deliberate and cold-blooded drowning of a help-less blind deaf-mute in the sight of a bound girl.[40]

The distaste evident here is further indication of the status of the horrific shocker within British film journalism at the time. And *Dark Eyes of London* has probably been neglected in standard film historiography because, as the only British 'H' certificate film before the Second World War, it seems to be a one-off oddity; the story of the British horror film is too often thought to begin only with Hammer in the 1950s.

The horrific or horror film presented a violent disruption of the normal patterns of life through malevolent and sometimes supernatural forces which cannot be contained within the restrictive boundaries of the orthodox realist aesthetic. This is the reason why the genre has been overlooked in most accounts of 1930s British cinema. Another trend within the broad umbrella of the shocker which has also been neglected, though perhaps for different reasons, is what might be termed the great detective/master criminal narrative. If the horrific is impossible to reconcile within the terms of the realist critical discourse, the great detective/master criminal narrative is now simply unfashionable because it represents an out-dated, old-fashioned idea of 'Englishness' and national identity. Films based on the adventures of characters such as Bulldog Drummond and Sexton Blake shared common generic ground. The characterisations are situated in relation to a particular ideology of national identity in which the heroes are always English gentlemen who represent the traditional values of honesty, sportsmanship, chivalry and patriotism and who are allied unambiguously to the preservation of the existing social and political order. The villains, in contrast, are usually foreigners, are depicted as fiendish and underhand, and are equally committed to overthrowing the established order for reasons of profit or power. The popular patriotism of the genre was very much a product of the time when Britain saw itself as a leader in world affairs and as an upholder of the status quo at a time when revolutions in Europe (particularly in Soviet Russia) were bringing about a tumultuous re-organisation of the social and political order. The ideology of the thriller can therefore best be understood in a wider historical context.

The archetypal hero of this type of narrative was Bulldog Drummond, who first appeared in novels by 'Sapper' after the First World War. Drummond is a demobbed army officer who finds civilian life dull and takes up amateur detective work as a way of amusing himself; he regards it as 'sport in a land flowing with strikes and profiteers; sport such as his soul loved'.[41] Drummond's opponent is Carl Peterson, head of an international criminal syndicate whose aim is to bring about a revolution in Britain and profit from the collapse of the British economy. Drummond is now a highly unfashionable character because of his undisguised xenophobia and anti-Semitism; although he is described as a 'sportsman and a gentleman' he sometimes seems little more than a fascist bully with a polished accent. However, as Michael Denning points out, 'Drummond is an important popular construction in a period of intensified class struggle, in a land which was indeed flowing with strikes and profiteers'.[42] Drummond's adventures came to the screen in both

Hollywood and Britain during the 1930s. Ronald Colman had starred in two good Hollywood films – *Bulldog Drummond* (1929) and *Bulldog Drummond Strikes Back* (1934) – but the occasional British Drummond films are widely regarded as cheap quickies which are too parochial to have any lasting appeal. Critics have also detected in them traces of the fascist elements which have made the character so unfashionable. In the view of most commentators, *The Return of Bulldog Drummond* (1934), starring Ralph Richardson, was the closest to the original stories. Jeffrey Richards, for instance, writes: 'Ralph Richardson as Drummond came nearest of all the screen incarnations to the physical and psychological make-up of the character'.[43] It was based on the second Drummond novel, *The Black Gang*, in which Drummond leads a secret society dedicated to the assassination of Bolsheviks, though the extreme violence of the novel was substantially toned down for the film. Richardson gave way to the now-forgotten John Lodge for *Bulldog Drummond at Bay* (1937), a film which has rarely attracted the attention of any critics. Those who do comment upon it are usually entirely negative. Peter John Dyer, for example, said: 'one reel of John Lodge in polo-neck and breeches guying a country yokel, torturing an intruder and carrying on a very British line in twin-bedded badinage with a fox-furred vamp, is enough to test any addict's tolerance.'[44]

Again there are veiled hints of the thuggish and unpleasant side of the Drummond character, which as much as anything else may have caused the film's neglect, but what is interesting in hindsight is the distinct anti-pacifist position which the narrative adopts. Drummond's enemies are a group of spies from an unnamed foreign country who use a peace club as a front and conspire to steal a new radio-controlled aeroplane. Although this plot device was not in itself unusual – Hitchcock used it in his American thriller *Foreign Correspondent* (1940), where Herbert Marshall's villain poses as the leader of a peace league – its use in *Bulldog Drummond at Bay* is significant in that it was made several years before the Second World War at a time when appeasement was still a credible and popular foreign policy and when there was strong pacifist sentiment, particularly on the left. Paul Rotha's *Peace Film* (1936), for example, had called for a halt to the National Government's rearmament programme. Ideologically, *Bulldog Drummond at Bay* can therefore be located on the right – another reason why such films are unfashionable and critically neglected.

The most polished and entertaining of the British Drummond films of the 1930s was in fact not a straight thriller but a pastiche. Walter Forde's *Bulldog Jack* (1935) was a vehicle for the light entertainer Jack

Hulbert. Most critics have seen it foremost as a comedy – Dyer describes it as 'a parody of Sapper's parody of a hero'[45] – but the film has enough genuinely exciting sequences and certainly the right narrative structure to be regarded as appropriate for inclusion here. Indeed, some of the contemporary reviews singled out its thriller elements above its comedy ingredients. *Film Weekly* remarked: 'Apart from the fact that the central character is burlesqued, the plot might easily be mistaken for a genuine Bulldog Drummond adventure.'[46] Drummond (Atholl Fleming) is injured in a car crash with Jack Pennington (Hulbert), a first-class cricketer (and, therefore, unquestionably a gentleman), who agrees to impersonate the detective in order to help the heroine (Fay Wray) whose father has been kidnapped by arch-criminal Morelle (Ralph Richardson). Assisted by Drummond's silly-ass friend Algy (Claude Hulbert), Jack saves the girl and foils a plan to steal a priceless jewelled necklace from the British Museum. Along with the slapstick and puns, the film includes some nice touches of irony which are reminiscent of Hitchcock: threatened by villains in the London Underground, Hulbert is at one point framed beneath an advertising poster of a sinister deathly face and the question 'Have You Insured Your Life?' The atmospheric robbery sequence in the British Museum recalls Hitchcock's *Blackmail* (1929), while the climax aboard a speeding underground train is as exciting as a straight thriller. Richardson turned in a giddy performance as the criminal mastermind which film historian Marcia Landy, detecting a deliberate reference in the film, suggests was based on Fritz Lang's *Dr Mabuse* (1922). She writes that Richardson's villain 'is modelled on the German archcriminal, and the setting of the film recalls Lang's use of the metropolitan setting'.[47] As the art director was Alfred Junge, the film can once again be located in terms of the European influence on British cinema during the decade.

The character of Sexton Blake, a sort of poor man's Sherlock Holmes, also made the transition to the British screen during the 1930s. Blake had been devised by the Harmsworth Press and had appeared in both comic-strip and book form, his adventures being the work of a group of writers rather than one author. He was at the height of his popularity during the interwar period, due to the success of the Sexton Blake Library (which ran until 1963). George Curzon played Blake in three films: *Sexton Blake and the Bearded Doctor* (1935), *Sexton Blake and the Mademoiselle* (1935), both produced by Fox British, and finally George King's *Sexton Blake and the Hooded Terror* (1938). Although it was very much a poverty row production, the latter film is interesting in that it cast Tod Slaughter as the master criminal, a sort of Moriarty character to Blake's Holmesian detective hero. It was an unusual vehicle for Slaughter in that it was contemporary rather than historical and was not based on one of his stage successes.[48] The film exemplifies two themes which were typical of the great detective/master criminal narrative: the superiority of the gentleman-amateur hero and the role of disguise and false identity. Sexton Blake, the famous private detective, is described as 'the only man who can deal with the Black Quorum – the greatest crime organization of the century'. Blake naturally succeeds where Scotland Yard have failed, even though his assistance is continually refused by Inspector Bramley (Norman Pierce). The English amateur Blake also saves the life of the professional French secret service agent Mademoiselle Julie (Greta Gynt), thus proving both his national and his gender superiority. The other theme, disguise and false identity, is illustrated through Slaughter's role as Michael Larron, ostensibly a suave millionaire stamp collector, who is really The Snake, leader of the Black Quorum. The idea that a respectable façade could conceal a master criminal is a common one in the shocker where outward appearances are often deceptive. The film itself has all the paraphernalia and plot devices of the genre – secret codes written in invisible ink, poison darts, hidden trapdoors and a death chamber full of snakes – while the villain's Chinese henchmen recall another master criminal of the shockers, Sax Rohmer's Fu Manchu.[49]

Towards the end of the 1930s a trend can be discerned towards another variation of the film shocker, the spy or espionage narrative. This type of film was a close relation to the great detective/master criminal narrative, particularly in the way in which the same national ideologies were foregrounded. The main differences were that secret spy rings replaced flamboyant criminal masterminds as the enemies of England and the villains were acting not for personal gain but rather through political and ideological commitment. As a literary genre, the spy thriller had emerged at the turn of the century when increasing tension in international relations had provided the context for writers such as William Le Queux and Erskine Childers to fashion stories which drew upon invasion scares and paranoia. As a film genre the spy narrative flourished again during the late 1930s when another international crisis was looming on the horizon. Whereas relatively few spy films had been made in Britain during the first half of the decade, their numbers increased noticeably during the second half. They drew upon the fears engendered by the rise of aggressive dictatorships in Europe, rearmament, and growing uncertainty over the policy of appeasement. During the course of 1939 a plethora of spy films were made in Britain, including *The Four Just Men*, *Traitor Spy*, *An Englishman's Home*, *Spies of the Air*, *Q Planes* and *The Spy in Black*. In December 1939 Mass-Observation remarked upon the proliferation of both British and American films with a spy theme. A report into film trends said:

> All these films were ready or released just before the outbreak of war. To a psychologist this simple fact would give a good picture of the mentality of the sort of people producing films at that time and of the general atmosphere of inferiority which the American [*sic*] democracies were unconsciously feeling towards aggressive Germany. This inferiority so accentuated by Munich was released by the fact of war and we at last showed ourselves able and ready to stand up to this sinister enemy with his humanity-eliminating Gestapo.[50]

It was Nazi Germany in particular which was identified as the 'enemy' in the spy films produced prior to the outbreak of war. Although the British Board of Film Censors forbade the naming of the country, the films hinted strongly through the Teutonic accents of their villains and the iconography of Gestapo-style leather overcoats and SS-style military uniforms. Given that most films in this cycle of spy films were made in the period between the Munich Agreement of September 1938 and the outbreak of war a year later, a time when it was being realised that Germany's aggression could not be contained by diplomacy, it is tempting to interpret them as a critique of appeasement. For example, in *Q Planes*, directed by the American Tim Whelan, a British secret service agent Major Hammond (Ralph Richardson) is investigating the disappearance of several models of a new secret aeroplane, the E-97. Although he cannot prove it, Hammond suspects that the cause of the disappearance is sabotage rather than an accident. Hammond is always seen wearing a bowler hat or a trilby and carrying a rolled-up umbrella. Marcia Landy suggests that his umbrella 'seems to be a satiric allusion to Chamberlain. His dogmatic insistence on being right constitutes a further parallel'.[51] However, on closer investigation this interpretation proves to be rather unsatisfactory in that Hammond is the only member of British officialdom who suspects sabotage. Thus, rather than being blind to the foreign threat, he is one of the few actually to realise it. The umbrella is less an allusion to Neville Chamberlain than it is a signifier of Hammond's Britishness. It transpires that the missing aeroplanes have been intercepted by a radio-beam mounted in a salvage ship which is manned by agents of a 'foreign power'. Hammond teams up with a test pilot (Laurence Olivier) to uncover the enemy conspiracy and capture the spy ship.[52]

The most interesting of the eve-of-war spy films in terms of constructing an ideology of national identity was Ealing's film of *The Four Just Men*, directed by Walter Forde. This was based on Edgar Wallace's first novel, written in 1905, which had already been filmed as a silent picture by the Stoll Film Company in 1921. A comparison of the novel and the 1939 film shows that in the transfer from page to screen, and in the updating of the story, a significant realignment of the story's ideological position has occurred. In the novel the Four Just Men are a secret society comprising men from various European countries – Manfred, Gonzalez, Poiccart and Thery – who act as vigilantes in dealing out rough justice to people who have escaped from or are beyond the normal reaches of the law. When the British Foreign Secretary, Sir Philip Ramon, introduces an 'Aliens Political Offences Bill' which will make it more difficult for foreign nationals to find political asylum in Britain, the Four Just Men undertake to assassinate him unless the measure is withdrawn. Ramon is characterised as stubborn but honest and a man of integrity who firmly believes that the measure is necessary to protect Britain from an influx of undesirables. He insists on going ahead with the bill and is subsequently killed when his telephone is electrocuted by the Four Just Men. The novel's ideological position is problematic, as David Glover points out: 'there are no outright heroes and villains here, for much of the novel's tension and suspense is due to the implacable opposition between two irreconcilable and equally sincerely held positions'.[53] In the later novels, such as *The Council of Justice* and *The Law of the Four Just Men*, the Just Men become less ambiguous crime-fighters who fight against foreign anarchists and international criminals, sometimes even on the side of the British police. There was seen to be something 'unEnglish' about secret societies. Jeffrey Richards remarks, albeit perhaps with his tongue slightly in his cheek, that they were 'really frightfully bad form and thankfully appeared rarely in the cinema of Empire'.[54] Ealing's 1939 film gets around the problem in an ingenious way: instead of the cosmopolitan group of the novel the Four Just Men are Anglici.ed so that they now comprise three Englishmen – Humphrey Mansfield (Hugh Sinclair), Brodie (Griffith Jones) and Terry (Frank Lawton) – and one Frenchman, Poiccard (Francis L. Sullivan). It is made abundantly clear that they are devoted to protecting Britain against foreign threats. The patriotism and national ideology of the film is nowhere better illustrated than in Brodie's remark to his girlfriend (Anna Lee) that he is 'in love with all the roads and rivers, the fields and woods and hills that make up this funny old island'. Thus the traditional pastoral image of England as a quiet and pleasant land is put forward as the one which the Just Men seek to protect. Ealing's press release emphasised that 'the story has been brought up to date – so much so that the first shot of the film shows a prisoner's escape (contrived by the "Four Just Men") from a political prison in middle Europe'.[55] The escapee, Terry, has unearthed details of a plot by an unnamed continental power to block the Suez Canal and thus cut off the movement of British troops and supplies to India prior to an attack on the Empire. The plot would lead to 'world domination in one man's hands', which at the time of production was clearly a reference to Hitler's territorial ambitions. It transpires that the enemy are being fed secret information by a Member of Parliament, Sir Hamar Ryman (Alan Napier), a pacifist and an appeaser. Charles Barr remarks that 'the film enforces, irresistibly, the inference that appeasement *is* treachery'.[56] Significantly, it transpires that Ryman is British only by naturalisation. Unlike the novel, where the Just Men's target is an honourable if stubborn man, in the film he is clearly marked as a traitor which thus legitimises his assassination. Ryman is electrocuted in his bath, whereupon Mansfield, an actor, then disguises himself as Ryman and delivers a stirring speech in the House of Commons urging Britain to rearm against the threat of foreign dictators. The film ends with shots of defence preparations being made by the Army, Royal Navy and Royal Air Force. The ideological positioning of the film in the context of the post-Munich era is clear: appeasement has been discredited and a firm stand has to be taken against foreign aggressors. These themes were evident to critics at the time: the American trade paper *Motion Picture Herald* remarked that the film 'has hit Britain's current mood of defensive-defiance in one crack' and exemplified 'Britain's self-appointed characterization of defier of Dictators'.[57] Yet even without its political context the film is a first-rate example of the shocker. It is fast-paced, exciting and contains a number of effective cinematic moments: for example, the camera's semi-circular movement around Terry in a telephone box at Victoria Station, just before he is poisoned by an enemy agent, is a technique of creating suspense which Hitchcock used on numerous occasions. A sequel was planned, and Ealing announced that Forde would direct *The Return of the Four Just Men* in 1940. Although this did not arise, the original film was re-released in 1944 with a new epilogue linking the Just Men to all those keeping alive 'the light of Liberty' alongside 'the illimitable forces of the Americans'.[58]

To conclude, where can the celluloid shockers of the 1930s be located in relation to the wider context of a British national cinema and film culture? There are two ways in which the shocker can be placed within the history of the British cinema, one which identifies it as a genuinely British alternative to the dominant Hollywood cinema of the 1930s, and another which sees it in a longer perspective as part of a particular trend or undercurrent within British film-making tending towards the sensational rather than the realist aesthetic which has been so important to orthodox criticism and standard historiography. During the 1930s the shocker was a uniquely British film genre, drawing upon an indigenous cultural tradition, that had no direct equivalent in Hollywood. It was a form of product differentiation from American genres such as the western, the gangster film and the big-budget musical which the Hollywood studios produced in such large numbers during the 1930s. Even such crime films as Hollywood produced were not the same, for they tended towards the classic detective story (represented by the long-running Charlie Chan series and the *Thin Man* films) rather than the thick-ear thriller. As Peter John Dyer remarked: 'there was a school of British thrillers as effective as Hollywood's Chans and Motos and as national as Duvivier's *Tête d'un Homme*'.[59] For all the critical disrepute in which it was held, the shocker was nevertheless as British as warm beer and fish-and-chips, and perhaps for that reason (with a few remarkable exceptions) the genre did not go down as well abroad. Moreover, with its low-brow origins and overt sensationalism, the shocker can be placed within that largely unmapped area which Julian Petley has described as the 'repressed side of British cinema, a dark, disdained thread weaving the length and breadth of that cinema, crossing authorial and generic boundaries, sometimes almost entirely invisible, sometimes erupting explosively, always received critically with fear and disapproval'.[60]

This trend is usually characterised in terms of the Gainsborough costume melodramas, the Hammer horror films, and the work of maverick directors such as Michael Powell and the American *émigré* Joseph Losey. It is a trend in which the shocker – a genre which made no pretence of realism and which routinely foregrounded the sensational and the extraordinary – can also be located. For instance, a film such as George King's *The Case of the Frightened Lady*, with its Gothic country house, imperilled heroine and Thuggee murders, has elements in common with both the Gainsborough and the Hammer cycles. The shocker can therefore be seen as part of a tradition of film-making which has long been marginalised in writing the history of the British cinema, but which is an important part of that history none the less.

5. Jack Buchanan and Anna Neagle in *Goodnight, Vienna*

CHAPTER 5

# Calling All Stars: Musical Films in a Musical Decade

*Stephen Guy*

I N the 1930s the British film industry produced a substantial number of musical films which were a popular element of the cinema-going habit of those years. Out of a total of just over 1,500 full-length feature films made in that decade, at least 220 can be described as musical films. They range from the film with the odd song-and-dance routine to the full-blown 'musical' in which music is at the heart of the film. They include variety and revue shows, musical comedies and romances, operettas, and films about dance bands and orchestras. Some are adaptations of staged shows and radio productions, others screen originals. They feature a firmament of popular entertainers: some are well known like Jessie Matthews, famous for her glitzy 'all singing, all dancing' Hollywood-style musicals; or Gracie Fields and George Formby, renowned for their comedies with music. Other stars are less well known today, but in their day were household names: all-round entertainers Jack Hulbert, Cicely Courtneidge and Jack Buchanan are examples. Famous classical singers are also to be found starring in the films, such as Richard Tauber and Gitta Alpar, as were celebrity dance band leaders like Jack Payne and Henry Hall. And behind the screen was an array of contemporary musical and writing talent, including Noel Gay, Vivian Ellis, L. Arthur Rose and Douglas Furber. Common to most of them was the linkage of musical entertainment to romance, comedy and laughter. British musical films of the 1930s are seldom melodramatic or brooding, sad or tearful, but happy and optimistic, relentlessly striving in their self-appointed task of making audiences Cheer Up![1]

Musical films, led by Hollywood productions, burst on to cinema screens with the arrival of sound at the end of the 1920s. The British film industry, unlike Hollywood, did not exploit the novelty of sound by disproportionately concentrating on musical films; indeed, Britain's first 'all talking' film was a thriller, Alfred Hitchcock's *Blackmail* (1929). Musical films formed a fairly constant proportion of total film output over the decade, averaging out at one in every six or seven films made. In terms of production costs, values and target markets, they were typical of the range of film productions as a whole, covering the spectrum of cheap quota quickies, medium-priced films designed for domestic consumption, and expensive prestige productions aimed at the world market. Most studios had a go at making them, as did most film-makers.

Sound technology had dramatic consequences for the cinema industry, not least of which was the necessity to rethink film language. With its dependence on image alone to tell a story, the silent film was primarily a visual art, but sound technology rudely changed the rules by introducing the new dramatic potential of synchronised dialogue, sound effects and music. Film actors who had become adept at communication through physical expression had to learn to utilise their voices and deal with dialogue. Many could not make the transition and fell by the wayside. But if sound killed off some careers, it also opened up opportunities for others. Film-makers, struggling to feed the audience's appetite for 'talking' pictures, were only too keen to recruit a veritable army of hitherto untapped stage talent, and as a result a new generation of theatrical performers entered the film business. It was an exciting, if uncertain, time for the film industry: not only had sound opened up new opportunities, but the Cinematograph Films Act of 1927 had given a boost to film production and there was a rapid expansion in the volume, if not necessarily the quality, of films made.

Rather than develop the 'talkie' in a new cinematic direction, however, British film-makers were largely content to exploit an existing theatrical heritage, and this was particularly true of the musical film. Film studios relied heavily on the theatre for inspiration, freely adopting its codes and conventions, form and style, employing its stars, writers and composers, and, frequently, borrowing acts and plays that had already established themselves on stage. And as so often in British cinema history, film-makers were also indebted to Hollywood, whose ideas and practices they all too easily followed.

Although British musical films were a landmark on the cinematic landscape of the 1930s, they have received scant attention from film historians.[2] A reason for this omission is that so many musical films are beyond the pale of aesthetic scrutiny, and consequently film writers have dismissed them. However, if the intention is to understand film as part of the popular culture of the period, these films need to be accounted for. The way to achieve this is not to see them from the limited perspective of aesthetics, but to assess them alongside the entertainment culture from which they derived and to which they remained inextricably tied. The first section of this essay evaluates films in terms of their theatrical context, selecting some typical examples for extended discussion. The second section contextualises the musical films within the broader musical culture, especially as embodied in the mass entertainment industry which included radio, gramophone recording and sheet music sales. The overall line of argument to be pursued is that the 1930s was a particularly musically inclined decade and that the musical film was a product of that prevailing climate.

## The theatrical context

Three film types can be classified on the basis of their musical-theatrical origins: music hall, European operetta and the imprecisely termed English musical comedy or musical revue. (While these theatrical strands are reasonably distinct, it should be noted that there was considerable overlap and cross-flow of influences and artists.) Without seeing all the films, it is difficult to quantify how, and to what extent, these theatrical traditions were adopted, especially as many films are an amalgam of theatrical references. Nevertheless, a number of films can be clearly related to a stage type, whether identified through film reviews or by viewing, and in the interests of clarity these will be the focus of attention here.

Music hall, which flourished in the latter part of the nineteenth century, had a lineage going back to the wandering jesters and singers of the seventeenth century. A working-class entertainment, music hall comprised a series of 'turns' or acts of a musical character. In the Victorian years it had a reputation for vulgarity, but by the 1930s music hall had transmuted into the more respectable form known as 'variety'. While losing its raw edge, it still retained its basic format as an entertainment constructed around self-contained acts.

As Andy Medhurst has argued, adapting variety for the screen presented a problem for film-makers: how could an entertainment based on a series of ready-made acts be transferred to a medium conventionally structured around the telling of a story?[3] The simplest solution for studios was to film the acts and invent a covering story to explain the linkage, however flimsy. These 'backstage' storylines frequently revolve round broadcasting stations, recording studios and stage shows, for the perfectly sensible reason that they offer a credible pretext for the assemblage of artists. It was a formula tried and tested by Hollywood and, according to Medhurst, British studios slavishly imitated it, assuming that the musical was a purely American genre and therefore imitation was the 'way to success'.[4] (The subject of Hollywood's effect on the British musical will be returned to later.)

There are numerous examples of the flimsily plotted 'revue' film: one of the earliest *Elstree Calling* (directed by Adrian Brunel, 1930) is little more than the presentation of a number of musical, dance and comedy performances, some from musical comedy.[5] They are introduced by a compere, Tommy Handley, and there is a slim plot revolving round an attempt to catch them on television. Another example, *Calling All Stars* (directed by Redd Davis, 1937), has more plot, being set in a gramophone recording company, and the stars are present to record their acts. In case watching them perform in the recording studio became too tedious, the scriptwriters introduced a twist: a porter at the studio drops the entire pile of newly pressed records, smashing the lot, with the predictable result they have to be recorded all over again. Actually, it's huge fun because by then the artists have dispersed over the globe, and the comic duo Flotsam and Jetsam, who represent the studio, take a police car and spend the rest of the film hunting down the diaspora of stars over the world, while intermittently singing the title song 'Calling All Stars'.

Judged as cinema, these films are crude, amounting to no more than badly filmed acts, even when the action occurs beyond the stage in the 'outside' world. The appeal of these films, though, lay in the individual performances, which also offer an insight into the kind of music-hall and variety acts seen by contemporary audiences. Furthermore, they throw up fascinatingly perverse absurdities and bizarre bedfellows when wildly different sketches are knitted together in rapid succession. *Calling All Stars* is a good example, cramming into its 79 minutes an astonishingly large and eclectic mixture of established entertainers and unrelated locations. The stars include musical-hall acts such as Flotsam and Jetsam, Billy Bennett and comic duo Ethel Revnell and Gracie West, who are juxtaposed with accomplished American singers such as Elisabeth Welch and singer-comedian Evelyn Dall. Tap dancers, strange acrobats and grotesques appear alongside musicians like Larry Adler and well-known orchestras such as that of Ambrose. The orchestras do popular numbers and perform with guest singers and some bizarre acts, such as the peculiar Gimble with his Cymbal. Once out of the Supertone Gramophone Company's recording studios, different background settings whizz by with alarming speed, including an army kitchen, a London street, the Savoy Hotel, a Hungarian nightclub, and the Cotton Club in Harlem.

Rather than giving equal status to a 'parade of stars', another strategy of variety adaptation was to focus on one or two stars or acts. This was the format, for example, of the 'Jack and Jim' musical comedies starring Arthur Riscoe and Naunton Wayne, and most famously the films of Gracie Fields. By the start of the 1930s Fields was a celebrated music-hall star and a prime target for studios seeking to exploit established names. Such was her fame and talent that from her first picture onwards, *Sally in Our Alley* (directed by Maurice Elvey, 1931), studios built films around her. Her films are basically a series of linked sketches, but they make considerable gestures towards cinematic conventions: in *Sing As We Go* (directed by Basil Dean, 1934) for instance, Gracie's singing and joking are woven into a relatively complicated narrative, and there are occasional cinematic flourishes, such as imaginative camerawork, the use of montage and the speeding up of the film in the chase sequence at Blackpool.[6]

The weaving together of variety acts into a continuous revue was not only found in film, but also on the stage. For film-makers, such shows offered variety entertainment in a ready-to-use format. Easily the best example of this is *Okay for Sound* (directed by Marcel Varnel, 1937), which is a 'lock, stock and barrel adaptation'[7] of the Crazy Gang's Palladium success of the same name. The highly successful Crazy Gang stage shows linked the talents of a core of music-hall performers into a single, narrativised, show. In *Okay for Sound*, which features Nervo and Knox, Flanagan and Allen, and Naughton and Gold, the gags and turns are knotted together into a lunatic plot about a bankrupt film magnate who unwittingly allows his studio to be infiltrated by out-of-work musicians.

*Okay for Sound* is a funny, nicely-made film aimed at the domestic market; but at the cheap, quota quickie end of the revue adaptations there are, judging by contemporary accounts, some appalling films. For example, *Song in Soho* (directed by A. Hopwood, 1936), a filmed version of the Windmill Theatre 'Revudeville', was tersely dismissed by the *Monthly Film Bulletin*: 'the performances are poor, some of the turns vulgar, the photography bad and the film as a whole dreary.'[8]

Perhaps a third of musical films in the 1930s can be attributed to the variety and music-hall heritage, with about 25 to 30 in the 'parade of stars' format. It is tempting to assume that this kind of stagey film was a convenient and cheap stop-gap in the early 1930s when studios were struggling to find enough sound material, but they are quite evenly distributed over the whole decade. While there was undoubtedly a percentage of tiresome, unpopular quota quickies, such as the 'Revu-devilles', the continual production of this type of variety film suggests they remained crowd-pullers throughout the entire decade, a point borne out by numerous positive reviews. *Elstree Calling* is an example of an early hit, as the *Bioscope*'s glowing review indicates: 'the whole revue is a very successful attempt to present together so varied and brilliant a collection of popular artists.'[9]

By the mid-1930s, the novelty had not worn off: *Kinematograph Weekly*, for instance, summed up the appeal of *Stars on Parade* (directed by Oswald Mitchell, 1935), as 'big variety cast, names that lend to exploitation, and popularity of musicals'.[10] Likewise, another trade assessment rated *Calling All Stars* 'very good' for 'entertainment value', with the endorsement that 'the like has done well before and there is not the slightest reason why this should not follow suit and prove a very sound general book-ing'.[11] Even right at the end of the decade there was still enthusiasm for these films, as the *Monthly Film Bulletin*'s assessment of *Music Hall Parade* (directed by Oswald Mitchell, 1939) shows: 'A number of first class Variety acts introduced by means of a slender story ... the direction of the film is so well handled that all the varied elements blend into a smooth continuity which results in excellent entertainment.'[12] The reason for the ongoing popularity of variety is clear: as intimated by these reviews, audiences clamoured to see their favourite variety performers and acts on screen, the vast majority of whom had made their names on stage before transferring to film.

Less numerous than the variety-sourced films were the musical films springing from the Viennese operatic tradition of composers such as Johann Strauss and Franz Lehar. About half were originally written for the screen, a handful based on the classics, and the rest developed from novels, plays and the odd radio production. It was not uncommon for film-makers to fuse music from different operettas with contemporary and classical compositions in the same film. Most of the films are not true operetta – the songs are interludes to the story rather than being intrinsic to the narrative – but they adopt the style, historical settings and values of the tradition.

For film-makers, the Viennese style had the ingredients for the kind of 'escapist' musical entertainment audiences seemed to want in the 1930s. Faced with films with evocative titles like *Princess Charming* (directed by Maurice Elvey, 1934) and *Two Hearts in Waltztime* (directed by Carmine Gallone, 1934), and described by such phrases as 'Ruritanian

musical comedy' and 'Viennese romance', audiences clearly knew what
to expect. The films conjured up a historical world of magical kingdoms
furnished with castles and sophisticated cafés, and inhabited by waltzing,
singing, champagne-drinking aristocrats for whom the quest for true
love over-rode questions of class and matters of state. Audience familiarity with the formula is evidenced by the *Monthly Film Bulletin*'s wearied
review of *The Lilac Domino* (directed by Fred Zelnick, 1937), a film based
on a well-known operetta about a romance between a poor Hungarian
Hussar and a baron's daughter. The film has all the 'usual boy-meets-
girl complications, with the usual happy ending. This is in every detail
a rubber-stamp film … The artificial singing and dancing sequences, the
"gay Hungarian" atmosphere, the interspersed comedy elements – all
are exactly according to the book.'[13]

Around thirty films were made in the Viennese style, with production
peaking in the mid-1930s and virtually disappearing by 1938. At the
start of the decade, the style was seen as a good proposition for Anglo-
German productions, and as a suitable subject for the European market.
Jeffrey Richards also observes that 'the constant stream of frothy
operettas set in Old Vienna [and] Old Heidelberg' was the hallmark of
German *émigré* film-makers settled in Britain.[14] Aside from theoretically
appealing to continentals, Viennese-style films were also good bets for
the domestic market and there were some notable hits, such as *Blossom
Time* (directed by Paul Stein, 1934) and *Goodnight, Vienna* (directed by
Herbert Wilcox, 1932). A range of film-makers and studios had a go at
making them, including Alfred Hitchcock with *Waltzes from Vienna* (1934),
and the commercially shrewd Herbert Wilcox who made four (*The Blue
Danube*, 1931; *Goodnight, Vienna*; *Bitter Sweet*, 1933; *The Queen's Affair*, 1934).
*The Blue Danube*, Wilcox's first foray into the musical film, was not a
box-office success, although Rachael Low does describe it as 'an interesting attempt to get away from the ceaseless talking of theatrical films and
make music the centre of interest'.[15] The film was originally scripted (or
'concocted' as Low says) by Wilcox and a colleague, but for his next
attempt, *Goodnight, Vienna*, he built on existing material, a radio play
with music by George Posford and Eric Maschwitz. *Goodnight, Vienna*
was one of the most successful films arising from the operetta tradition.

Set in the summer of 1914 in Vienna, the story begins with the
burgeoning romance between a wealthy and elegant army officer,
Captain Max Schlettoff (Jack Buchanan), and a poor but beautiful flower
girl, Viki (Anna Neagle), who is also an outstanding singer. Schlettoff's
father, an army general and intimate of the Emperor, is opposed to the
romance and expects his son to marry Countess Helga. Putting love

before parental wishes, Schlettoff decides to elope with Viki, but before they can escape they are separated by the outbreak of war. A lost message, and subterfuge by the general, results in Viki spending the war years under the impression that Schlettoff has deserted her for the Countess. When peace comes, Schlettoff and others from his regiment are thrown into poverty, and he is forced to earn his living as a shop assistant. By contrast, Viki emerges from the war rich and famous as a singer. They meet by chance, but Viki, still believing that Schlettoff has spurned her, wants nothing to do with him. Schlettoff, unaware of the reason for Viki's animosity, is confused by her hostility, but pursues her anyway. By the end, the misunderstanding is cleared up and they are reunited in love.

The film contains the classic ingredients of Viennese operetta. Located in a swirling upper-class world of military officers, countesses and emperors, magnificent balls and musical gaiety, romance is central to the lives of the protagonists and the search for true love an all-encompassing ambition transcending class boundaries, political considerations, and the sensibilities of parents. Another symbol of the Viennese tradition, mistaken paternity or a character not being what he appears to be, is a motif present here: on the surface Viki may only be a flower-seller but underneath she is a great singer; similarly, when Schlettoff is reduced to penury and lowly shop work, the audience knows that really he is an aristocrat. The formula, though, has been given an interesting contemporary twist in this film with a departure into realism: wartime images of buxom barmaids cavorting with drunken soldiers in bier-kellers, and half-starved veterans wandering and begging in the streets in the war's aftermath sit oddly with the fairytale world of waltzes and champagne. The realism, though, is merely an interlude in a fairytale; the story comes full circle and ends where it started in a magical café with the star-crossed lovers serenading each other with 'Goodnight, Vienna'.

*Goodnight, Vienna* is a solidly crafted film, and has some good melodies, especially the title song which became a big hit, but it suffers from that flat, stilted quality so common to Wilcox's films (and many British films in general). It was a problem not helped by some exaggerated acting more suited to a silent film. For all its weaknesses, though, it was a 'huge box-office success',[16] and propelled Anna Neagle on to her highly successful screen career under the guidance of husband-to-be Wilcox.

According to Rick Altman, the attraction of Viennese operetta had always been its 'willingness to deal openly with society's favourite topic – sex, adultery, infidelity, innuendo, double-entendre'.[17] Audiences

certainly responded to the frivolous, romantic atmosphere at the heart
of the majority of these films as, significantly, the few that deviated
from this convention into melodramatic mode seemed more likely to
fare badly at the box-office, *Pagliacci* (directed by Karl Grune, 1936) and
*Bitter Sweet* being examples. The latter film, a weak adaptation by Wilcox
of Noël Coward's worldwide stage hit, is really neither better nor worse
than Wilcox's highly successful *Goodnight, Vienna*, and so its lack of
commercial headway suggests that audiences were put off by the tragedy
of its tale of elopement and death. As Wilcox ruefully posited, the story
was perhaps 'rather too sad for a film'.[18]

A key attraction for audiences was also the presence of stars, and the
success of *Goodnight, Vienna* was underpinned by Jack Buchanan. As *Film
Pictorial* made quite clear in its review: 'Jack Buchanan and music; more
Jack Buchanan and romance – and more Jack Buchanan, in a setting
which is as like Vienna as we who never have been there probably
conceive it. Maybe you've guessed it's Jack Buchanan's picture?'[19]

Glasgow-born Buchanan, a self-taught comedy actor, singer and
dancer, achieved fame on the smarter, more sophisticated end of the
London musical stage. Renowned on both sides of the Atlantic for his
urbanity and immaculate dressing ('"Fix me a Buchanan" says the really
dress-conscious dude in the States'),[20] he was also tantalisingly reclusive,
which led Fay Wray to label him 'a male Garbo'![21] By the early 1930s
he was at the height of his fame; apart from a string of stage successes
in London and New York he had appeared in silent and talking films,
the most important being Ernst Lubitsch's *Monte Carlo* (1930), co-starring
Jeanette MacDonald. Buchanan was acquired by Wilcox in 1931, and
went on to make a number of films for Wilcox after *Goodnight, Vienna*.
Buchanan remained a top-rank box-office attraction till the end of the
1930s, when his star began to fade.

While Viennese-style films could be vehicles for artists from musical
revue, they were often designed as showcases for popular classical
singers, many imported from central Europe, such as the Hungarian
operatic soprano Gitta Alpar, Austrian tenor Richard Tauber and Polish
tenor Jan Kiepura. This trio was notably popular with cinema audiences,
all big enough draws for inclusion in the *Motion Picture Herald*'s 1936
gallery of top-selling British and American players. Rachael Low describes how Tauber was British International Pictures' 'biggest celebrity'
and how *Blossom Time* 'was carried by its distinguished star'.[22] The fan
papers offer an insight into the kind of mass following these classical
singers generated: their pin-up photographs were offered for sale, and
they were regularly the subject of star profiles and projections. In 1933,

for instance, *Film Weekly* hailed Kiepura, star of *Tell Me Tonight* (directed by Anatole Litvak, 1932), 'the supreme singing star of the moment. He has thousands of admirers, all waiting for his next film'.[23]

Like music hall, the ancestry of the English musical comedy tradition can be traced back to the seventeenth century when plays were first set to music, but more specific landmarks in its lineage can be found in the early eighteenth century with John Gay's *The Beggar's Opera*, and later in the works of Gilbert and Sullivan, and European operetta. Another influence, according to one account, was music-hall burlesque which, via the refinement of the Gaiety Theatre in the 1860s, gave 'birth to the English musical comedy'.[24] Exactly what was meant by musical comedy/revue was debatable, and the productions that came under its umbrella ranged from the sophisticated works of Noël Coward such as *Private Lives* to low-brow musicals like *Me and My Girl*. As sanctioned by usage, it described a musical and comedy tradition distinct from variety; whereas variety was based around a programme of acts, musical comedy was a conventional theatrical production based on the work of a composer and playwright. There were also overtones of class snobbery too, with musical revue having middle-class pretensions over the working-class culture of the music hall.

Film-makers drew energetically on the English musical comedy tradition, and freely exploited the pre-existing fame of its leading players. Jack Buchanan has already been mentioned, but the list of top-billers includes artists such as Jessie Matthews, Jack Hulbert and Cicely Courtneidge. Anna Neagle was also from this background, but unlike the others was one of the tiny handful of British cinema stars actually created by cinema itself rather than coming from theatre. There was a string of immensely popular films indebted to musical revue; most famous are the films of Jessie Matthews, such as the excellent *It's Love Again* (directed by Victor Saville, 1936). Less well known are hits emanating from husband-and-wife Hulbert and Courtneidge, who made a series of films (not always together) on the back of their theatrical fame, including the huge critical and commercial hit *Jack's the Boy* (directed by Walter Forde, 1932).

Many of the films that emerged from musical comedy have a pervading theatrical atmosphere. The predisposition towards theatre is most literally indicated by the willingness of studios to rely on stage productions for material, and to film them as faithful reproductions. Two better-known examples of this tendency are the stagey adaptations of the long-running musical hit, *Chu Chin Chow* (directed by Walter Forde, 1934), and Gilbert and Sullivan's *The Mikado* (directed by Victor

Schertzinger, 1938), which is really a set-piece performance from the D'Oyly Carte Company. Less well known is *The Lambeth Walk* (directed by Albert de Courville, 1939), the retitled film version of the 1930s smash-hit show *Me and My Girl*.[25]

*Me and My Girl*, written by prolific authors L. Arthur Rose and Douglas Furber with music by Noel Gay, was produced by Lupino Lane, who was also its star. Lane, a popular entertainer and member of the extraordinary Lupino showbusiness family, was the driving force behind the show. After an uncertain start *Me and My Girl* became a phenomenal success running continuously from December 1937 until the war interrupted it in March 1940. The King and Queen made a well-publicised 'surprise visit' in May 1939, and went on to see it twice more; it was the first comedy musical to be televised; and in the autumn of 1939 it was taken to France to entertain the troops.

*Play Pictorial* explained the appeal of the show: 'This bright and breezy musical show provides one of the finest tonics to be found anywhere in town. Packed with funny lines and situations with plenty of catchy tunes and lively dances, it arouses more laughter to the minute than any piece of its kind for years last.'[26] Even high-brow newspapers were obliged to acknowledge it was fun, the *Sunday Times*, for one, conceding that 'only a very superior person indeed could survey this bold spectacle without thawing into a smile'.[27] By common consent, the two magical ingredients were Lupino Lane's sparkling performance, and the dance numbers, notably 'The Lambeth Walk'. A boisterous dance, with its foot stamping and climactic chorus of 'Oi!', it became a firm favourite. As one columnist wrote, it 'destroyed the tyranny of the foxtrot or a waltz which for twenty years made the ballroom an unsociable place'.[28]

It was inevitable that such a legend would end up on celluloid. Called *The Lambeth Walk* to exploit the dance's fame, the film retained Lupino Lane and his brother Wallace, but recast the other roles with well-known and popular actors. Unfortunately, little information is available about the process of adaptation; Lane's biographer, James Dillon White, for instance, refers to it only in passing, not even deigning to mention its title. Dillon does record that the film was made in tandem with the show, and describes how for 'several weeks Lupino Lane had to sleep at Denham, film from 7am to noon, and motor up to London for the two stage performances'.[29] (Such a gruelling schedule was not uncommon for actors trying to fulfil stage and film obligations, prompting one theatre historian to complain that the exhaustion of actors 'resulted in much dull and listless acting on stage'.)[30] If contemporary accounts are anything to go by, *The Lambeth Walk* followed closely in the footsteps of the original play. The fan paper *Film Pictorial*, for example, complained it used 'the old and worn-out technique of transferring the stage show almost intact to the screen'.[31] There were some alterations, such as the insertion of a street scene at the beginning, and the reduction of the number of songs to two, the keynote songs 'Me and My Girl' and 'The Lambeth Walk'.

Revealing one of musical comedy's ancestral roots, it is in the form of a classic fairytale. Bill Snibson (Lupino Lane), a cheery Cockney and bookie's runner from working-class Lambeth, learns he is really a lord, heir to an estate, and a member of an eccentric aristocratic family. But Bill can only take up his inheritance if he is groomed into the manners and bearing of the nobility. Initially Bill is dazed by the enormity of it all ('but you're all nobs', exclaims Bill, 'I don't fit in'), and wants to return to his native Lambeth. However, his steely aunt, the Duchess (Norah Howard), is determined he should stay and learn how to be a duke, ingenuously invoking a sense of *noblesse oblige* by arguing it is his duty. While the toffs tolerate Bill, they cannot stomach his girlfriend Sally (Sally Gray), who arrives at Barford Hall with all the rawness, dropped aitches and gutter habits of a Lambeth resident. As the Barfords plot her departure, Bill, in best fairytale convention, puts romance first and refuses to stay without her. Stalemate ensues until the situation is resolved by affable Sir John (Seymour Hicks) who, unbeknown to anybody else, whisks Sally off for a Professor Higgins-like reconstruction of accent and behaviour (which confusingly seems to take place in twenty-four hours compared with the six months in the stage version). When she reappears it is as an elegant, posh-speaking lady-to-be. Having acquired the guise of the upper classes, the gentry are content with them, and allow the marriage and Bill's inheritance of the dukedom.

The film/play was intended as an affectionate send-up of the aristocracy and sentimentalising of the Cockney, the well-worn tale providing a hanger for a simplistic comedy of class manners. The jokes are generated by juxtaposing the highly stereotyped lifestyles of the working and ruling classes. On one side are the cheeky, streetwise Cockneys (the Cockney being generic shorthand for working-class Londoners, as Lambeth was never the home of Cockneys), and on the other the toffs – wealthy, stuffy, eccentric, plummy-voiced and firmly entrenched in dusty tradition and antiquity. The laughs are predictable and one-sided, invariably gained at the expense of the gentry; Bill is shocked to learn, for instance, that the toffs have servants to help them bathe ('and no peeping', Bill orders his new valet as he jealously shuts him out of the bathroom), and he faints in disbelief at the sheer scale of the inheritance. Bill is the hero, the little man who outwits his social superiors, and humanises them in the process. The film's sentiment is embodied in the lyrics of 'The Lambeth Walk': as the first verse illustrates, the Cockneys are proud of their working-class community in defiant opposition to the gentry:

> Lambeth you've never seen.
> The skies ain't blue,
> The grass ain't green.
> It hasn't got the Mayfair touch
> But that don't matter very much.
> We play the Lambeth way.
> Not like you but a bit more gay,
> And when we have a bit of fun, oh, boy ...

It is quite an enjoyable film; there are some neatly integrated musical effects, the orchestration is good, and the singing and dancing brisk and enjoyable. The editing is quite sharp and the film moves along at a reasonable pace complementing to some extent Lane's quickfire one-liners and acrobatic agility. As with the stage version, Lane is the star of the film, and without him the film would falter. Lane's Cockney, with his pencil moustache, bowler hat, chequered jacket and tie, and exaggerated expressions, is a Chaplinesque figure, and the best elements of the film are the comic sequences set in motion by Lane. Overall, though, the film has the stilted quality of statically shot stage productions, lacking the vitality and spontaneity evidently enjoyed by the theatre audience. With Albert de Courville directing, such an uninspired approach was to be expected; de Courville, a masterful producer of theatrical revues, was never destined to be a front-rank film director.

*The Lambeth Walk* provides an interesting commentary on contemporary class consciousness, touching as it does issues similar to those in *Pygmalion* (directed by Anthony Asquith, 1938) which, Roy Armes argues, is a 'culminating point of British 1930s cinema because it deals consciously and explicitly with the underlying but often concealed themes of the decade – class, morality, accent'.[32] By plucking a bookie's runner and depositing him in a manorial home, the film pinpoints the vast social and cultural chasm that existed between the lowest and highest classes, and the importance of appearance and accent as a measure of birth and background. Moreover, the underlying logic of the film is that classes can never meet; Bill and Sally can join them only on condition they become like them. As Bill argues at one stage: 'East is east, and west is west ... we can no more walk the Mayfair way than they can walk the Lambeth way.'

However, while class difference drives the plot and inspires the jokes, the conflict between the classes is narratively resolved through class understanding. It was a point noted at the time, as evidenced by the *Observer* when it remarked that by the end (of the play) 'the clash of class is satisfactorily solved'.[33] The meeting of the classes is symbolised, ironically enough, by 'The Lambeth Walk', and the consensual message it symbolised was emphasised by making this scene the centrepiece of the film. When the crowd of lowly folks from Lambeth spontaneously perform the dance in Barford Hall, the incredulity and reserve of the Mayfair toffs gradually melts away, and one by one they join in, and everyone is united. In a decade of perceived social and political division, it was an important ideological message, and one the royals were only too happy to be associated with. When they saw the stage version the king and queen were widely reported as having enthusiastically joined 'with the rest of the audience, cocked their thumbs and shouted Oi!'[34]

This class reading of *The Lambeth Walk* serves to raise the issue of the social and political relevance of the musical film. Whatever their origins and format, musical films were invariably seen as bright and breezy musical tonics for depression audiences. Often described as 'escapist' entertainment, the implication was that they had no social relevance, were somehow non-political and isolated from real life. But as has been shown by successive studies, even the most trivial film was loaded with social meaning. Jeffrey Richards, for example, concludes that even 'apparently innocuous films conveyed a definite message ... in particular with regard to the political *status quo*, attitudes to peace and war, and responses to the class structure.'[35] It is not a theme to be developed here beyond making the generalisation that musical films, like *The Lambeth Walk*, were seldom oppositional or antagonistic, and that their underlying values and assumptions promoted an acceptance of the political and social status quo. An implication here is that audiences endorsed that message, and a reason they enjoyed musical films was because they offered a cheery reassurance about contemporary society.

Reviewers of *The Lambeth Walk* were mostly lukewarm, the exception being the *Monthly Film Bulletin* which praised it as 'an excellent film version of the Victoria Palace stage success'.[36] While some critics were bothered by the pedestrian direction, others disliked the banal, predictable humour – a criticism they presumably also applied to the original show. *Kinematograph Weekly* was in this category: 'the fault with this picture is not in the teamwork, not in the technical presentation, it is that most of the gags, all of which get their laughs the easy way in allowing the cockney to score off the aristocracy, are not only hackneyed but overplayed.' Despite the slating, *Kinematograph Weekly* predicted it a certainty at the box office on account of its star values and the irresistible 'Lambeth Walk'.[37] As it turned out, the prediction was off-target as the film had an unremarkable box-office career judging by its absence from box-office surveys and popularity polls, not to mention its cursory treatment in Lane's biography.

Apart from the film's debatable lack of merit and the depressing effect of negative reviews, its prospects were probably damaged by a decline in the popularity of the all-music type of musical film at the end of the decade. In May 1939, for instance, *Film Pictorial* ran a lively article about how 'we are in the throes of the greatest musical movie slump since the "all talking, all singing, all dancing" boom that ushered in talkies collapsed'.[38] Two causes for the decline can be speculated: first, that they fell victim to the growing demand for more 'realistic' films and the concomitant drift from 'escapist' films as epitomised by most musical films. Second, that audiences became more critical of film quality as the years wore on, and the appearance of favourite stars singing and dancing was no longer adequate compensation for otherwise mediocre films. Films framed around variety artists did remain popular in the war, but significantly their production quality improved, and they increasingly touched on social issues.

If film-makers were firmly rooted in theatrical traditions, then so were audiences, who, as Ernest Betts wrote, 'were still theatre-minded and accepted with enthusiasm whatever they were given'.[39] As the production and popularity of so many innately theatrical musical films suggests, audiences must have had some degree of rapport with them. There was often a sense that audiences saw the films as convenient substitutes for live theatre, enabling them to enjoy a theatrical experience and see theatrical stars they might otherwise be unable to see on the stage itself. The *Monthly Film Bulletin*'s recommendation of *Variety Parade* (directed by Oswald Mitchell, 1936) was couched in those terms: the film, it stated, would 'please and entertain those … who rarely have the opportunity of seeing the artistes who appear in the film.'[40] For some fans, the film was clearly a poor second choice to seeing stars perform in the flesh, as this fan argued about Gracie Fields: 'the old controversy is on again: why can Gracie Fields pack a west end variety house for twelve performances a week and yet one of her films runs for barely a week at a cinema less than a quarter of a mile away? … it is Gracie who brings in the crowds … the insurmountable difference between a flesh and blood artist and an animated photograph.'[41]

Although audiences for musical theatre had declined by the 1930s, live stage entertainment, especially variety, remained very popular. John Stevenson, for example, notes now variety provided 'the bread and butter for a host of musicians, artists, and performers'.[42] Indeed, the first half of the decade experienced a resurgence in variety, which was no doubt fostered by filmed (and broadcast) variety performances. Another trend revealing the 'renewal of public interest in the flesh and blood theatre'[43] was the growth of live acts in the cinema programme. As an optimistic variety trade journal reported in its end of year round-up in 1933: 'more independent theatres and cinemas are playing variety acts than in any year since the war, and that in itself is sufficient proof of our optimistic outlook for 1934.'[44] The demand for variety acts in cinemas was also registered in a survey of cinema-goers in 1931 which found that the live turn was 'universally popular'[45] and at least one new super-cinema, the Troxy in London's Stepney, was unsure whether films alone would fill its seats without the aid of stage artists.[46]

The notion of cinema as a branch of musical theatre was also signalled by the friendly attitude of the variety profession towards it (unlike radio, which it saw as a menace killing off theatre audiences and offering a paucity of poorly paid work by compensation). For variety artists the cinema was seen as a good potential source of employment, as well as being generally beneficial for the profession. The sense of integration between variety and cinema was symbolised by the launch in 1931 of *Variety, Music, Stage and Film News* (later renamed *Variety, Cabaret and Film News*), a professional journal whose title self-evidently equates film with theatre. The whole ethos of theatre and cinema also coincided as both were seen as places of 'escapist' entertainment, with the result that theatre, like the cinema it inspired, was dominated by 'musical comedy, farce, and revue'.[47]

## Film and other musical media

Although steeped in a theatrical heritage, many musical films were also, of course, sponges for American cultural fashions, not least Hollywood musicals. As has already been mentioned, British studios frequently imported Hollywood personnel – writers, actors, choreographers and so forth – and often imitated Hollywood style and conventions. Storylines might involve an American and be structured around the 'backstage' format, synonymous with Hollywood musicals, and try to imitate the complex, extravagant choreography of Busby Berkeley. There are numerous examples of the 'Hollywoodisation' of musical films, and they cover the spectrum of theatrical traditions. *Calling All Stars*, with its American settings and performers, is an example of American influence in a variety film. Some bizarre hybrids were thrown up by the marriage of Hollywood and British conventions: the musical comedy *Everybody Dance* (directed by Charles F. Reisner, 1935), for instance, features the quintessentially English comedienne Cicely Courtneidge playing an American-style cabaret artist in a transatlantic, backstage plot, complete with pale imitations of Berkeley choreography, glitzy costumes and extravagant set design. For all Hollywood's influence, though, it is worth recording that the Hollywood musical was itself indebted to Broadway, which in turn was fuelled by European theatrical traditions.[48]

In its early years, radio too was theatrically orientated. When broadcasting started in 1922, radio had the same basic problem as film: how to accommodate an existing form of entertainment into the format of a new medium. As with film-makers, broadcasters' solutions were uninspired. They failed to exploit the creative opportunities offered by radio, making instead straightforward relays of shows from theatres, giving 'the impression that Broadcasting House was situated at the end of an Edwardian sea-side pier'.[49] From the early 1930s, policy changed and instead of depending on outside relays the BBC recruited artists and began to produce its own shows in-house. But while these shows were more distinctly the products of radio, they were still founded in theatre. It was not until *Bandwagon* in 1938 that a show truly exploited the medium, and would, as George Nobbs says, 'have been meaningless on a stage'.[50]

Radio broadcasting soon gained a huge following, and by 1939 one in ten homes was licensed.[51] With such a massive audience, radio was soon a powerful force in the generation and promotion of stars and theatrical shows, with all the commercial implications that this entailed. Without a fortuitous radio relay of highlights from *Me and My Girl*, for instance, the show would have gone under after its first uncertain weeks.[52] The BBC was a major player in the presentation of variety: although variety did not become a pillar of the broadcasting schedule until the early 1930s (a policy consolidated by the formation of a separate variety department in 1933), even its early variety broadcasts were popular enough to propel performers into stardom. Singer and comedian Tommy Handley, for instance, was by the end of the 1920s 'one of the first on the road to exploit the popularity of artistes who had gained fame via the microphone'.[53] With such fame, it was no coincidence that he was recruited as compere for the pioneering *Elstree Calling*, and throughout the rest of the 1930s much-loved radio stars were sought by film-makers. There was no question they sold films, as any number of reviews indicate, such as the *Monthly Film Bulletin*'s comment that *Radio Parade of 1935* (directed by Arthur Woods, 1934) 'should be a popular film as so many radio stars appear in it. There are songs, dances, comic turns'.[54]

Its audiences were theatrically minded, they were also musically minded: the 1920s and 1930s were notable for a boom in the popularity of all kinds of music. The centrality of music in the nation's life is alluded to by several historians. Stephen Jones, for example, observed: 'musical activity was a very popular working-class recreation, ranging from the Welsh male voice choirs, the Yorkshire and Lancashire brass bands and the workers' jazz of the North-East, to the new dance music and gramophone records of the capitalist leisure industry.'[55] Stevenson argues that there was also a tremendous expansion in the 'performance and appreciation of serious music' and, in support of his argument, he cites the education reformer Sir Henry Hadow who in 1932 proudly claimed that 'the spread of musical education, and the interest which it encourages is wider and deeper at the present day than it has ever been', and that this wave of music-making and appreciation was 'flowing to floodtide'.[56]

Apart from musical films, musical hallmarks of the 1930s included the reopening of Sadler's Wells Theatre in 1931 and the founding of Glyndebourne in 1934. In terms of mass culture, there was the mushrooming of dance halls and the concomitant proliferation of dance styles, sometimes indigenously fashioned, as with 'The Lambeth Walk', but more often imported from America together with American music. It was an era when dance band leaders could be celebrities, the most famous being 'able to command large salaries at the top hotels and clubs',[57] and to have films anchored round them, such as top-biller Jack Hylton in *She Shall Have Music* (directed by Leslie Hiscott, 1935). Music and song-sheet sales were big business, the piano being a common feature in even modest homes. Music also reached a vast home audience through a massive volume of gramophone record sales: for instance, (British) Columbia Co. turned out over four million records in one month in 1929.[58]

Radio broadcasting emphasised music: for example, the *Radio Times*' projected listening for a week in January 1939 was listed under eight category headings, five of which were for musical relays: 'Variety and Musical Shows', 'Brass and Military Bands', 'Ballad Concerts and Light Music', 'Concerts, Recitals, Opera' and 'Chamber Music'. (The three non-musical headings were 'Outside Events and Sports', 'Plays and Features', and 'Talks and Readings'.)[59] Some of the most famous names

produced by radio were band leaders, most notably Jack Payne and
Henry Hall, both of whom also made films featuring their bands, Payne's
*Say It With Music* (directed by Jack Raymond, 1932), and Henry Hall's
*Music Hath Charms* (directed by Thomas Bentley, 1935).

Musical films were enjoyed for their musical qualities, even by high-
brow music fans. A consistent line of criticism in the *Monthly Film Bulletin*,
for example, was that although in cinematic terms the films might leave
much to be desired, in musical terms they offered the chance to see and
hear classical compositions, performed by accomplished musicians and
singers. *Gypsy Melody* (directed by Edmond Gréville, 1936), for instance,
was described by the *Monthly Film Bulletin*: 'a Ruritanian musical comedy
... the music constitutes the film's major appeal and it is almost worth
seeing the film just for the performance of Liszt's Second Hungarian
Rhapsody, which is extremely well rendered by Rode and his orchestra,
and excellently recorded'.[60]

Similarly, films were sold on the strength of their songs: the advertisement for the best-selling *Jack's the Boy*, for instance, promotes the film
via Jack Hulbert's reputation as a singer, reproducing the lyrics of the
songs and trumpeting how 'he has sung his way to success'.[61] The
significance of the musical content of films is also illustrated by the huge
sales of film-related song sheets and gramophone records that were
frequently marketed in conjunction with the film.

Music was the common denominator in a number of entertainments
including both the performing arts and the industrialised mass media.
Theatre, radio, song-sheet publication and gramophone recording were
all culturally and commercially interlinked, the interface being music. It
was a connection embodied in a journal called *Popular Music and Film
Song Weekly*, first published in 1937 and headed by Henry Hall. It was
dedicated to popular music regardless of the means of reproduction. As
the leading editorial explained:

> For fourpence per week you are receiving the dancing, film, and song
> 'winners' of the popular music world ... Every week there will be a film
> song and pages of articles dealing with the gay world of dancing, of film
> entertainment, and of personalities behind the broadcasts and the big
> bands of the day. This is a wonder paper of melody that gives you the
> music of the day in the cheapest way.[62]

## Conclusion

Musical films of the 1930s were firmly rooted in traditions of musical
theatre whose histories went back centuries. When sound technology

forced film-makers to rethink film language, rather than think originally in terms of pure cinema they readily fell back on the well-oiled techniques and creative talent of the musical stage. They drew predominantly from variety and the stage musical traditions of Viennese-style operetta and English musical comedy, as represented most clearly in the films chosen for discussion, *Calling All Stars, Goodnight, Vienna* and *The Lambeth Walk*. While drawing heavily on theatre, film-makers also freely borrowed ideas and style from Hollywood musicals leading to the 'Hollywood-isation' of many British musicals, although this has not been the focus of attention here. Whatever the individual influences on a particular film, almost all shared the common characteristic of being an entertainment based on laughter, fun and romance. Regarded as 'escapist' entertainment, the implication was that they lacked contemporary relevance but this was seldom the case, as the class reading of *The Lambeth Walk* indicates.

While film-makers can be criticised for displaying a lack of imagination in their reliance on a theatrical perspective, they do seem to have struck a chord with audiences, quota quickies apart. As has been argued, the appeal and significance of these often stagey films for audiences lay in their close relationship with other cultural forms. Audiences, still predisposed towards musical and variety theatre, could relate to the musical film as an offshoot of it. Featuring stars whose reputations had mostly been secured on stage before entering pictures, the films provided a cheap and convenient means of seeing and hearing a stable of favourite stage stars and performances – a sort of precursor of the television variety show. Radio too, was a crucial factor in the projection and creation of stars (many of whom similarly originated from the stage), and the appearance of radio personalities in film was a major selling point.

The musical film, and the musical theatre from which it largely derived, was also the product of, and testament to, a decade when musical entertainment *per se* was immensely popular. This popular interest in music covered a surprisingly varied selection of tastes from low-brow to high-brow, and was enjoyed through the spectrum of mass media as well as through live performance. While musical entertainment had always been popular, enthusiasm for it was undoubtedly fostered in the interwar decades by the technologies of mass reproduction and the commercialised entertainment industry that grew up around them. Once the film had found its voice it became an increasingly important link in a complex entertainment chain promoting and marketing musical entertainment to a keen and appreciative audience.

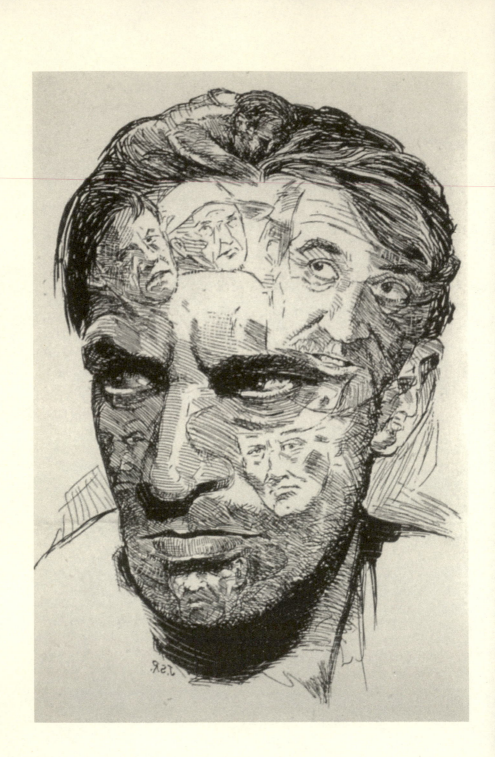

6. Poster for *King of the Damned* featuring Conrad Veidt

CHAPTER 6

# 'Thinking Forward and Up': The British Films of Conrad Veidt

*Sue Harper*

F OR British audiences of the 1930s, the star was a major determinant in their choice of film. Very few viewers were influenced by the producer or the director, though they might have favourite genres (the musical, the costume film) or even favourite cinema chains (the Odeon, the Gaumont),[1] but the mass audience's choice was mainly predicated on the pleasure expected from, and conferred by, the star. The main problem confronting the historian of star styles is the tension between the appearance of the stars (their manner, their arrangement of features) and the management and marketing of that essence. That tension is raised with some urgency in Michel Mourlet's celebrated essay on Charlton Heston: 'his eagle's profile, the imperious arch of his eyebrows, the hard, bitter curve of his lips, the stupendous strength of his torso – *that is what he has been given, and what not even the worst of directors can debase*' (my emphasis).[2] The relationship between the 'given' and the 'constructed' star image is a complex one. It can alter radically over quite short periods of time, according to industrial conditions or shifts in audience taste.

Clearly, patterns of star popularity are intimately connected to deep-seated social needs. Before 1936, British cinema audiences of the early and mid-1930s favoured the Hollywood product, with gentlemanly actors and ladylike actresses such as Ronald Colman and Norma Shearer. As Jeffrey Richards notes: 'the aura of gentility surrounding the lists is almost overpowering.'[3] After 1936, British stars such as Gracie Fields, George Formby, Robert Donat and Jessie Matthews took the field, with transatlantic child stars such as Shirley Temple and Deanna Durbin much in evidence.[4] However, lists of favourites are something of a blunt instrument when it comes to fine-tuning a version of British film culture in the 1930s. 'Minor' stars may often tell us a great deal about popular taste, and in order to excavate forgotten imaginary habits, we need to reconstitute a map of culture which gives due cognisance to stars such as Elisabeth Bergner, Nova Pilbeam, John Loder or Conrad Veidt. Some of them have enduring power; Veidt, for example, although born over a hundred years ago, still has a fan club, whose motto is 'Courage, Integrity, Humanity'.[5]

With the entry of Conrad Veidt into the country in 1932, the British film industry gained a star who was, according to Michael Powell, 'one of the greatest names in European cinema, and one of the most romantic and magnetic men alive'.[6] Veidt possessed fabulous good looks, a sardonic manner and a voice which he could moderate from rasping steel to silky purr. He had extraordinary physical control, and was able, for example, to make the vein in his forehead throb at will for any key film scene.[7] He left Germany for good in 1933 because his wife was Jewish and because his own liberal views made further residence in Hitler's Germany impossible. On a brief visit home between his British films, Veidt was forcibly detained by the German authorities for his supposed involvement in anti-Nazi propaganda. Michael Balcon, then head of production at Gaumont-British, had to intervene for him to return to England.[8] Veidt never went back to Germany, and began applying for British naturalisation in 1937. The Home Office was impressed with Veidt's contribution to the British film industry, and (unusually) it interpreted immigration regulations in a very liberal manner to facilitate the quota conditions for his *Under the Red Robe*; it cancelled Veidt's landing conditions and allowed him to 'count' as someone of British domicile rather than as an alien.[9] It was not until February 1939 that Veidt received his British naturalisation papers.[10] At the outbreak of war, he put his personal fortune at the disposal of the British government.

Veidt made a range of films for British companies in the 1930s: *Rome Express* (Gaumont-British, 1932), *I Was a Spy* (Gaumont, 1933), *The Wandering Jew* (Twickenham, 1933), *Bella Donna* (Twickenham, 1934), *Jew Süss* (Gaumont, 1934), *The Passing of the Third Floor Back* (Gaumont, 1935), *King of the Damned* (Gaumont, 1936), *Dark Journey* (London Films, 1937), *Under the Red Robe* (New World, 1937), *The Spy in Black* (Harefield/ Columbia, 1939), *The Thief of Bagdad* (London Films, 1939) and *Contraband* (British National, 1940).[11] Veidt won substantial favour in leading film magazine polls for his performances in *I Was a Spy, The Wandering Jew* and *Jew Süss*.[12] The *Kinematograph Weekly* listings, which began in 1937, indicated that many of his films were box-office hits, and mentioned *Under the Red Robe, The Spy in Black, The Thief of Bagdad* and *Contraband*.[13]

He was, therefore, an actor who was a bankable asset, and who was marketed by all his British producers as a major star. However, they had problems finding appropriate vehicles for him. In 1934, Michael Balcon was forced to abandon a project called *I Serve*, which was ideal for Veidt (a romantic tale of the love and murder in 1903 of King Alexander of Serbia), because of the recent assassination of King Alexander of Yugoslavia.[14] Balcon also toyed with the idea of casting Veidt in a major role in *Anna Karenina*, but was foiled when the Americans staked a claim in the novel first.[15] When Alexander Korda had Veidt under contract he, too, was hard pressed to make the best of his talents, and he tried out various abortive projects such as the lives of Liszt and Nobel.[16]

Veidt's entry into British cinema was part of a larger influx of continental workers into the industry. Designers such as Alfred Junge and Oscar Werndorff, producers such as Paul Czinner and Erich Pommer, and directors such as Lothar Mendes and Berthold Viertel entered Britain as a consequence of events in Hitler's Germany. They found a niche in the industry and managed to do innovatory work. It was more difficult for performers. Elisabeth Bergner was handicapped by her excessively winsome style, Richard Tauber by his portliness. Only Conrad Veidt, of all the continental acting imports, was used to artistic and box-office effect. His accent was an asset rather than a drawback, and it was the selling point of a very popular record released in 1933.[17] Veidt's charismatic manner evoked a frisson which was not provided by other British or indeed American stars of the period. However, his image was modulated by the various production companies by which he was employed and marketed.

Veidt, of course, came to British cinema with an outstanding reputation as a major actor in German cinema; he was second only to Emil Jannings in reputation (and possibly to Hans Albers at the box office). Veidt had appeared in *Das Kabinett des Doktor Caligari* (1919), *Das Wachsfigurenkabinett* (1924), *Orlacs Hande* (1925), *Der Student von Prag* (1926) and others, as well as making some films in Hollywood.[18] In all these films, Veidt deployed the full repertoire of the expressionist actor, and his body was asymmetrically presented; its two halves (left and right, upper and lower) were in constant opposition to each other, and in a state of muscular disarray. His patterns of gaze in the German and early American films were unpredictable and unfixed, and the overall impression is of a dystopian persona riven by contradiction.[19] Indeed, Freud's remarks on psychopathological drama are precisely applicable to this part of Veidt's acting career.[20] As an *unheimlich* character, Veidt was a source of inspiration to those who had their own axe to grind. The surrealist painter Clovis Trouille painted two important pictures of Veidt as the hero of *Caligari*, 'Csare, sort un instant de ton profond nuit', and 'Je vous presente Csare, Le Somnambule'.[21] Veidt featured in Irmgard Keun's famous Weimar bestseller *Das Kunstseidene Mädchen*, and both Kracauer and Benjamin wrote portraits of him. Veidt's silent film about homosexuality (*Anders als die Anderen*) caused him to become, albeit fleetingly, a gay icon in 1920s Berlin.[22]

All that changed with Veidt's British films. To be sure, he still played exotic figures. But Veidt's physical *Haltung* changed radically between the 1932 *Rome Express* and the 1933 *I Was a Spy*. After 1933, Veidt carried himself quite differently and this profoundly affected the social meaning which could be encoded in his body. Of course, the physical components remained the same; the sensual lips, the vulpine teeth, the spatulate fingers, the spare frame. But attention to Veidt's physical demeanour shows that the skeletal alignment had altered completely, such that the muscle tone was symmetrically distributed and the head and neck were loose and free. His pattern of gaze had altered too, and was full and still. The energy signalled by Veidt's body was no longer demonic (self-contained and self-destructive) but charismatic; the body was relaxed because its power could be discharged. Veidt shifted from representing deviant figures to marginal ones, which contained different social meanings.

It is very tempting to attribute this change to the teachings of F. M. Alexander, founder of the Alexander technique. This is based on the principle that the individual's life can be transformed by the correct alignment of head, neck and back; 'think forward and up' was the key maxim of the technique. Alexander himself insisted that the whole posture be upright but relaxed so that energy could be appropriately released: 'You learn first to inhibit the habitual reaction to certain classes of stimuli, and second to direct yourself consciously in such a way as to affect certain muscular pulls.'[23] Alexander was teaching in Hampstead during the 1920s and 1930s, and his technique was popular then (as it is now) with singers and actors wishing to improve their performance. Alexander's most influential book, *The Use of the Self*, was published in 1932, and it aroused considerable interest, prompting George Bernard Shaw, Aldous Huxley, Stafford Cripps and Archbishop William Temple to become his pupils.[24] Veidt was living in Hampstead from 1933 and, if his physical behaviour on film can be adduced as evidence, may well have been Alexander's pupil too. But this must remain at the level of surmise.[25]

So it looks as though a series of domestic coincidences (living in Hampstead in 1933, moving in liberal/bohemian circles) transformed Veidt's manner on screen and enabled him to interpret roles in a new way. But there were other determinants on Veidt's image. The British production companies employing him had widely differing policies. Under the aegis of Michael Balcon, Gaumont-British had an agenda of producing up-market entertainment, occasionally with a radical or propagandistic edge and always with a commitment to quality and craftsmanship.[26] Balcon was interested both in appealing to international markets and in providing employment for German/Jewish refugees from UFA.[27] The Foreign Office actively supported Gaumont-British during the first half of the decade. Balcon had assembled an unparalleled ensemble of foreign designers and cameraman, and the Foreign Office felt that he could make films which, since they were artistically acceptable by international standards, would express the epitome of British culture. Accordingly, the Foreign Office sent photographs and scholarly information to Balcon to help him select appropriate styles.[28] So Gaumont represented the best (and the most 'European') of the British film companies.

*Rome Express* was the first film to be made at the Lime Grove Studios in Shepherd's Bush, and this was a key selling point in the film's publicity material: 'Only unlimited expenditure could produce such an epic of cinematic art'.[29] Walter Forde directed, Günther Krampf was cameraman, Sidney Gilliat worked on the script and Andrew Mazzei (who later designed such Gainsborough blockbusters as *Madonna of the Seven Moons*) was art director. The narrative dealt with the robbery of a Van Dyke painting, and its subsequent discovery on board the Rome express, on which the whole film is set. The British Board of Film Censors made no objection to the scenario, because it was carefully pruned of explicitly violent or erotic elements.[30] The script itself was tightly constructed, with plenty of narrative vignettes, and a sense of circularity and closure. There is a rueful sense of British grundyism, and a powerful argument in favour of European sophistication; it is suggested that 'we do these things [adultery] a little better in France'.

Veidt was cast as Zurta, the villain, and the script gives plenty of hints that he is both dangerous and unfathomable; he is 'a crook, probably of German citizenship, ruthless and dominating but possessing a certain fund of grim humour'. When he raises his eyebrows, his expression is 'baffling'.[31] Veidt's performance replicated the habits of his earlier German films, in that the angular gestures and unpredictable movements inhibited any sense of the character's motivation. But anyway, technical matters swamped the impact of Veidt's performance. The camerawork was so exuberantly varied (very mobile camera, lots of dolly shots and tight framing of objects) that the close-ups at which Veidt excelled did not occur until half-way through the film. The *mise-en-scène*, too, inhibited Veidt's performance. Forde was newly obsessed with the technique of back projection, and was too involved with replicating the jiggling motion of the train to concern himself with making a narrative space for the newcomer.[32]

Balcon thought that he had made 'quite a coup' in co-opting Veidt for *Rome Express*.[33] But Veidt could not flourish in completely deviant roles, in an English context at any rate. *Rome Express* did allow him, as Daniela Sannwald has noted, to deploy his talent for the depiction of social and sensual hungers.[34] But the director's and art director's infatuation with the technical challenges of the project overshadowed Veidt's contribution to the film.

Veidt's next film, *I Was a Spy*, was a different case. This was based on the reminiscences of a Belgian woman spy in the First World War, and was directed by Victor Saville, with art direction by the great Alfred Junge. At Welwyn Junge constructed massive sets, such as the square of Roulers, because there were no adequate facilities at Shepherd's Bush. These sets determined the lighting values of the film, which in turn influenced the presentation of the stars.

The film's script is preoccupied by the sacred and profane aspects of Teutonic culture. On the one hand it presents two Germans thus: 'They are an unprepossessing pair. One is trim and cadaverous, the other is big, fat and thoroughly unpleasant.' On the other hand, German culture is represented by *Die Meistersinger* and by a doctor who says, 'I'm afraid I am a bad (that is to say good) German'.[35] The Veidt character is constructed and acted in such a way as to neutralise the conflict between the negative and positive Germans. The film mounts a powerful argument in favour of a civilised and pacifist Europe, and manages that by framing the narrative within brackets of authenticity and authority. It begins by quoting letters from Churchill, and ends by using a messianic sermon about the coming of peace. *Picturegoer* noted 'a recrudescence of the war atmosphere in films which may or may not be a sign of the perturbed time through which we are passing'.[36] And indeed, *I Was a Spy* is an index of the anxiety felt in some intellectual and industrial circles about the right and wrong types of European.

The script suggested that the heroine (played by Madeleine Carroll) has a liaison with the Uhlan commanding officer (played by Veidt). This suggestion was intended to raise the film's emotional temperature and to enhance the sexual clout of the two stars. But the recent Youssupoff libel case caused problems for Balcon, who felt obliged to protect his studio from litigation, and so the completed film was more sexually anodyne than the original plan.[37] This reduced the erotic charge Veidt was able to carry.

Undismayed, Gaumont pushed ahead with a publicity campaign for the film which urged cinema managers to exploit Veidt's sexual charisma: 'While there is a powerful war background to this production, we think it best to subordinate it to the selling campaign. The glamour of the central character in the story is much more attractive as selling material and has the extra advantage of being attractive to women.'[38] And it was probably at the behest of the studio that Veidt wrote (or had ghost-written) an article in *Film Weekly* about his 'pulling power' entitled 'Women Who Wanted to Marry Me'.[39]

Veidt's performance in *I Was a Spy* demonstrates (as I have already suggested) a radically different use of the body. In his previous films he had represented neurotics destroyed by self-generated tensions, and his physical demeanour was jagged and asymmetrical. Now Veidt's body and gaze evoked a balanced composure, and he portrayed someone torn by an external and social conflict. He was able to appear as a kind of battleground, in which the forces of desire and duty were acutely at issue. This is particularly highlighted in the trial scene, in which he feels compelled to act as the prosecutor in the trial of the woman he loves. Because of the controlled nature of his performance, his sexual yearning for the heroine seems coterminous with his zeal for honour. Honour, of course, has to triumph, since its rewards are less evanescent than those of desire. Veidt's performance dominates the script and the *mise-en-scène* is powerful because it evokes the existence of a European officer class which is dignified, principled and above all stylish.

The success of this film led Balcon to offer Veidt a longer-term contract.[40] Balcon considered that he himself had masterminded Veidt's British career and had first recognised his promise, ruefully noting that 'Veidt is a dominant personality. Every time I go out with him in the West End I am mobbed'.[41] But there was a hiatus in Veidt's involvement with Gaumont-British. Before the contract for *Jew Süss* and the other Gaumont-British films came into operation, Veidt made two films for Julius Hagen at Twickenham Studios.

Twickenham was a small-scale independent operation of minimal status, and it is likely that Veidt signed his two-picture deal with them out of sheer financial need. The studio made a fair profit in the years 1931–34 from quota films, studio rental and low-budget melodramas, and could afford to take the odd risk such as *The Wandering Jew*. The head of production, Julius Hagen, had no clear policy on matters of class and gender representation or on the social function of film, as Balcon or Alexander Korda did. Hagen was more entrepreneurial and took more risks, often with disastrous consequences.[42] Moreover, Hagen was attached to old-fashioned texts and procedures. His favourite novelist was Ethel M. Dell, and his favourite scriptwriter H. Fowler Mear, an extremely lurid writer who made Dell seem like Tolstoy by comparison.[43]

Hagen's fondness for residual forms is clearly evident in his two Veidt films. *The Wandering Jew* was directed by Maurice Elvey and scripted by Mear, with art direction by architect James Carter, who was Hagen's right-hand man. Based on a stage play, the film deals with a Jew who lives through the ages and, through good works, is finally granted death.[44] The film's sets are packed with detail, and the music (Chopin, Dvorak, Wagner) is clearly intended to evoke a popular type of high culture. The script of *The Wandering Jew* is flamboyant. The words are reminiscent of the captions in silent film: 'What does it matter, so the days are peaceful and the nights gay?' and 'It would go hard with Christ, to know his own again'.

Veidt's performance overcomes the limitations of the script. He slows the pace of his delivery, modulating his voice so that the lower registers are more audible. The body language augments the sense of stateliness and power; it is deliberate, and the movements are flowing and integrated. The facial expressions are lingering, and shown to best advantage by some extremely sympathetic camerawork and lighting. The overall impression of the Jew is of an individual stoically suffering the pains of immortality, and attaining enlightenment and transfiguration. Veidt's sublime performance was intensified by his political engagement with the role. In an important interview with *Picturegoer* he indicated: 'the part I am playing is at once the most beautiful and the most complex one for which any actor could wish ... the very fact that in this man is concentrated the history of a great people who can trace their history right back to biblical times only enhances its fascination.' He insisted that his relationship with Elvey was unusually harmonious – 'there is no question of one having to defer to the other' – and that this enhanced the coherence of the performance.[45]

In contrast, the role offered to Veidt in *Bella Donna* was of minimal interest to him. The film was directed by Robert Milton, and otherwise staffed by Twickenham regulars. It was adapted from a well-known novel by Robert Hichens, had been a stage play with Mrs Patrick Campbell in the lead, and silent film starring Pola Negri.[46] Hichens was a novelist enamoured of the mysteries of the East, and his 1904 *Garden of Allah* was a meditation on the desert. *Bella Donna* (meaning 'beautiful woman' as well as Deadly Nightshade) deals with a married woman infatuated with her exotic Egyptian lover (Veidt, in a large fez). She attempts to poison her husband, is foiled, and is abandoned by both husband and lover.[47] The moral rigour of the tale is combined with the reprise of a key motif in British popular culture: the insatiable nomad. He appears as early as Byron's *The Giaour*, and surfaces again in *The Sheikh* by E. M. Hull, filmed with Rudolph Valentino. This contains the immortal exchange (in a tent) between the heroine and her desert lover:

'Why have you brought me here?'
'Are you not woman enough to know?'

Veidt was hired to play this character, and the casting indicates that Hagen had no understanding of the new directions in his work. Hagen wanted an exotic predator, whereas Veidt was now working from within on marginal characters, and was in the process of establishing that they were not extraordinary at all.

As with *The Wandering Jew*, Veidt was able to transform unpromising material by sheer technique, and his interest in Jewish and liberal/humanitarian issues intensified his delivery and enabled him to invest socially marginal figures with dignity and power. Veidt's first project when he returned to Gaumont was *Jew Süss*, another film whose racial politics were well to the fore. The original novel of *Jew Süss* had a five-part narrative structure which permitted a radical interpretation of socially marginal groups.[48] No attempt was made in the film to reproduce this plurality of class interest. The film is exclusively concerned with the Jewish group, and its propagandist message is unusually near the surface. The script suggests that if atrocities were permitted in 1730, 'then they can do it in 1830 and they can do it in 1930'. The film ends, unusually for its period, with a caption pleading for religious tolerance: 'Perhaps, one day, the walls will crumble like the walls of Jericho, and the world will be one people.' The film concentrated, with an intensity absent from the book, on the compensations for the lack of official status; 'real power' suggests the Jewish moneylender 'lies in never showing it'. It is tempting to interpret this emphasis as a covert message from radical and/or Jewish intellectuals; that although they did not have a place in the machinery of state, they could still influence the hearts and minds of the audience.

*Jew Süss* was very expensive to make. It was directed by Lothar Mendes, the art direction was by Alfred Junge, and the script by Dorothy

Farnum and A. R. Rawlinson.[49] The production was cumbersome (47 different sets overall, 1,000 different lighting operations every day), and the logistics were complex. Balcon viewed the film as a high-status priority; he and Mark Ostrer booked it at the prestigious Radio City Music Hall in New York, and gained the outright sponsorship of Albert Einstein.[50] In addition, Balcon arranged a simultaneous première in Paris.[51]

A lesser actor would have been swamped by such high production values and brouhaha. Veidt rose to the challenge, and turned in a performance of remarkable subtlety. In addition to his political commitment to the role, he was now developing a new technique of interiorising character. The fictional Jew Süss is consumed first by the desire for power, and then for vengeance; fuelled by anger at being consigned to the margins, he unleashes his rage on society and is himself destroyed in turn. Veidt's performance brings a stillness and a vulnerability to the role; his control of feature is such that, in key scenes, we actually see the mask of the social persona slip to reveal temporarily the 'real' person of the Süss beneath. Veidt's method was based on profound humanist beliefs, which he now had the skill to convey with his body. He noted of Süss: 'Even if he is cold and remorseless in his endeavours, and feeling for those around him dwindles out of existence, even if such a state comes about; there is still some spark of soul, of human nature within him, maybe crushed or hidden within some outer crust or box, but nevertheless there, vibrating, living, always ready to break out if its covering should weaken.'[52]

Veidt was thus vitally instrumental, in both *The Wandering Jew* and *Jew Süss*, in constructing an image of Judaism which was a marked innovation, and an advance on contemporary literary representations.[53] Furthermore, this innovation was achieved in the face of enormous practical difficulties. The execution scene in *Jew Süss* took place in a snowstorm, for which a malodorous mixture of naphtha, soap flakes and solidified spirit was used on set. The technicians all wore surgeons' masks, but Veidt soldiered on.[54] According to Christopher Isherwood, who was on set at the time, Veidt's technique never faltered. There was a hiatus in filming the scene, and an assistant offered him a sweet:

He remained Süss, and through the eyes of Süss he looked down from the cart upon this sweet Christian girl, the only human being in this cruel city who had the heart and the courage to show kindness to a condemned Jew. His eyes filled with tears. With his manacled hands he took the candy from her and tried to eat it – for her sake, to show his gratitude to her. But he couldn't. He was beyond hunger, too near death. And his emotion was too great. He began to sob. He turned his face away.[55]

During this period, film journals published a number of articles prompted by Veidt's growing charisma. Some of these were doubtless a means of preparing the way for *The Passing of the Third Floor Back*. But they are an interesting index of growing awareness in the profession that Veidt's acting skills were taking an unusual turn. *Picturegoer* suggested that 'in this country, Class 1 consists of Conrad Veidt', and *Film Weekly*'s chief critic John Gammie called him 'one of the half-dozen leading exponents of his art in the world'.[56] Veidt himself gave a series of interviews. He described his particular skill as a form of self-effacement – to give way to the persona being represented, to empty the mind of egotism and to allow the new self to live, albeit temporarily: 'You become a dead man ... you feel this shadowy alter ego appealing, in a mood that was once yours, to the sympathy of others.'[57] These are typically Romantic formulations, but powerfully expressed, and Veidt tempers them with the suggestion that the great actor receives and condenses the feelings of the audience: he is 'a human wireless set which can pick up the waves radiated by other human persons'.[58] The actor is an energy field who will facilitate the transformation of the picture by the spectators.[59]

Veidt attempted to put these views into practice in his next film for Gaumont, *The Passing of the Third Floor Back*. This was based on a play by Jerome K. Jerome, which dealt with the entry of a mysterious, Christ-like figure into a suburban guesthouse. Jerome's play, however, was loosely constructed, and its notions of human agency were obscure. The Gaumont film improved on the play; it was scripted by stalwarts Alma Reville and Michael Hogan, who had to implement the purifications demanded by the BBFC.[60] More importantly, the film was directed by Berthold Viertel, who was a close friend of Veidt's. Viertel was a Marxist of sorts, who had worked with Murnau and at the Vienna Volksbühne. In 1936 he went on to develop a bleak theory of historical necessity while working on *Rhodes of Africa*.[61] The rigour of class analysis which obtains in *The Passing of the Third Floor Back* should probably be attributed to him.

The narrative strategy of the film is quite simple. A stranger – cosmopolitan, elegant and magical – transforms the lives of the inhabitants of a guesthouse by awakening them to a sense of moral beauty. His presence forces them to acknowledge the paltriness of their everyday desires, and the inequities of the social system. The film expresses a visionary humanism, since the stranger represents everyone's best self: 'I came because you wanted me.'[62] The ideas in the film script were very much to Veidt's humanist tastes. He noted: 'In the silent film … a light shone from behind the Stranger's head. In this current production there is no such mumbo-jumbo. I am just a stranger, human, natural, benevolent. Yet I must convey to the audience the potentialities in my presence, and here beings my difficulty.'[63]

Veidt as the stranger achieves the impossible; he makes goodness interesting. He does it by deploying the resources of hand and eye in a way which recalls the practice of hypnotism; indeed one of the inhabitants calls him 'mesmeric'. Veidt has refined his technique until the performance is minimalist; the gaze is still, and the movements are tiny but resonant with meaning. Because the face is ambiguous, it is able to function as the site of everyone's desires. The performance was aided by very sympathetic *mise-en-scène*. Werndorff designed the sets, and in every particular they augment Veidt by throwing him into relief. When he is in shot, the composition within the frame is always symmetrical, and the lighting functions as a metaphor for his power. The script suggests that 'he opens the curtains and a streak of sunshine crosses the room, making a subtle difference to the chamber'. It is rare that the consonance between an actor and the other signifying elements of the narrative is as complete as this. With *The Passing of the Third Floor Back*, Veidt reached the apotheosis of his acting career. Because of subsequent mismanagement, lack of opportunity, industrial difficulties and the political situation, from then on it was to be downhill all the way.

Veidt's last film for Gaumont was *The King of the Damned*, about a penal colony in the tropics, in which a revolt is led by Convict 83 (Veidt). The sordid conditions in the camp, and the subsequent violent riots, caused profound problems with the BBFC, who refused permission for a subplot about a half-caste girl and insisted that the film be set in an undefined 'somewhere' so as not to offend anyone.[64] Walter Forde directed, Werndorff was art director and Sidney Gilliat contributed to the script. The problem was that the film was 'overcooked'. It was over-designed and fussy, and the camerawork rarely had any depth of field. The action scenes were badly orchestrated too. Balcon realised with hindsight that they had misjudged: 'we perhaps concentrated on the large-scale mob scenes and convict riots to the detriment of the personal issues in the story.'[65]

The 'personal issues', of course, were the powers inherent in the Veidt role. Veidt deployed his by now habitual slow gaze, upright posture and firm but slow movements, which concur with the demands of the script: '83's eyes are compelling. We play this mental fight for all it is worth.' On the whole, though, they were inappropriate for what was essentially an action part. To be sure, Veidt as Convict 83 expresses humanitarian values: 'Perhaps a day is coming when the horrors and evils of this place will be swept away ... a day when men will work side by side for the common good, respecting each other and themselves.'[66] But the fine speeches accord ill with the pace of the film.

Gaumont used Veidt to sell the film. Its most arresting poster was a drawing of Veidt's head containing the faces of all the other convicts; he was clearly meant to surround and supersede their suffering. The image is curiously redolent of those nineteenth-century drawings of phrenology and pathology, in which the individual's body represents social ills. But *The King of the Damned* was an inappropriate vehicle for this. Veidt could no longer flourish at Gaumont and, when his contract ended, he signed with Alexander Korda's London Films in the summer of 1936.

Korda also had difficulty finding the right roles for Veidt. In addition, Korda was experiencing financial problems which affected his forward planning. Veidt himself noted that he played in *Dark Journey* and *Under the Red Robe* as a special favour to Korda, since neither of them were strictly London vehicles.[67] *Dark Journey* was made by Victor Saville Productions; it was directed by Saville and staffed by old Korda hands such as Biro and Wimperis. The narrative was set in 1918 Norway, and dealt with the German Baron Marwitz, who was an undercover head of the Secret Service. He falls in love with a French spy, played by Vivien Leigh, and is instrumental in capturing her. The film was preoccupied with European unity and with the threat posed by 'bad' Germans:

'Is it a crime to be a German?'
'It's worse – it's a vulgarity.'[68]

On the face of it, the project of *Dark Journey* seems identical to the Gaumont *I Was a Spy*. But there are two vital differences, and both reside in the role Veidt was required to play. First, Marwitz is an aristocrat. This, doubtless due to Korda's team, which throughout the 1930s, as I have shown elsewhere, had traditionally used aristocratic symbolism as a means of carrying debates about class confidence and social power.[69] Secondly, he is a womaniser, and his amatory techniques are widely deployed. Both the aristocratic and the philandering aspects of the role were deeply alien to Veidt as an individual, and to 'Veidt' as a star. First, he was uxorious, and second, he had come to be associated with the flower of European high bourgeois values. He was, therefore, uneasy with the flamboyant aristocratic style. To add to these problems, the lighting and decor practices in the film did not favour him.

The same problems obtained for *Under the Red Robe*. This was made by New World Pictures, which had a very close relationship with London Films; personnel were paid by London Films through the covert agency of Rock Pictures.[70] Besides using a range of London personnel, other workers of the highest calibre were drafted in; Victor Sjöstrom directed, and James Wong Howe collaborated with Georges Périnal on the photography. Veidt, as the star, received £4,700 plus a percentage of the takings, which was a high salary in British pictures then.[71] Since he *was* the star, the sets, costumes and lighting favoured him, though he was handicapped by an extremely unbecoming wig.

*Under the Red Robe* dealt with court intrigues in early seventeeth-century France, and Veidt was required to play Gil de Berault, an aristocratic adventurer whose swordplay earns him the soubriquet of 'The Black Death'. He is an amatory adventurer too. Like other London costume films, *Under the Red Robe* was preoccupied by the nature of kingship (it deals with the just overthrow of Richlieu) and the definition of aristocratic style. Veidt had to act with nonchalance, which was quite different from his customary elegance. To be sure, Veidt was technically fit enough to run up and down staircases waving a rapier, but it was a problem of style. He had come to excel in portrayals of minimalist stillness, and de Berault was a trampoline role. There is some evidence that Veidt himself wanted to try a swashbuckling part: 'As a young man, I was not dashing. I was always in those very sinister parts … now, in *Under the Red Robe*, I fight, swim, ride … I am enjoying it all immensely!'[72] But it was an ill-judged desire, and his performance suffered accordingly.

By 1938, Veidt was feeling uneasy about the roles Korda had provided, and he was seeking finance for other vehicles which were more to his taste. Veidt's interest in the hypnotic aspects of acting had led him to Mesmer and Charcot. This developed in turn into a pre-occupation with Freud, and Veidt wished to make a film about a Freudian psychotherapist practising in Harley Street. This would open up the issues of symbolism in dreams, the Oedipus complex and the theory of sexuality: 'Most people … are eager to know just how much their own lives are influenced by dreams and subconscious thoughts.'[73] The European intellectual in Veidt was losing touch with his audience's taste. He was unable to raise funding or interest in the project. Instead,

Veidt made another spy film for Korda, who had a contract with Columbia outside London Films.

This time Veidt was fortunate in having Michael Powell as director of *The Spy in Black*. The film did very well at the box office, probably because of its topicality. The narrative was set in 1917 in the Orkneys, and dealt with the relationship between a British double agent (Valerie Hobson) and the German Captain Hardt (Veidt). Emeric Pressburger reconstructed the original so as to 'provide a stunning part for a great star' and Veidt collaborated on the script.[74] Powell and Pressburger recognised Veidt's worth: 'For us, he *was* the great German cinema. For us, he was invention, control, imagination, irony and elegance. He was the master technician of the camera, and knew where every light was placed.'[75] Fortunately for Veidt, Powell at that stage disliked master shots and favoured close-ups.

The problem was that Powell had an over-simplified notion of the tendency of Veidt's work: 'I know your work, and the theme as I see it, is about a man who is completely devoted to his duty.'[76] But, as I have suggested, Veidt by that time excelled in portraying men who were torn apart *by* their duty; he specialised in evisceration. However, Powell and Pressburger had the whip hand, and accordingly it is Hardt's gallantry which is to the fore as he chooses to go down with the ship he has commandeered.

Another problem was that the narrative had to be nuanced to accord with the mood in Britain, which was on a war footing. The balance between the good and bad Germans which had informed Veidt's earlier 1930s films was no longer welcome. Accordingly the script was much less ambiguous:

> 'You are English! I am German! We are enemies!'
> 'I like that better!'
> 'So do I! It simplifies everything!'[77]

Ambiguity, however, had become Veidt's stock-in-trade, and his performance attested to the strain.

Veidt's last film for Korda was *The Thief of Bagdad*, which was partly directed by Powell. He plays the magician Jaffar, who is able to afflict his rival with blindness, turn his enemy into a dog, summon up a hurricane and make a clockwork horse which can fly. Veidt *looks* wonderful; deeply tanned, with a turban, pearls, and thick gold gauntlets; his piercing blue eyes flash a lot, to excellent effect. But the fantasy genre within which the film is firmly located gives Veidt very little opportunity to *be* wonderful. Veidt tried to internalise the part as usual, but it was a struggle since the script constructed it in a one-dimensional way. Veidt noted: 'It is impossible to make such a character appear as a credible human being. He must be a fairy story character, yet at the same time it must be clear that he has come from Hell and he must go back to Hell.'[78]

Veidt had no appropriate explanatory model for the role, and so his performance suffered. It is powerful without being subtle. It is possible that Powell prompted Veidt to act in such an over-blown manner because he himself identified so strongly with the magus/artificer figure. Although *The Thief of Bagdad* is brilliant as a work of popular cinema, Veidt is only the chief ornament of its *mise-en-scène*.

Veidt's last British film, *Contraband*, was also directed by Powell, but this time they were under contract to British National, a less ambitious studio. The story deals with the contraband cargo of a Danish merchant captain (Veidt) and his relationship with a British spy (Valerie Hobson). The tone of the film is light-hearted, and it is firmly set within the chase genre. Powell noted that Pressburger's script concocted 'an amusing thriller in a wartime setting ... it was all pure corn, but corn served up by professionals, and it works'.[79]

The script requires Veidt to be able to order a meal in a restaurant and to wriggle out of some complicated rope knots. It makes no use of his talents, and it is rather like watching a racehorse pull a milk cart. The vehicle glides along, but a donkey would do the job just as well. *Picturegoer* was savage with Veidt for squandering his talents:

> How are the mighty fallen! The actor who once refused to consider playing the towering little monster of the French Revolution is now content to be a Danish sea captain, who is led up the garden by a pack of tuppeny-hapenny spies. The man who is built by nature to petrify kings and emperors with a look, rot the marrow of their bones with a sibilant whisper, is bent on setting himself down in your memory and mine as a commonplace, well-meaning ninny.[80]

What *Picturegoer* failed to recognise was that at this stage in his career, and in the war, Veidt had minimal control over the parts he was offered, and there were many humiliations. He had been bamboozled, presumably by his publicity agent, into giving absurd advice to women about the best types of maquillage and shampoo.[81] But worse, the powerful Board of Trade began to doubt Veidt's honesty. Official investigations of *Contraband* suspected that Veidt's fee had been artificially inflated so as to get the film into the double-quota class, and that he was involved in a loan arrangement or capital investment scam which he had not declared.[82] What seems more likely, given Veidt's personality, is that he loaned his own money to the production company. But he must have felt his honour was impugned, and soon he left for Hollywood, where he turned in a few competent but perfunctory performances such as Major Strasser in *Casablanca*. Shortly afterwards, Veidt died of a massive heart attack at the age of 50.

In conclusion, the acting career of Conrad Veidt contains interesting lessons for the historian of 1930s British cinema. It is clear that there were a number of determinants on the development of Veidt's new acting style in 1933. His radical change of physical demeanour was probably due to the Alexander technique, which had a profound effect on the type of social roles he was able to play. More importantly, Veidt was able to flourish only in a narrowly defined production context. He worked best for Michael Balcon, whose bourgeois seriousness most accorded with his own. He also worked best on projects to which he was intellectually committed, such as *The Wandering Jew*. A craftsman of superlative talents, Veidt was eventually inhibited by producers or directors who marketed him as an exotic rather than as his real specialism: a visionary, functioning powerfully from the margins.

7. Tod Slaughter and company in *Maria Marten or the Murder in the Red Barn*

## CHAPTER 7

# Tod Slaughter and the Cinema of Excess

*Jeffrey Richards*

I N the heyday of British films, there was always a tension between 'respectable' and 'unrespectable' cinema. In each decade there were films which conformed to a dominant critical aesthetic of documentary realism, quality literary sources and moral uplift and films which flouted these canons at every level, exalting unreality, hedonism, pulp fiction and melodramatic excess.[1]

In the 1950s these tensions can be seen to exist classically between the British war film, which re-created in black and white episodes from the late war, featuring almost exclusively the exploits of officers and gentlemen and enshrining a moral code based on restraint, service, sacrifice and self-deprecating good humour, and the Hammer horror film which explored in vivid Technicolor the contrast between the ordered bourgeois normality of Victorian England and the forces of unreason and excess lurking below the surface.[2] Hammer films celebrated the single-minded gratification of their desires by outlaw anti-heroes. In film after film the conscienceless, fanatical dandy Baron Frankenstein pursued his scientific experiments in defiance of the laws of God and Man, and the virile, arrogant, indestructible Count Dracula slaked his sexual desire on the bodies of a succession of female victims who subsequently became his willing confederates in the pursuit of sensation. Initially symbols of a ruthless and exploitative upper class, they had been transformed by the 1960s into the anti-heroes of an era of sex, style and instant gratification.

The 1940s saw a similar polarisation of styles and values. On the one hand there were the critically respected films about 'the people's war', black and white, semi-documentary features with realistic contemporary settings, ordinary people both in the services and on the home front, and the foregrounding of emotional restraint, service and sacrifice. On the other hand there were the critically excoriated Gainsborough melodramas, with their spectacular costumes, conspicuous consumption and extravagant goings-on. They were peopled by whip-wielding lords, bosom-heaving ladies, highwaymen and gypsies and consisted of abductions and seductions, duels, plots and murders, with a succession of anti-heroines who were independent, aggressive and single-minded in their pursuit of wealth, status and sexual gratification.

The 1930s also had its cinematic alternatives. The dominant value systems of the decade were contained in Alexander Korda's imperial epics, with their location shooting in the colonies, their celebrations of an upper-class officer caste dedicated to service, duty, self-sacrifice and emotional restraint, and the regional working-class comedies of Gracie Fields and George Formby which were about carrying on, making the best of things, overcoming all odds with a smile and a song and winning through by decency, hard work and good humour. What they had in common with each other and with both the 'people's war' films and the post-war war films was the downplaying of sex and sexuality and the playing up of duty and self-denial.[3]

Their unrespectable counterpart was the work of Tod Slaughter which has almost no critical standing in film history. His films were ignored by the establishment culture of the 1930s. *The Times*, for instance, reviewed only one of them, *The Face at the Window*, observing loftily:

> In the early days of the cinema there was always an audience ready to hiss the villain, weep for the heroine, and cheer the hero, and this film presumably has been made with this intent ... In any audience, no doubt, there will be some ready to cheer this diluted fare of melodrama, perhaps one or two to weep, and not a few to stifle an apathetic yawn.[4]

If noticed at all by later commentators, his films tend to be dismissed as antique, crude, barnstorming exercises, mere filmed stage plays rather than cinematic experiences.[5]

But this judgement is profoundly mistaken on several grounds. First, it fails to recognise the crucial role of stage melodrama in the shaping of British cinema and the significance of Slaughter's films in the historic transposition of Victorian melodrama to the cinema screen, where it is the matrix and precursor of both Gainsborough melodrama and Hammer horror, which can be grouped together with Slaughter's films as a 'cinema of excess'. Both Gainsborough and Hammer have received respectful critical attention in recent years.[6] It is time that Slaughter joined them in receiving similar critical recognition.

Interestingly, there were one or two unexpected voices raised in Slaughter's defence during his lifetime. *World Film News*, flagship journal of 1930s cinema intellectuals, ran an interview with Slaughter, describing him as 'the last outstanding representative of the real people's theatre'.[7] The rise of the cinema had turned the theatre into a middle-class institution. Touring melodrama was the last vestige of working-class theatre. It was very likely this which endeared it in principle to the largely left-wing intelligentsia who would probably have rejected it on artistic and aesthetic grounds.

Graham Greene, then writing film criticism for *The Spectator*, published an unusually enthusiastic review of *The Face at the Window*:

> It is one of the best English pictures I have seen and leaves the American horror films far behind. You go to laugh, but find yourself immediately – from the ingenious titling on – in the grip of the fine firm traditional dialogue, the magnificent casting, sets and camerawork which plonk you surely back into that vague Victorian period, when anything might happen ... Mr. Tod Slaughter is certainly one of our finest living actors ... that dancing sinister step, the raised shoulder and the flickering eyelid. What makes this kind of melodrama so ... convincing ... Perhaps it is that the author really believes ... in good and evil, in a morality which has the tradition of a thousand years behind it.[8]

Melodrama was indeed the people's theatre, developed in the 1790s and dominating the repertoires of popular theatres until the First World War. In his pioneering book on melodrama, Michael Booth gives a classic definition of the form:

> Essentially melodrama is a dream world inhabited by dream people and dream justice, offering audiences the fulfilment and satisfaction found only in dreams. An idealization and simplification of the world of reality, it is in fact the world its audiences want but cannot get ... an allegory of human experience dramatically ordered, as it should be rather than as it is. In this world life is uncomplicated, easy to understand and immeasurably exciting. People are always true to their surface appearances and always think and behave in the way these appearances dictate. One of the great appeals of this world is clarity: character, conduct, ethics and situations are perfectly simple, and one always knows what the end will be ... The world of melodrama is a world of certainties ... where vice and virtue coexist in pure whiteness and pure blackness ... where good triumphs over and punishes evil, and virtue receives tangible rewards. The superiority of such a world over the entirely unsatisfactory everyday world hardly needs demonstration, and it is this romantic and escapist appeal that goes a long way to explain the enduring popularity of melodrama.[9]

Melodrama certainly did contain stock characters, sensational setpieces and moral absolutes. It did emphasise plot over characterisation. But it would be wrong to dismiss melodrama as mere escapism. For one thing, melodrama was characterised by fidelity to contemporary reality in its settings, and for another it often dealt with specific social issues such as crime, factory conditions, alcoholism and gambling as well as more general class and gender issues in ways to which audiences could relate directly. This is increasingly recognised by historians of the genre.[10]

A major revaluation of the genre was made by Peter Brooks. Brooks focused specifically on melodramatic excess not as a cause for criticism but for appreciation and understanding of how melodrama operated:

> The desire to express all seemed a fundamental characteristic of the melodramatic mode. Nothing is spared because nothing is left unsaid; the characters stand on stage and utter the unspeakable, give voice to their deepest feelings, dramatize through their heightened and polarized words and gestures the whole lesson of their relationships ... the world is subsumed by an underlying Manichaeanism, and the narrative creates the excitement of its drama by putting us in touch with the conflict of good and evil played out under the surface of things.[11]

So, strong emotions, overt villainy, moral polarisation, extreme behaviour and extravagant expressions are all part and parcel of the form. Brooks claims further that melodrama becomes the principal mode for 'uncovering, demonstrating and making operative the essential moral universe in a post-sacred era', in recognising and confronting, combating and expelling evil to purge the social order.[12] Melodrama thus functions as ritual and catharsis. The style of acting and diction in particular is inflated and unreal. Brooks argues that 'melodramatic rhetoric, and the whole expressive enterprise of the genre, represents a victory over repression. We could conceive this repression as simultaneously social, psychological, historical and conventional ... The melodramatic utterance breaks through everything that constitutes the reality principle, all its censorship, accommodations tonings-down. Desire cries aloud its language ... Desire triumphs.'[13] The critical resistance to and embarrassment about melodrama may derive, he suggests, from its rejection of censorship repressions. One of the great appeals of melodrama is thus the possibility of saying the unsayable, resisting control and accommodations, and rejecting the class system or sexual repression. This interpretation could be applied directly to the films of Tod Slaughter.

It is worth recalling that the melodramatic style of posturing, gesture and extravagance developed for functional reasons. Originally melodrama was mime with music. The patent theatres had a monopoly of straight dramatic performances until the stage was opened up by the abolition of the patents in 1843. But the style persisted as a way of gaining attention from and controlling the large, noisy, enthusiastic audiences in the working-class theatres. It had become accepted. These original elements of stage melodrama – mime acting, extravagant gesture, musical accompaniment – transferred easily and naturally to the silent screen. The stage had been evolving steadily towards cinema, with flashbacks, split screen and spectacle all having their stage precursors.[14] It is no coincidence that the old stage melodrama theatres in the poor inner-city districts were among the earliest to be converted into cinemas. The staples of the melodrama stage naturally became the staples of the cinema, both in Britain and America. *East Lynne*, the classic stage melodrama of mother love, based on Mrs Henry Wood's novel, was filmed in 1902, 1908 (twice), 1909, 1910, 1912, 1913 (twice), 1915, 1916, 1921, 1922, 1925 and 1931.[15] The popular stage hits of the leading nineteenth-century melodramatists George R. Sims and Dion Boucicault were filmed and refilmed for the British silent cinema: Sims's *The Lights O'London*, *The Harbour Lights* and *In the Ranks* in 1914, *The Romany Rye*, *The Nightbirds of London*, *Master and Man* and *The Trumpet Call* in 1915, *The Ever Open Door*, *The Great Day*, *The English Rose*, *The Lights of Home* and *The Lights of London* in 1920, *His Other Wife* in 1921 and the *The Harbour Lights* in 1923; Boucicault's *After Dark* in 1915, *The Colleen Bawn* in 1924 and *The Streets of London* in 1929. H. B. Irving, son of Sir Henry Irving, starred in a 1916 film version of his father's celebrated melodrama, *The Lyons Mail*, from the play by Charles Reade. The last great representatives of stage melodrama in the 1920s, Sir John Martin Harvey and Matheson Lang, appeared in British silent versions of their stage hits.

Plays like *East Lynne* and *The Lyons Mail*, recurrently revived on the stage in their heyday and subsequently filmed and refilmed for the cinema, constitute a popular folk memory, a hinterland of the imagination shared by the mass of the population who recognised the familiar characters, themes and setpieces when they recurred and which depended for their impact on the recognition and operation of a shared value system which gave the action of the drama meaning and purpose.

The arrival of the talkies in the late 1920s might have suggested that the days of filmed melodrama were over. But in fact it received a new lease of life with the addition of dialogue. In 1931 Donald Calthrop starred in a film version of Irving's virtuoso vehicle *The Bells*, with a score by Gustav Holst. This is currently a lost film.[16] In the same year,

Sir John Martin Harvey made a sound version of *The Lyons Mail* in which he had acted with Irving at the Lyceum when a young man. Larger-than-life melodramatic villains featured in British screen adaptations of Dickens such as *The Old Curiosity Shop* (1935) with Hay Petrie as the malignant dwarf Daniel Quilp and *Scrooge* (1935) with Sir Seymour Hicks in the title role. The latter was based on a long-running stage adaptation of Dickens's story.

For 1930s British cinema, however, Victorian melodrama meant essentially Tod Slaughter. Tod Slaughter was born Norman Carter Slaughter in Newcastle-Upon-Tyne in 1885 and educated at Newcastle Royal Grammar School. He made his stage debut in 1905 in West Hartlepool and was soon managing a touring company specialising in melodrama, performing such plays as *No Mother to Guide Her*, *A Warning to Women* and *A Wrecker of Men*. In 1913 he became lessee of the Hippodrome theatres at Richmond and Croydon, relinquishing the leases when, on the outbreak of war in 1914, he joined the army. He served for the duration, latterly in the Royal Flying Corps, and was demobilised in January 1919. He resumed his theatrical career, running the Theatre Royal, Chatham, for nearly four years. In 1922 he took over the Elephant and Castle Theatre and there put on a series of classic Victorian melodramas including *Maria Marten*, *Sweeney Todd* and *Jack Shepherd*. He later recalled:

> The people loved them. Visitors began to come from the West End and I had distinguished people every other night. Some of them candidly said they came for amusement, but one and all they forgot to laugh ... They found that melodrama was damned good drama, and they felt the power of the company. It was like a drug and they yielded to it. They began to see that this old stuff is not just something antique, left over from the last century. They began ... to see that it's very much alive, in fact, and will never die.[17]

He believed that melodrama gave people what they wanted: 'The real theatrical thrill; crime and punishment; mystery; the villain brought to justice ... The revival of the old popular drama after the war is what I regard as my most important work. I always play them straight, you know, I have never burlesqued them. That would be madness.'[18]

On giving up the Elephant and Castle after three years, Slaughter toured the London suburbs with a repertoire that included *Maria Marten*, *Sweeney Todd*, *The Face at the Window*, *The Lights of London*, *The Silver King* and *Springheeled Jack*. This was to set the pattern for the rest of his career, touring the provinces and the suburbs with his Victorian melodrama repertoire. He claimed in *Who's Who in the Theatre* (1952) to have appeared in 500 different plays and gave his hobby as 'work'. He died in 1956 aged 70 at Derby after appearing in a production of *Maria Marten*. The fact that he went bankrupt in 1953 suggests that the public's theatrical taste had finally begun to change and that Victorian melodrama was no longer acceptable as a viable element of continuing theatrical fare.

Slaughter made his screen debut at the age of 50 in 1935 and between then and the Second World War appeared in seven filmed melodramas. During the same period, he played in three other films. He had supporting roles, as the heroine's father in *Darby and Joan* (1937, MGM-Rock), a romance based on a novel by the popular writer 'Rita', and as a showman in *Song of the Road* (1937, Sound City), a characteristic populist drama from John Baxter about an old farm labourer in search of work. He also appeared with distinction as millionaire criminal mastermind Michael Larron, head of the Black Quorum, in George King's pulp thriller feature *Sexton Blake and the Hooded Terror* (1938, MGM-King).

George King, who produced all of Slaughter's Victorian melodramas, was one of the 'quota kings' of the British cinema. A former agent, he produced 150 films between 1928 and 1945, many of them to fulfil the 'quota' introduced by the Cinematograph Films Act of 1927, which required 20 per cent of films shown in Britain to be of British origin. According to Derek Threadgall, where other producers made this type of film for 15 shillings a foot and sold them for £1 a foot, King made his for 14 shillings and 6 pence and sold them for £1 a foot and this margin gave him a nice profit.[19]

It cannot only be the quota which explains Slaughter's films. From 1935 to 1938 the Slaughter films were produced at Shepperton Studios and released by MGM as part of their British quota. After the Cinematograph Films Act of 1938 revised the quota and imposed a minimum cost limit to improve quality and eliminate the 'quota quickies' which had earned derision from critics and audiences, George King moved his base of operation to Beaconsfield Studios and set up Pennant Productions to make films for British Lion release. Among the earliest Pennant productions were two further Slaughter melodramas, *The Face at the Window* and *Crimes at the Dark House*. This suggests that they were profitable in themselves; nevertheless, they never became respectable. H. F. Maltby, the veteran actor and dramatist, who scripted or coscripted five of them, makes no mention of the Slaughter films in his autobiography, *Ring Up the Curtain*, published in 1950.

Their success with the public may be explained by the fact that they are part of a shared folklore with deep roots in popular culture. The first Slaughter film, *Maria Marten or Murder in the Red Barn* (1935) was based on fact. The true story of Maria Marten was a sordid one. Maria was nearly 26, the good-looking daughter of a farm labourer at Polstead, Suffolk. She had three illegitimate children by three different fathers and was pressuring the father of the third child, 24–year-old squire's son William Corder, for money. He agreed to marry her but they quarrelled, he killed her on 18 May 1827 and buried her in the Red Barn. Corder disappeared to London, advertised for a wife and married, a respectable schoolteacher in Ealing who stood by him when he was tracked down by the Bow Street Runners and arrested for Maria's murder. Eventually he confessed and was publicly hanged on 17 August 1828. The story, which was extensively reported in the press at the time, seized the public imagination on account of three elements: Maria's mother was said to have dreamed on three successive nights that her missing daughter was buried in the Red Barn, giving it a supernatural aspect; the murderer was pursued and captured by Bow Street Runner Pharos Lee, making him an early detective hero; and there was the class element of the illicit liaison of farm labourer's daughter and squire's son with the latter failing to 'do the decent thing'.

These elements secured the enduring success of the story. According to Michael Kilgarriff, only one version of the story was published in the nineteenth-century – an 1877 version performed at the Star Theatre, Swansea – but there were many different stage versions of the story in the nineteenth century, beginning with *The Murder in the Red Barn*, played at the Royal Pavilion, Mile End, in 1828.[20] There have even been three new stage versions in the twentieth century, in 1928, 1964 and 1969. Inevitably, the Victorian dramatisations transformed Maria from an unmarried mother of three into a wronged innocent, a beautiful country maiden seduced and murdered by the wicked squire, who becomes in the stage versions an older rather than a younger man. There had already been four film versions (1902, 1908, 1913 and 1928) when George King chose it as the subject of his first Tod Slaughter production. Nevertheless, he took the precaution of submitting the script to the British Board of Film Censors (BBFC). It was approved but King was told to eliminate the procession of Corder to the gallows and his hanging. These scenes were filmed none the less and when the film was submitted for approval on 27 February 1935, it was passed with an 'A' certificate on condition that procession and execution were deleted. As it stands now, the procession and actual hanging were cut. We see Corder standing on the scaffold and a roll of drums signals his end.[21]

*Sweeney Todd, the Demon Barber of Fleet Street* (1936) was the second of

George King's Slaughter vehicles. Sweeney Todd was not an historical character but a Victorian urban myth. He first appeared in a serial, *The String of Pearls*, by Thomas Peckett Prest, a prolific writer of 'penny dreadfuls', in *The People's Periodical* in 1846. It was adapted for the stage by George Dibdin Pitt, resident playwright of the Britannia Theatre, Hoxton, in 1847. Subsequent adaptations appeared by different authors during the course of the nineteenth century and there have been three new adaptations since the Second World War as well as a musical version by Stephen Sondheim.

Peter Haining has tracked down three sources for the story.[22] The name and the cannibalism element in the story probably derive from the career of the sixteenth-century Scottish cannibal Sawney Beane, 'The Maneater of Midlothian', whose story had appeared in a magazine edited by Prest in 1835. A recurrent French urban myth centres on a barber who kills his customers and has them disposed of by a neighbouring pie merchant in his pies. A story dated *circa* 1800 appeared in France recounting this tale, but Haining has discovered a fourteenth-century French ballad on the same theme. However, Haining also notes that Prest dates his story precisely to 1785 and contemporary newspapers carried an account of a murder by a barber in Fleet Street of a young gentleman visiting London. Blended together, these elements gave us the legend of Sweeney Todd, the demon barber of Fleet Street. There had been one previous film version, in 1928 and starring Moore Marriott as Todd, before George King's 1936 production. Once again King submitted a script to the censors. They noted that the silent version had been submitted to them on 4 September 1928 and had at first been turned down. After considerable cutting, it was passed. The cutting involved deleting the actual murders and all references to human remains in pies. King was adjured to observe the same rules, and when making the film he bore these strictures in mind. The actual murders were not shown. Slaughter merely approached his victims with a razor, cackling. There was no explicit mention of the human remains in the pies. But the piemaker, Mrs Lovett, is Todd's accomplice, her pies are regularly eaten during the film and the audience's knowledge of their contents is quite rightly presupposed by the film-makers and underlined with nudges and winks.[23]

*The Crimes of Stephen Hawke* (1936) was not a Victorian original but was scripted by Paul White, Jack Celestin and H. F. Maltby from a story by Frederick Hayward, written in the style of Victorian melodrama. In an interview preceding the film Slaughter describes it as 'a new old melodrama'.

It was back to a Victorian original for *It's Never Too Late to Mend* (1937). Charles Reade's novel, published in 1856, was an exposé of Victorian prison conditions and was directly inspired by the regime of Lt. Austin, chief warder at Birmingham Gaol, whose brutalities in 1851–53 led to his conviction and imprisonment. After several unauthorised stage adaptations, it was successfully adapted for the stage by Reade himself and Arthur Shirley. This version was revived in London in 1874, 1878, 1881, 1885 and 1891, and became a staple of stock companies. It was filmed in 1917 and scenes from the play appeared in a silent film series, 'Tense Moments from Great Plays', in 1922. *The Ticket of Leave Man* (1937) was based on a celebrated melodrama by Tom Taylor, first performed in 1863, and much revived thereafter. It was filmed in 1918. *The Face at the Window* (1939) was based on another much performed melodrama by F. Brooke Warren, first seen in Salford and Blackburn in 1897. It had already been filmed in 1920 with C. Aubrey Smith in the lead and in 1932 with Raymond Massey.

The final Slaughter melodrama in this cycle was *Crimes at the Dark House* (1940), adapted from Wilkie Collins's *The Woman in White*. Serialised in Dickens's journal *All the Year Round*, it was an enormous hit in 1859 and in book form in 1860 enjoyed a great vogue. There were several unauthorised adaptations before Collins himself successfully adapted it for the stage in 1871. It ran at the Olympic Theatre, London, from 9 October 1871 to 24 February 1872 and then toured. There had been a British silent film version, *The Woman in White* (1929), directed by Herbert Wilcox and starring Blanche Sweet and Cecil Humphreys, and three Hollywood versions (1912, 1914, 1917). With the exception of *The Crimes of Stephen Hawke*, then, all the subjects chosen as film vehicles for Tod Slaughter were familiar, well established and well loved.

The seven Slaughter melodramas stand together as a distinctive body of work. They were all produced by George King who also directed five of them. The other two were directed by Milton Rosmer (*Maria Marten*) and David MacDonald (*It's Never Too Late to Mend*). Five were scripted or co-scripted by H. F. Maltby and three by Frederick Hayward. Four of them were photographed by Hone Glendinning and four were designed by Philip Bawcombe. Slaughter of course starred in all of them and his wife Jenny Lynn supported him in one of them. Marjorie Taylor played the female lead in four of them; John Warwick the hero in two, and Eric Portman the hero in two. Regularly returning character actors included D. J. Williams (four films), Aubrey Mallalieu and Ben Williams (three), Robert Adair, John Singer, Ben Soutten, Margaret Yarde and Stella Rho (two). They function as a cinematic repertory company.

There are, however, significant differences between the Slaughter films and their Victorian theatrical progenitors. Where the Victorian melodramas were contemporary stories in contemporary settings, they were by the time Slaughter came to film them costume dramas. Their distance from the present was specifically emphasised in the first three. *Maria Marten* began with the actors in costume being introduced on stage by a nineteenth-century theatre manager and each taking a bow to the audience. *Sweeney Todd* was contained within a flashback as a modern-day barber tells the story to a client who at the end flees from the shop. *Stephen Hawke* is framed by an edition of the popular radio show *In Town Tonight* featuring a duet from the singing team Flotsam and Jetsam and interviews by a dinner-jacketed announcer with a Cockney catsmeat man and with Tod Slaughter talking about his new film. The rest of the films had no such introductions, it being apparent that by now audiences were willing to accept the films for what they were.

It should be stressed, however, that while *Maria Marten* openly acknowledges its theatricality, what follows is not a case of placing the cameras in the front row of the stalls and photographing the action. Although the music, acting style and some of the sets recall the theatre, the film is staged, lit and cut to give it cinematic life and dramatic flow. While much of the film is done in medium shot with few close-ups, the camera tracks on movement, dollies in at key moments and the murder is done in full-blooded Gothic style, with bold close-ups, atmospheric longshots and effective use of shadow, thunder and lightning. The successful cinematisation of the story is presumably attributable to the director Milton Rosmer, a veteran character actor but also a director under contract to Gaumont-British for whom he made *Channel Crossing* (1933) with Matheson Lang, *The Guvnor* (1935) with George Arliss and *The Great Barrier* (1937) with Richard Arlen. He was borrowed from Gaumont for this project. George King was a more functional and rudimentary director than Rosmer but his work still stands as distinctively cinematic rather than merely photographed theatre.

Just as the melodramas have become self-consciously historical, they have also lost their specific contemporary relevance. *It's Never Too Late to Mend* was specifically intended as a protest against mid-Victorian prison conditions. The Slaughter film version begins with a preface, needed to meet the requirements of the censor forbidding criticism of contemporary British prisons, carefully distancing the film from the present. It points out that when the book was first published in 1856 it caused a sensation and Queen Victoria ordered an investigation which led to wide-ranging prison reform and 'the universally high standard prevailing today'. *The Ticket of Leave Man* was based on a social problem drama, illustrating the plight of paroled prisoners. As David Mayer has pointed out, the play, adapted by Tom Taylor from a French original, addressed four issues of current concern in 1863: the introduction of the ticket of leave system for convicts, concern about police spies with the creation of an official plain-clothes detective division in the Metropolitan Police, the 'surveillance' system for monitoring parolees and the garrotting scare of 1862–63 which was attributed by many to paroled convicts.[24] Few of these specific concerns was still relevant in 1937 though the plight of paroled prisoners remained a timeless issue.

They have also been slimmed down and simplified to meet a cinematic running time that was usually less than half the running time of the original plays. The film *Maria Marten*, for instance, eliminates both the supernatural (Mrs Marten's dreams and the appearance of Maria's ghost to haunt Corder which was a feature of the Victorian plays) and the detective element (Pharos Lee is cut). The film retains the gormless maid and her bumpkin admirer as comic relief counterpoint to the tragic main story and adds a gypsy lover for Maria plus all the romantic paraphernalia of gypsy encampment, gypsy fortune-teller and gypsy curses. But the cutting and restructuring has the effect of foregrounding sex and class as central themes, and this in the last resort is what all the Slaughter films are about.

In addition, and equally significant, is the fact that in all the Slaughter films the villain's role is built up to make him the centre of the action. Slaughter gives more or less the same performance in each film and it conforms exactly to Brooks's definition of melodramatic acting, externalising emotions, expressing forbidden desires and rejoicing in his wickedness. It is a cinema of excess in which Slaughter is in his element, gleeful in his villainy, leering, cackling, eye-rolling, hand-rubbing, revelling in lechery and murder but doing it with such eye-twinkling relish that he makes the audience his accomplices. It is impossible not to warm to him as he repeats his catchphrases in *Sweeney Todd*: 'I'll polish him off', and, caressing the throats of his victims, 'I love my work'. In *The Crimes of Stephen Hawke* it is revealed from the outset that genial, elderly, bespectacled Regency money-lender Stephen Hawke is in fact the iron-gripped housebreaker and robber 'The Spinebreaker', and so throughout his delicious double-entendres can be enjoyed by the audience. He is first seen casing a house for a robbery and is discovered by a priggish small boy who threatens to expose him. 'Come here, my little man,' wheedles Hawke. The boy approaches and off screen there is the sound of a scream and a spine being broken. The audience are made complicit with Slaughter's joyful execution of his 'work'. 'I promised to make you a bride – you shall be a bride,' he hisses as he murders Maria Marten, 'a bride of death.' It is a line he repeats as he murders the maid in *Crimes at the Dark House*, confirming the continuity of character and style throughout the films.

In *Maria Marten*, Slaughter plays William Corder, the Squire of Polstead, pillar of respectability on the surface but underneath that veneer an aristocratic cad. He seduces innocent farmer's daughter Maria Marten (Sophie Stewart) with the aid of strong drink. He then abandons her and flees to London. There he loses a fortune gambling and becomes engaged to a wealthy, psalm-singing spinster. Back in Polstead, he is confronted by a pregnant Maria demanding marriage. He lures her to the Red Barn, murders and buries her. When her disappearance is reported, Corder denounces Carlos the gypsy (Eric Portman), who loved Maria, and puts up a reward for his capture. Carlos is tracked to the Red Barn but there Corder's dog disturbs Maria's grave and at the sight of Maria's body, Corder goes mad and confesses, is arrested and hanged, with Carlos as volunteer hangman.

The film can be seen to be working on three different levels. At one level, it is the classic Victorian morality tale. It warns girls of the danger of getting pregnant outside marriage. Maria, once exposed as pregnant, is expelled from the house by her father ('I disown you. Go and never come back') in a classic Victorian tableau. Subsequently she is murdered by her false lover. At another level the film shows sympathy to outsiders. It is set firmly in the context of the community. The film opens in the Red Barn with a vigorously-staged and cheerful barn dance with the whole village, including the Squire, participating. Later, that sense of community is violated as the Squire uses the barn for the murder. The film is structured around a succession of exclusions from the community. Carlos the gypsy and the gypsy fortune-teller are expelled from the dance simply for being gypsies. Carlos is rejected as a suitor for Maria's hand by her father and later accused of the murder by Corder – both events unjust. Maria too is excluded because of her pregnancy. At the end the community gather to see Corder hanged and Carlos acts as hangman, one outsider avenging another. Moral order and justice are simultaneously restored.

On a third level, thanks to the centrality and power of Slaughter's performance, it is a celebration of excess. Corder seduces Maria, subsequently rejecting her as 'the village slut'. He gambles recklessly ('I'd play him if the Devil himself were perched on his shoulders'). He hypocritically woos a spinster, joining in the singing of psalms with an ostentatiously fake piety. He persecutes a minority, the gypsies. He even cheerfully gulls a country bumpkin out of his money. Finally, having gone mad, he defies the world in his cell: 'Yelp, you curs, I'll beat you yet.'

The film of *Sweeney Todd* is a simplified version of the story as dramatised by George Dibdin Pitt, with the order of events rearranged, some supporting characters eliminated, the ghosts of Todd's victims dispensed with, and some episodes reworked: in the film it is the hero Mark Ingestrie and not, as in the play, the magistrate Sir Richard Brown who goes to Todd's shop disguised as a farmer to trap him. But the familiar melodramatic elements of secret passages, disguises and star-crossed lovers are all there.

Slaughter plays Sweeney Todd, the Fleet Street barber who kills off his wealthy clients and has their bodies disposed of by his neighbour and accomplice, Mrs Lovett, the pie-maker. When the film opens, he has already disposed of eight apprentices before Tobias Wragg, a parish orphan arrives, escorted by the beadle, in an episode not in the original play and interpolated from *Oliver Twist*, adding to the Dickensian flavour of the proceedings. Todd terrifies and ill-treats Tobias who eventually escapes to throw in his lot with the hero and heroine. We see Todd successively dispose of a returning Indian merchant, Findlay, his fence Parsons who tries to blackmail him and his accomplice Mrs Lovett, whom he suspects of betraying him. Eventually Mark Ingestrie exposes him. Todd sets fire to his shop and prepares to flee but after a struggle with Mark topples to his death in his tip-up barber's chair which precipitated his victims into the cellar.

Like *Maria Marten*, the film contains two pairs of lovers: the romantic couple, the poor but honest sailor Mark Ingestrie, played as a gentleman by Bruce Seton, who loves ship-owner's daughter Johanna Oakley (Eve Lister), and their working-class comic counterpoints, Mark's comrade Pearley and his lover, an adenoidal, open-mouthed, vacant-eyed lady's maid (Davina Craig). Both couples are united at the end. The crimes of the arch-villain and his ultimate exposure and destruction and the trials and tribulations of star-crossed lovers and their eventual happy resolution are standard elements in Victorian melodrama, but the film version contains an added capitalist/imperialist dimension not in the original play. In the play, Oakley is a spectacle-maker. In the film, he is a ship-owner and this gives the story a whole extra resonance. Sweeney Todd plans to use the proceeds of his murders and robberies to become Stephen Oakley's partner in his ship-owning business. At the same time, he has designs on Johanna. When his investment appears to be lost,

Todd demands Johanna in marriage as compensation. Mark, arriving with his ship on the coast of West Africa, helps drive off the natives besieging the trading post of Scottish trader Patterson. Mortally wounded, Patterson bequeaths to Mark a bag of pearls. Mark is robbed and almost murdered by Todd, just as Todd appropriated the profits of Indian nabob, Findlay. Mark, enriched by his imperial plunder, plans to marry Johanna. So there are legitimate profits to be made from free enterprise capitalism in the Empire (Mark, Findlay) but illegitimate profits to be made at home by Todd.

*The Crimes of Stephen Hawke* centres on the murders and robberies committed by Hawke, apparently a respectable money-lender but in reality the feared burglar and murderer 'The Spinebreaker', who murders a small boy who threatens to expose him, an aristocratic guest at his party whose emerald ring he covets, and a neighbour, shipping agent Joshua Trimble, who suspects him. He departs each murder scene cackling with glee.

He has, however, a soft spot for his adoptive daughter Julie (Marjorie Taylor), who loves Matthew Trimble (Eric Portman), the son of Joshua. Unmasked by Matthew, posing as his dead father, Hawke flees and to escape capture gets himself arrested and imprisoned for stealing bread. When he learns that, in order to protect him, his daughter is being forced to marry the brutal and lecherous prison governor Miles Archer, who has uncovered the identity of 'The Spinebreaker', Hawke breaks gaol and kills Archer. Pursued to his own house, he falls to his death from the roof. Unusually in Slaughter villains, this one has been able to inspire genuine love from his daughter and his one-eyed, one-legged associate, Nathaniel.

Charles Reade's novel and play *It's Never Too Late to Mend* intertwines two stories. One is that of poor but honest farmer George Fielding who goes to Australia and works in the goldfields to earn enough to marry the woman he loves, Susan Merton. The other centres on a thief, Tom Robinson, who is gaoled and terribly ill-treated before being transported to Australia where he is befriended by Fielding, redeems himself and becomes an honest member of society, proving the truth of the old adage 'It's never too late to mend'.

The film similarly intertwines the two stories, though eliminating the Australian section of the book which is merely reported on by the characters. However, it replaces Tom Robinson as the central character by Squire John Meadows, played by a moustache-twirling, cackling and eye-rolling Slaughter. In the film, as in the book, he wants to get his hands on Susan Merton. So he does everything he can to separate the lovers and bring about his will, foreclosing the mortgage on both her father and Fielding through his tool, lawyer Crawley, and then when Fielding leaves for Australia, intercepting their letters by blackmailing the postmaster, and when Fielding returns rich, drugging and robbing him. His treachery is eventually exposed by Robinson.

The long central section of the film, however, deals with his role as visiting magistrate at the county gaol, where he is revealed as a sadist. He orders the use of solitary confinement in the black hole, bread and water diets, the treadmill, straitjackets and floggings. He personally flogs prisoners, taking down the cat o'nine tails with evident relish and talking constantly of the prisoners as his 'naughty children'. The boy Matthew Josephs, who stole bread for his dying mother, dies of the ill-treatment he receives. Tom Robinson is saved from going mad by the intervention of the prison chaplain, Mr Eden, who embodies Christian compassion and is present at the climax of the film to stand in front of Meadows with a crucifix to protect his victims from his machinations. In the end, Meadows goes mad and ends up on the treadmill himself, with the words of the parson ringing in his ears: 'It's never too late to mend.' In the book, Meadows does not appear at all in the prison section of the book. It is the prison governor, Hawes, who is responsible for the horrors there. By substituting Meadows for Hawes, the film allows Slaughter to dominate the proceedings and redoubles his villainy.

The film of *The Ticket of Leave Man* is based mainly on the first three acts of the play, largely omitting the fourth in which Bob Brierly's prison record stops him getting a job as a navvy. There are two major alterations from the play. The first is an upwards social revaluation of hero and heroine. In the play Bob Brierly is described as 'a Lancashire lad' and he speaks with a North Country accent. Experiencing the delights of big city life for the first time, he falls into the toils of criminal 'Tiger' Dalton. He befriends a street singer, May Edwards, and their love later develops during his three years in prison. In the film, Brierly (John Warwick) becomes the usual well-mannered and well-spoken poor but honest gentleman hero of all the Slaughter melodramas and May (Marjorie Taylor) is transformed into a genteel singing star in the pleasure gardens. They are also already engaged at the outset of the film.

More significantly, the cuts in the text and the elimination of minor characters lead to the building-up of the role of the villain, called simply 'The Tiger', and played by Slaughter in his customary eye-rolling and cackling manner. The film opens with him robbing a house in Peckham and garrotting two policemen, something only referred to in the play.

Thereafter it traces his nefarious schemes: he frames Bob Brierly for passing forged banknotes in order to get his hands on May whom he desires. When Brierly is released and gets a job at a bill discount office, 'The Tiger' reveals his prison record and gets him sacked. He then seeks to recruit him to help rob the office safe but Brierly informs the police and 'The Tiger', fleeing through a churchyard, falls into an open grave and breaks his neck.

'The Tiger' garrottes two policemen, and an ex-convict who recognises him. He garrottes his associate, a cunning, hook-nosed, hand-wringing, 'Oi Veh' Jewish stereotype, Melter Moss, who is pawnbroker, money-lender, fence and forger. But the scriptwriters have added another dimension to the film which is not in the play: 'The Tiger' has a double life, masquerading as the saintly Mr Pybus, head of the Good Samaritan Aid Society, which purports to help released prisoners. He uses the Society's office as his base of operations, eventually setting fire to it with his other associate, a thug called 'Ugly', trapped inside. 'Ugly' is burned to death.

The lecherous pursuit of an innocent maiden and a criminal double life by an apparently respectable figure lie also at the heart of the action in *The Face at the Window*. The setting is Paris in 1880 and the city is terrorised by a series of murders and robberies committed by a mysterious criminal called 'The Wolf', whose crimes involve a hideous face at the window, a blood-curdling howl and a knife in the back. Slaughter plays the wealthy Chevalier del Gardo, complete with cape, slouched hat and monocle. He has fixed his lecherous designs on Cecile (Marjorie Taylor), the daughter of banker Brisson. After the bank is robbed by 'The Wolf' and faces a crisis, del Gardo offers to become a partner in return for Cecile's hand. When Cecile resists his advances, professing her love for well-born but penniless bank clerk Lucien Cortier (John Warwick), del Gardo has him framed for the robbery and he is dismissed from the bank by Brisson who does not inform the police out of memory of his friendship for Lucien's father. When Brisson begins to suspect del Gardo of framing Cortier, he is murdered by 'The Wolf'. Cortier now accuses del Gardo of being 'The Wolf' and challenges him to a duel but, before the duel can take place, del Gardo's henchmen carry off Cortier and throw him into the Seine, bound hand and foot. He is rescued by the comic servants who have observed the proceedings from a hiding place.

Cecile is lured to 'The Wolf's lair, a splendid low dive, 'The Blind Rat', peopled by prostitutes, crooks and Apache dancers and presided over by the majestic Margaret Yarde as La Pina It is here that del Gardo has decoyed a succession of young girls for his pleasure. Cecile, brought there to see the allegedly injured Cortier, is subjected to del Gardo's advances, but Cortier turns up, rescues her and escapes. He asks the police to allow his friend Professor Le Blanc to perform his new electrical experiments that animate murdered corpses who then write down the name of their murderer. It will be done with Brisson's body. Del Gardo agrees to attend the experiment, but before the agreed time he turns up, preceded by 'The Face', and stabs Le Blanc to death. Cortier takes over and substitutes his servant for the corpse. The 'corpse' writes del Gardo's name during the experiment and del Gardo confesses he is 'The Wolf', defies the police and escapes by diving into the Seine. The police and Cortier chase him to his home where in the cellar they find him preparing to dispose of a cage containing 'The Face', his hideously deformed foster brother, whom he uses to terrify his victims. As he prepares to slide the cage into the Seine, 'The Face' grabs him round the neck and they both end up drowning in the Seine.

*Crimes at the Dark House*, credited to George King but completed without credit by David MacDonald after King fell ill, is a film which concentrates on the exploitation of women. Largely filmed in interiors, underlining its innate theatricality, it focuses directly on the bravura performance of Slaughter as Sir Percival Glyde, promoting the character who is Wilkie Collins's secondary villain to the primary position in this version. The memorable chief villain of the novel is the enormously fat and hypnotically charming Count Fosco, who was given a definitive interpretation by Sydney Greenstreet in the stylish 1948 Hollywood adaptation of *The Woman in White*. In this version, he is reduced to a supporting role and shrunk into Dr Fosco, the dandified, diminutive keeper of a private madhouse, who blackmails Glyde and is eventually murdered by him. The role is played with relish by Hay Petrie.

*Crimes at the Dark House* takes several key scenes from Collins's novel and around them weaves an exposition of the villainy of Sir Percival Glyde. He is first seen driving a tent-peg through the head of a sleeping companion in the Australian goldfields and assuming his identity as Sir Percival Glyde. He returns to England to take over as squire of the heavily mortgaged family estate, Blackwater Hall, and to marry heiress Laura Fairlie (Sylvia Marriott). Glyde, cackling with gleeful laughter at every excess and crime and licking his lips lecherously at the sight of pretty women, impregnates the chambermaid Jessica and strangles her when she demands marriage. He strangles Mrs Catherick, who had been secretly married to the real Sir Percival. When Ann Catherick, the woman in white, is found ill with pneumonia, he pushes her bed close to the open window and removes the bedclothes to ensure that she dies. He has his wife Laura locked up in the asylum as Ann and claims Laura is dead, in order to inherit her fortune. He tries to rape Laura's sister Marian ('Wenches like you want taming'). Having finally gone mad, Glyde is burned to death in the church while trying to destroy the register containing evidence of his marriage to Mrs Catherick by setting fire to it. Almost none of this is in the original novel apart from the plot to lock Laura up as Ann and take her fortune, and Glyde's death destroying the marriage register, which in the book attests to his illegitimacy and not a secret marriage.

The subordinate position of women in Victorian society is highlighted by the film. Laura is compelled to marry Glyde by her self-centred guardian Frederick Fairlie, although she loves the young drawing master Walter Hartright (Geoffrey Wardwell). Her wedding night is graphically depicted by the film. Glyde forces drink on her and then sends her to bed. The director intercuts close-ups of her tear-stained, trembling face and close-ups of his feet on the stairs. There is a close-up of the door slowly opening and his cackling laugh is heard and the screen goes dark. It is a powerful demonstration of 'first night' or wedding night fears which the censors normally forbade. Glyde, who declares that 'marriage is a business proposition', tries to browbeat her into signing over her money to him but when encouraged by her spirited sister Marian to resist, he has her carried off to a private asylum in place of Ann Catherick, whom she resembles. Ann had been confined because of her obsessive hatred of Glyde who had abandoned her and her mother. Laura is rescued from the asylum by Walter and not, as in the book, by Marian.

*Crimes at the Dark House* was the last of Slaughter's first cycle of films. During the war, he resumed his touring theatrical career, playing in such vehicles as *Jack the Ripper, Landru* and *Dr Jekyll and Mr Hyde*. In 1945 he did a season of Grand Guignol plays at the Granville Theatre, Walham Green. His film career resumed after the war, at the primitive Bushey Studios working for Ambassador Films. They had been reissuing Slaughter's pre-war films throughout the war and they had presumably found them profitable enough to want to add to them. *The Curse of the Wraydons* (1946), based on the play *Springheeled Jack or The Terror of London*, which featured Slaughter as a mad inventor who is the head of a French spy ring in Britain during the Napoleonic War, was one of his poorest films, badly plotted, technically limited and handicapped by some long, dull expository scenes. *The Greed of William Hart* (1948), though, was one of his best. It retold the story of Burke and Hare with

Slaughter and Henry Oscar as a priceless pair of black comedy 'Oirish' graverobbers and murderers in a film which took advantage of its low budget and cramped sets to create a sense of claustrophobia and vivid horror by the use of bold close-ups.[25] Subsequently there were two crime films with Slaughter as master criminal Terence Riley, *King of the Underworld* (1952) and *Murder at Scotland Yard* (1953). Coincidentally, Slaughter died in the year that Hammer remade *The Curse of Frankenstein* and launched a new cycle of British horror films.

At the most obvious level the Slaughter films fulfil both Booth's and Brooks's definition of melodrama as demonstrating a morality that preferred good over evil and virtue over vice and ensured the punishment of wrongdoing. But the dominance of Slaughter's characters suggests another interpretation: a celebration of excess. At a time when much of mainstream cinema was sexless, the keynote of the Slaughter films was lechery, the shameless and gleeful pursuit of sex. It governed the actions of almost all of the Slaughter characters, with William Corder seducing and murdering Maria Marten, Sweeney Todd obsessively seeking Johanna Oakley, 'The Tiger' pursuing May Edwards, Squire Meadows plotting to gain Susan Merton, Chevalier del Gardo lusting after Cecile de Brisson and Sir Percival Glyde seducing and murdering a chambermaid, marrying Laura Fairlie both for lust and money and seeking to rape her sister Marian. At the end of several films (*It's Never Too Late to Mend, Maria Marten, Crimes at the Dark House*), Slaughter goes mad, his mind snapping under the burden of excess. Feminist critics have argued that in the case of the so-called mad women of Victorian literature, madness is a label attached to those who reject the conventions of a repressive society. The same might be argued of Slaughter. He can with some justice be seen as an anti-hero like Margaret Lockwood's wicked ladies and James Mason's degenerate lords in the Gainsborough melodramas and Peter Cushing and Christopher Lee's aristocratic predators.

At another level, the films can be seen as a critique of Victorianism, forerunners of that series of 1940s British films which constituted a critique of nineteenth-century patriarchy (*Gaslight, Hatter's Castle, Pink String and Sealing Wax*). The films demonstrate a very modern sympathy for outsiders who are the victims of Victorian society: gypsies and unmarried mothers (*Maria Marten*), paroled prisoners (*The Ticket of Leave Man*), brutalised convicts (*It's Never Too Late to Mend*) and madhouse inmates (*Crimes at the Dark House*). The films regularly highlight the plight of women in a repressive patriarchal society. In virtually every film, women are forced to marry against their will or are denied by their fathers the right to marry men whom they love. The films also consistently expose hypocrisy, seen retrospectively as a cardinal Victorian vice, by showing 'respectability' in the middle and upper classes to be a mask for evil-doing. The 'respectable' squires in *Maria Marten* and *It's Never Too Late to Mend*, the 'respectable' businessmen of *Sweeney Todd* and *Stephen Hawke*, the 'respectable' aristocrats of *The Face at the Window* and *Crimes at the Dark House*, the 'respectable' charity worker of *Ticket of Leave Man*, are all leading double lives of criminality and/or illicit sexuality.

The links between the Slaughter films and the later genres of excess are both direct and symbolic. Bernard Robinson, art director on *Crimes at the Dark House*, went on to become a Hammer regular and John Gilling, who scripted *The Greed of William Hart*, did so too. Gilling even reworked his Slaughter script ten years later as *The Flesh and the Fiends* with Donald Pleasence and George Rose taking on the roles of the murderous bodysnatchers first played by Tod Slaughter and Henry Oscar. Although Slaughter never played Frankenstein or Dracula on film, his gentry anti-heroes, notably Squire Meadows, Chevalier del Gardo and Sir Percival Glyde, with their murders, seductions and other misdeeds, could be seen as direct precursors of the Hammer anti-heroes. It should also be noted in the context of melodrama that both Frankenstein and Dracula had long histories of stage adaptation and the celebrated 1930s Universal films of *Frankenstein* and *Dracula* were both based directly on stage versions.

Similarly, James Mason's Lord Rohan and Lord Manderstoke in the Gainsborough melodramas, roles which significantly made Mason the top male star at the British box office, while played more in the brooding, saturnine style of a Rochester or a Heathcliff than in the barnstorming manner of Slaughter's wicked squires, share values and attitudes in common with the earlier anti-heroes. Similarly, Gainsborough plots with their star-crossed genteel lovers, aristocratic seducers and double lives parallel the themes of the Slaughter films. Indeed, Margaret Lockwood moves sick persons close to open windows to ensure their deaths in both *The Wicked Lady* and *The Man in Grey* exactly as Slaughter does in *Crimes at the Dark House*. If one can with justice describe the Slaughter films as a series of variations on a handful of basic themes, it would also be true to say that those themes were refreshed and revisited both by Gainsborough and by Hammer in a continuing cinema of excess.

8. Nova Pilbeam facing execution in *Tudor Rose*

CHAPTER 8

# Jack of All Trades: Robert Stevenson

### Brian McFarlane

M OST people, if asked today about Robert Stevenson, would be likely to associate him with an extraordinarily successful run of Disney films from the mid-1950s for the next 20 years. In 1978, the journal *American Film* published an article entitled 'Who is the World's Most Successful Director?',[1] in which the author claimed: 'Throughout his [Stevenson's] career he has remained anonymous and stubbornly obscure.'[2] Disney, for whom he made such commercial hits as *Mary Poppins* (1965) and *Bedknobs and Broomsticks* (1971), in fact swallowed him up. It is worth remembering that, before this voluntary enslavement to family entertainment, he had had a decade of interestingly varied achievement in Hollywood, and that, in a still more distant decade (the 1930s) he had emerged 'into the front rank of English directors'.[3]

It may be that his very versatility worked against his acquiring in England the reputation he deserved. Victor Saville no doubt made more inventive musicals; Alexander Korda's imperial adventures were more spectacular; Alfred Hitchcock's thrillers clearly dominated that field; Anthony Asquith made a more stylish theatrical adaptation; Herbert Wilcox had more persistent success with costume drama; Michael Powell's regional melodrama, *The Edge of the World* (1938), had more vigour than Stevenson's venture in such territory; Carol Reed dealt more sharply with romantic comedy; and perhaps even Maurice Elvey outstripped him in science fiction. If none of these comparisons works unequivocally in Stevenson's favour, it may also be claimed that none of these comparators acquitted himself so ably, with such versatility, across such a *range* of genres. For Stevenson is the 1930s genre director *par excellence* in British cinema, and the range is paradigmatic of what was available in British commercial film-making in the decade. His work, even more so than is the case with that of some of his contemporaries (one thinks, for instance, of Reed's *Bank Holiday*), is almost untouched by the flourishing documentary strain of indigenous film production of the period. Apart from this, he might be confidently urged as the most representative director of the decade; his work embraces virtually all of its popular genres. If they are rarely the best of their respective genres, his films as a whole constitute the oeuvre which best instructs later generations about what British cinema was like in this still sketchily scrutinised decade.

Most of those other, better-known names seem to have been addicted to the idea of cinema from early youth. Not so Stevenson. Born in 1905, he was academically gif ed, went to Cambridge University on a scholarship, graduated in 1926 with a first-class degree in mechanical sciences, and the following year, as a graduate student in psychology, he edited *Granta*, the university's prestigious literary magazine. If this background distinguishes him from, say, Wilcox, who very early began in the distribution arm of the industry, or Elvey, who 'from an early age gravitated towards the world of show business',[4] or Reed, who in 1924 'walked on stage in his first acting role',[5] it no doubt helps to explain his attraction for Michael Balcon. Balcon, who produced *Tudor Rose*, the film which made Stevenson's name, famously liked to draw gifted university men into the business. He followed this practice at Gainsborough, which he had co-founded in 1924, and at Ealing, where, from 1937, he was chief of production until its closure 20 years later. 'We [that is, Balcon and Gainsborough producer Edward Black] ... recruited a number of promising young men from the universities – Ian Dalrymple, Derek Twist, Robert Stevenson, among others, all made their mark as directors,'[6] Balcon writes in his autobiography. Of the three named, Stevenson was the only one who really made a 'mark' as a director and he was the only one who made the transition to Ealing with Balcon, though Balcon was later to relate 'the pictures [*Young Man's Fancy* and *Return to Yesterday*] did not really come off'[7] – a judgement open to query.

Stevenson seems to have had no interest in the cinema until, at the age of 20, he 'decided to write a thesis on the psychology of the "ki-ne-ma"', and one day went to see Joan Crawford in *Sally, Irene and Mary*. He promptly fell in love with both Joan Crawford and the 'ki-ne-ma',[8] though he never completed the thesis. After working for a newsreel agency, he finally entered the film industry proper as a screenwriter for Gaumont-British in 1929. His earliest credit is on Sinclair Hill's musical, *Greek Street* (1930), in relation to which Denis Gifford's *The British Film*

*Catalogue 1895–1970* attributes the 'story' to Stevenson and the screenplay to two others. In the next few years, his name appears as co-author of the screenplay on a number of Gainsborough productions, most often in tandem with Angus MacPhail, who would later become a key figure at Balcon's Ealing Studios. These films have not been available for viewing for the purposes of this chapter, so that one can do little more than note that Stevenson wrote regularly for Balcon's top director, Victor Saville, and for major stars Herbert Marshall and Edna Best. These co-authored screenplays were drawn twice (*The Calendar* and *The Ringer*, 1931) from plays by the prolific Edgar Wallace, and from plays by A. A. Milne (Saville's *Michael and Mary*, 1931) and Monckton Hoffe (Saville's *The Faithful Heart*, 1932). As well, he was involved in the scripts of three films made for UFA in bilingual versions and distributed by Gaumont-British (*Happy Ever After*, 1932, with his later collaborator Jack Hulbert; *The Only Girl*, 1933, with German-based British star, Lilian Harvey; and *FP 1*, 1933, with Conrad Veidt and Jill Esmond), and a French-made production, *The Battle* (1934), with Merle Oberon and Charles Boyer. In the first four years of the decade, he has credits either as co-writer or as associate producer on no fewer than 15 films, many of them involving some of the most highly-regarded talents of the day. He was associate producer (Balcon himself usually assumed the producer credit, a practice he was to carry over to his Ealing period, where it earned some resentment) on *Little Friend* (1934), the moving and, for its time, quite daring drama of the effect of her parents' looming divorce on a young girl (Nova Pilbeam), and *The Camels are Coming* (1934), a Jack Hulbert comedy-adventure set in Egypt. The latter was partly filmed on location, though *Film Weekly* reported at the time: 'Sand got into the cameras; high winds prevented the recording of dialogue. So some of the authentic Egyptian sequences were finally re-filmed, prosaically, in the studios at Shepherd's Busi..'[9] On location for this film, Stevenson met actress Anna Lee whom he subsequently married and who starred in five of his 1930s films, before leaving with him for Hollywood in 1939.

*The Camels are Coming* is directed by the American Tim Whelan, who made many films in Britain in the 1930s, but the director's credit seems as irrelevant here as it does on *Falling for You*, on which it is shared by Stevenson and star Jack Hulbert. Hulbert's breezy persona, part silly ass, part song-and-dance man, able to cope with the romantic as well as the adventurous demands of his roles, belongs to what has been called 'the cinema of attractions'[10] and as such flourished regardless of directorial hand. The narratives appear to exist primarily for the display of Hulbert's talents as singer, dancer and comedian. As Andrew Higson has written of *Sing as We Go*: 'The attractions are the point of the film, not its flaws; the pleasures of this film are less the drama of narrative integration, and more the attractions of potential disintegration.'[11] Hulbert can seem tiresomely jaunty company today, as if his style really belonged to another medium, but he was very popular, at least with domestic audiences, in the 1930s.

Of the two films Stevenson co-directed with Hulbert, *Falling for You* and *Jack of All Trades* (1936), the most one can say is that the star is allowed to have his head. He is co-starred in the former with his wife, Cicely Courtneidge, who, much more than Hulbert, seems always to be playing to the circle of the music halls, nudging the audience in the ribs, as it were. The fact that she is marginally more restrained here than in some of her other 1930s films may say something for Stevenson's guiding hand, though her role as Minnie, reporter on the track of a vanished heiress, is secondary to Hulbert's; he is not merely a rival reporter, but also carries the romantic lead opposite Tamara Desni as the heiress. There is little attempt to integrate Hulbert and Courtneidge's musical and other numbers (e.g. a skating episode) into the plot; the film virtually stops while they do their stuff, which is presumably what their fans wanted from them. The film's opening sequence, set in the Swiss Alps, depicting Hulbert as an inexpert skier helped to his feet by a little girl who reappears towards the end of the film to repeat the comic scenario, is typical of the way in which Hulbert's comic talents are put on display; as are the skating sequence a little later, when he is watched by a beautiful woman, and the scene in which he sings 'You Don't Understand' as he gazes adoringly at her. These are essentially 'turns', having a tenuous connection with the plot, but the plot is always ready to stop for them. As an inexperienced director, Stevenson must have found himself in an intransigent mode: there are odd editing touches which suggest a wish to be doing something more obviously 'cinematic' with this material and some comic inventiveness in the staging which goes beyond the mere filming of comic set pieces; the songs by Vivian Ellis are pleasing enough and Vetchinsky's sets and Bernard Knowles's camerawork give the film an appropriately glossy look which completes its removal from reality.

*Jack of All Trades* (1936) is the firmest in narrative terms of the three films starring Hulbert. *The Camels are Coming*, which begins with a cod newsreel in which air ace Hulbert is heading for Egypt with a fleet of aircraft for the Egyptian government, is a spoof outpost-of-empire adventure, in which the story of drug-trafficking gives way to Hulbert's particular brand of clowning and loose-limbed song-and-dance. *Falling for You* spoofs the newspaper thriller genre, with the interruptions noted above. *Jack of All Trades*, on which Stevenson's name precedes Hulbert's on the credits, has a more robust comic underpinning: there is as before the series of turns, either song-and-dance numbers or comic set pieces, but the plot has its basis in an *idea*. Jack bluffs his way on to the staff of a bank and promotes a non-existent company while pursuing a romance with a rich girl, Frances (Gina Malo), who funds the factory which grows from Jack's invention. The plot grows ever wilder and ends with his ousting arsonists and with a lot of byplay involving a movable bridge and retractable fire hoses. Underlying these more or less absurd events is that very 1930s motif of the poor protagonist pretending to be rich and important; in passing himself off as such, he reinforces a comforting suggestion that anyone with enough drive can be as mobile as he. As well, the film offers a satirical picture of big business being taken in by 'the Merivale Plan', each successive banker or investor too self-important to admit he knows nothing about it. The ultimate effect is not exactly populist – Hulbert's persona is too upper-middle-class for that – but the overthrowing of the pompous and/or corrupt of the business world was a resonant theme of the 1930s as it emerged from the depression.

The film does avoid the emptiness of many comparable 1930s pieces which are no more than vehicles for a star persona. At its best, it moves swiftly and the musical numbers have an easy, relaxed quality, which on occasions recalls the style of *Top Hat*. In fact, the episode in which Jack meets Frances on the river by night and sings 'You're Sweeter Than I Thought You Were', leading to a dance in which others dance behind them silhouetted through lighted windows, seems modelled on the Astaire–Rogers triumph in terms of choreography, decor (Vetchinsky's work again) and lightly romantic tone. It is of course hard to be certain about Stevenson's contribution to such an enterprise, but it is not too much to claim that this film has a greater narrative fluency, that the 'attractions' are more carefully woven into the narrative, and the star seems more disciplined than in either *Falling for You*, Stevenson's first credit as co-director, or *The Camels are Coming*, in which director Whelan allows the tone to waver disastrously between the conventionally suspenseful and the merely facetious. Here, the plot is really no more than a series of strained comic business and the musical interludes are like discrete interruptions to a quite other enterprise. Hulbert, no doubt like other music-hall-nurtured performers, may have been largely director-proof, but *Jack of All Trades*, in its narrative fluency, in the inventive staging of the musical numbers, in the neat shorthand of its 'montage sequences' (the young Terence Fisher is the editor), and above all in the harnessing of the Hulbert persona to a stronger-than-usual storyline, is an agreeable entertainment. It is absolutely typical of its decade, but it is much more accomplished than many of the films with which it invites comparison, such as Graham Cutts and Austin Melford's *Car of Dreams* (1935) or Maurice Elvey's *Heat Wave* (1935) or Rene Guissart's *Sweet Devil* (1938), all with singing heroes (respectively John Mills, Les Allen and Bobby Howes) and all with less firmly structured comic plots.

It is his next film which really established Stevenson as belonging among the forefront of British directors. This is the costume drama *Tudor Rose* which, by comparison with Alexander Korda's landmark retelling of British history, stresses intimacy rather than pageantry. In the year of the tumult leading to the abdication of Edward VIII, it must have struck a resonant chord in its obvious respect for constituted authority and the designated lines of succession. Its opening sequence is focused on the deathbed of Henry VIII (Frank Cellier, recurring authority figure of 1930s Gainsborough); the dying King starts up to ask, with well-founded suspicions of the deviant watchers, 'What are those shadows?', before announcing the succession: 'Edward the Prince, my son, then my daughter Mary and her heirs, then Elizabeth and her heirs and, failing them, my sister's child Jane Grey.' He dies, laying his curse on 'any that should betray these children'. The drama of the rest of the film lies in precisely such betrayal, first of Edward, at the hands of his two conniving uncles, Edward Seymour 'The Fox' (Felix Aylmer) and Thomas Seymour 'The Peacock' (Leslie Perrins). They are characterised thus by another power-broking watcher, Warwick (Cedric Hardwicke) who, despite his disclaimer that 'I am no politician, I am a plain soldier', is largely responsible for the bypassing of Mary and Elizabeth and thereby bringing Jane Grey (Nova Pilbeam) to the throne. It is Warwick who insists that Jane's life be wrenched out of its natural course (echoing the life of George VI who would be forced to assume the throne on the abdication of his brother, exciting sympathy in the process). When Jane protests that she does not wish to be Queen, she is silenced with, 'It is not only your right [which, in the dying King's words, it is not] but your sacred duty'. She, like the unwilling King of nearly four centuries later, will accept the role for duty's sake, and on the understanding that there will be no more bloodshed. Her life, as every schoolchild once knew, was pitiably shortened by her compliance. The film no doubt offers a simplified (though not stupid) view of the tides of history, but on the level of romantic melodrama it is often very touching indeed, and, in some ways, superior to Korda's better-known epic.

The film's real strength lies in its articulation at a number of levels of the poignant contrast between vulnerable humanity and political expediency. If this is not an original premise it is certainly one of universal importance and it provides a firm structure for the film. Stevenson is by no means a flashy director, but he creates a succession of visually eloquent images which carry the film's theme. Jane and the boy king, Edward (Desmond Tester), are represented in ways which underscore their endangered youth. Edward is first seen playing at archery with a young friend and wondering about when guns will replace bows and arrows, and telling his uncle Edward Seymour that 'If I'm King, I can have a gun'. But he, as will be the case with his successor, Jane, is in fact quite powerless; the title is no more than a handle which ambitious schemers will turn for their purposes. There is pathos in the ways in which the physically frail but spirited Edward tries to fill the role of King: there is a shot of him copying the stance of his father, Henry VIII; he intermittently adopts the diction of monarchy – 'It is our royal command' – but a moment later he lapses into the informality of pleading for Thomas Seymour's life with, 'You mustn't do it. You must let him go.' The screenplay, by Miles Malleson (who also plays Jane's ineffectual father), in such shifts, enacts the contrast and contest between the political and the human.

In the case of Jane herself, Stevenson is fortunate in his choice of actress. Nova Pilbeam, not merely a fine unmannered young actress, was 16 at the time[12] and able to convey, on the one hand, the child's innocent wish to be allowed to get on with her studies and the pleasures of country living, and, on the other, the rapidly acquired dignity of the young woman forced to accept the throne she has not sought. In the sequence which introduces her, nearly 20 minutes into the film, she is seen doing her lessons. This opening image establishes her as a girl of studious pursuits, though she admits she would like to take a holiday from 'gravity of manners'. In another room her parents, ineffectual father (Miles Malleson) and dominant mother (Martita Hunt), disagree about her future, which immediately consists of her removal to London: 'A great chance', says the mother, but Jane's nurse, Ellen (Sybil Thorndike), warns that London is 'the devil's playground', the two views again echoing the film's major opposition. On every level, the film articulates the idea that politics cannot afford to be susceptible to human feeling; just as the great house of Seymour is fatally divided by political aspiration, so Jane's family and friends are divided between ambition for her and fear for her safety. The clash of these immiscibles is made apparent early to Jane when she enters a palace room where Edward Seymour is warning his brother Thomas that his interference will cost him his head.

The life of rural retreat in which Jane has been happy, and will be again in the scene in which she and her young husband, Warwick's son, Guildford Dudley (John Mills), go riding in the country, contrasts resonantly with those scenes of her life in London. In rendering the danger and confinement of this life, Stevenson employs the image of heavy doors bolted behind her and uses a long overhead shot as she moves towards the massive stairs of the council chamber which makes her appear as intensely vulnerable. This latter is a well-timed image because, with the defeat of Warwick as Protector, she is no longer Queen and she and Dudley are arrested. The scene fades to the Tower of London, symbol of political danger and punishment, where Jane feeds birds on the window sill of her cell. Jane is herself the embodiment of the film's governing dichotomy; where other political punishments have been signified by, say, an axe falling or a head on the gate to London Bridge, here Jane's innocence is symbolised by this image of her with the birds.

Structurally, the film offers a further commentary on the theme of the politically expedient or devious at the expense of human/humane impulses. Stevenson has not made a stiff historical pageant, but has sought to imagine and dramatise the play of these impulses at work behind the march of history. Above all it is those without aspirations to political power but who become caught in its web who provide the film's pathos, and Stevenson has maintained a judicious balance between these two kinds of episode. A key structural element is the entry late in the film of Mary Tudor (Gwen Ffrangcon Davies). Her claim to the throne, following Edward's youthful death, has been confirmed by Henry on his deathbed, but for his own purposes Warwick has chosen to bypass this dying command. Now Jane Grey and his own son will pay the human price for his political scheming, when Mary's army overthrows Warwick's force. Mary herself is not made to appear a monster but another victim of political necessity, though, as it happens, one powerfully placed to act her will. Mary is first seen at prayers when a horseman appears to warn her to raise the eastern counties to support her. This juxtaposition of images prepares us for Mary's subsequent appearance in the Tower. Seen here from the rear she is a dark, forbidding figure as she enters Jane's cell. There is a convincing weight of moral conflict in the scene between the two when she tells Jane she does not wish for her death, making the distinction that, 'Though I may feel pity, I can show no mercy'; if she spares Jane and Dudley, 'an army of protest will be raised and two thousand may die'. There may well be here the over-simplification of history of which Graham Greene complained about the film at large,[13] but in terms of drama it works very well as a precursor of the final and still very affecting scene of Jane's death. There is a touching mixture of youth and mature dignity as she reacts to Dudley's death, and, when she asks for her cloak because it is cold and 'I mustn't seem to shiver lest they think I'm afraid', there is a crystallising of the film's sense of the fragile strength of personal goodness in a politically controlled world. The film began with the sound of hoofbeats ushering in a new era and it ends with a steady roll of drums and the reciting of Psalm 121 ('I will lift up mine eyes unto the hills') on the soundtrack. The final poignancy is intensified as Stevenson's editor, Terence Fisher, cuts effectively from Jane to the Executioner begging for her forgiveness, to her response, to the Nurse removing her cloak, to Jane's face in close-up as she recalls moments from her past, to the final shot of the birds scattering on the parapet as the cannon rings out.

One is not making great claims for the film in finding it a more satisfying slice of humanised history than Korda's more famous predecessor. If it lacks the gusto of *The Private Life of Henry VIII* ('philistine romping'[14] as one account has it), it more than compensates for this by the restraint and sensitivity of Stevenson's handling of his young players in particular, and they are backed by one of those Gainsborough casts which seem almost profligate in their riches. In addition, in having an idea about political life and its potential for ravaging the personal, and in its persistent development of this idea at various levels of narrative and narration, it offers a dramatically coherent and involving experience. Its message to 1930s audiences must have been one of respect for the proper line of succession; the film clearly implies that nothing but harm can come from its disruption. In 1936 audiences were not to know how well the reluctant new king would conduct himself.

Stevenson's final 1936 release, the punningly titled *The Man Who Changed His Mind*, is a neat if minor piece of science fiction-cum-horror, which has the advantage of a charismatic display of obsession from Boris Karloff as Laurience, the scientist who believes in the possibility of taking 'thought content from the brain and storing it as you would electricity'. Karloff is able to deliver such poppycock with impressive conviction and his scientific zeal is supported by Vetchinsky's vision of the paraphernalia associated with such beliefs in cinema. A contemporary reviewer noted: 'The settings are thoroughly in tradition – full of strange glass tubes, metal coils and impressively sparkling and flashing masses of apparatus. The mind transpositions are cleverly handled.'[15] The special effects are of course light years away from what audiences have now become accustomed to; the point is, however, that they seem entirely adequate to their function in the narrative, rather than being designed to excite a collective indrawing of breath.

The gist of Karloff's research is that he wants to practise on humans the experiments he has already conducted on monkeys; that is, he wants to transfer the 'thought content' from one mind to another. He has chosen for the experiment his cynical, crippled assistant Clayton (Donald Calthrop) and Lord Haslewood (Frank Cellier), the newspaper magnate who has withdrawn his support from Laurience's research when it becomes clear it will not bring profit to his newspaper. As a result of pressing on with his work on switching human thought, Laurience causes the deaths of these two guinea pigs and only the intervention of Claire (Anna Lee), his increasingly suspicious medical assistant, saves her boyfriend, breezy reporter and magnate's son Dick Haslewood (John Loder), from being permanently endowed with Laurience's own mind – that is, in a sound young body. The fact that it is a woman who activates the denouement, engaging in the last-minute cerebrations and rescue work almost invariably the province of the hero, is perhaps the single most unusual aspect of the film, which for the most part draws on the familiar ingredients of the genre. These latter include its narrative impetus in the scientist's obsessive urge to pursue his research in the face of all kinds of opposition (moral, rational, opportunistic), the ideological concern with such issues as the right of the scientist to make accommodations with capital in the interests of furthering his work, and the characteristic imagery of laboratories and lecture rooms. As well, there are narrative borrowings from the 'old dark house' genre (when Claire gives up her work in a conventional hospital, she makes for Laurience's forbiddingly Gothic house where dogs are barking, and the cab-driver says, 'I don't go to that door') and from romantic comedy. With regard to the latter, there is some facetious battle-of-the-sexes sparring between Claire and Dick, but, as noted, there is a certain freshness in allowing her to be the dominant figure at the end.

In fact, in several of Stevenson's collaborations with Anna Lee, she is accorded a more positive role in impelling the narrative than was common. This is true of her function in *King Solomon's Mines* (1937), *Non-Stop New York* (1937), *Young Man's Fancy* (1939) and, to a lesser extent, their last pre-Hollywood film, *Return to Yesterday* (1940). As an actress she shows spirit and charm rather than intensity or range, but in general she is equal to the demands made of her across the genres in which Stevenson's British work is found. She is perhaps least satisfactory in *King Solomon's Mines* in a role never envisaged by Rider Haggard, though the *Film Weekly* reviewer considered she showed 'more acting ability in this picture than ever before' even if 'some conviction is taken from her portrayal by the perfection of her hairdressing, which neither sandstorms nor volcanic eruptions disturb'.[16] Graham Greene, referring to 'the weighty coquetry' of her performance, is predictably scathing about the film's 'introduction of an Irish blonde who has somehow become the cause of the whole expedition'.[17] Not only does she propel the narrative by insisting on pursuing her father who has gone off to find the legendary mines, thus causing the expedition headed by white hunter Allan Quatermain (Cedric Hardwicke) to follow her, but she is there of course to provide a conventional love interest, which may well have appalled Haggard as it did Greene. 'If you weren't a girl I'd give you the hiding of your life,' says Sir Henry Curtis (John Loder, regular leading man for Stevenson), a member of Quatermain's party, and the role of Kathy is no doubt more of a concession to the box office than to gender politics. However, intrusive as Haggard purists may regard the character, she is given important things to do in the plot, as Lee's characters are in all her films for Stevenson, and she is not in the final moments reduced to the status of mere appendage.

In fact, of course, the final moments belong to Paul Robeson as the African chief, Umbopa, who bids farewell to the white party whose cause he has unaccountably supported in opposition to his own people. The film uses Haggard's popular adventure story to promote the cause of Empire, using the conventions of the genre, as Marcia Landy points out, to 'mask colonizing attitudes':

> The idea of the journey into the interior is presented as the archetypal trial in the wilderness, stressing the dangers of nature and of hostile people who are presented as different, savage, and superstitious. The white men's superiority is signaled by their command of language (Quatermain keeps a journal), their superior knowledge of nature, their ability to harness the physical strength of the natives for their own purposes, and their desire for knowledge at any cost.[18]

The character of Umbopa inevitably seems contentious now. Robeson is given several melodious but entirely un-African songs to sing, including 'Climbing Up', a reprise of which concludes the film, and irresistibly suggests the colonialist view of the 'native' whose aspirations are the result of his contact with white superiority. In return for his help in leading them across the desert, they invoke their white magic (a lucky eclipse of the sun) to overthrow the witch-doctor, Gagool, and Twala, the chief who has wrongfully assumed Umbopa's throne. The film is a good deal less patronising in its representation of black–white relations than Zoltan Korda's *Sanders of the River* (1935), produced by Alexander Korda, but both Korda and Michael Balcon, Stevenson's producer and chief shaper of Gainsborough's policy, were, according to Jeffrey Richards, 'intensely patriotic and both were concerned with the favourable promotion of the national image'.[19] From this point of view, Umbopa is seen as an intermediary between ignorant savages and the wise benevolence of the white adventurers, the materialism of whose aims is played down. Where the more intellectual Stevenson stands in relation to this scenario is hard to determine, but it is arguable that his attention to Anna Lee's role reflects something more than either his personal or the studio's commercial interests. Despite the sometimes irritating coyness of the writing and playing of the role, she is allowed a surprising freedom as she talks to Umbopa. In fact, the sense of ease between Umbopa and the whites, especially a white woman, is perhaps the most 'liberal' aspect of the film, which in most respects is 'rousing, schoolboy adventure fare'.[20] Perhaps because of the excellence of Geoffrey Barkas's second unit footage shot in Africa, some of the studio-staged scenes involving the principals, none of whom left England, seem artificial by contrast. Again, Stevenson would be outdone by Korda in the imperial epic stakes, when *The Four Feathers* appeared two years later, but he was continuing to show his versatility across a range of 1930s genres, touching them with a suggestion of humanity that is not always to be felt in their other exponents.

His next assignment was a second feature, the comedy thriller *Non-Stop New York*, in which Anna Lee is once more a lively, resourceful heroine, unusually lower-class in origin if not in accent, and in which he maintains a brisk pace and makes good use of a witty, sometimes exciting screenplay. The latter is the work of Kurt Siodmak and Derek Twist and it involves movement back and forth between America and England. It opens in New York on New Year's Eve, 1938 (with some stock footage doing satisfactory duty), when an out-of-work English chorus girl, Jeannie (Lee), becomes the only witness to a gangland killing. On the ship returning to England, she is framed by the killer, and goes to prison. Surprisingly unembittered by these experiences, she stows away on a New York-bound aircraft to save the life of the man who has been wrongly found guilty of the murder. And so on. It is enough to say that Stevenson works this fairly improbable premise for enjoyable results. There is romance between Jeannie and Inspector Grant (John Loder again), who, along with the real killer, Brandt (Francis L. Sullivan), is also on board the eponymous flight, where much of the action takes place. How accurate a picture of transatlantic air travel in the 1930s the film offers is questionable (it was 'ridiculous' according to actor Desmond Tester)[21] – there are sleeping berths, cocktail lounges, a flight deck from which the intrepid Jeannie is almost pushed to her doom – but Stevenson makes excellent use of its confined spaces to build up the thriller element of the film. Also on board are a child musical prodigy Arnold (Desmond Tester), who prefers jazz, and his gushing aunt (Athene Seyler), whose private parachute will play its part in the film's denouement. This latter is reached after 72 breathless minutes in which Stevenson and his scriptwriters maintain an engaging balance between comedy and excitement, and within its modest limits the film is extremely well made. Though the fade is still the main means of inter-sequence punctuation, its potential for slowing the film's tempo is offset by skilful editing *within* sequences, especially in the climax, tensely shot by the great Mutz Greenbaum, in which Grant climbs over the top of the plane to get to the controls after the pilot has been shot by the decamping Brandt. Stevenson also makes confident use of 'montage' sequences for concise conveying of narrative information, as in the typical alteration of typewriters, newspapers printing and billboards with the headline appealing for 'MISSING ENGLISH GIRL' to come forward, and its parallel at the film's end about 'STOWAWAY WITNESS' and 'BOY PRODIGY'. Visually, Stevenson, abetted by Greenbaum, keeps the film tight and interesting, as in the striking moment when Jeannie, washing floors, 'sees' the face of the condemned man superimposed on the wet floor, and the image sends her to Scotland Yard.

As in the two preceding films, it is the initiative of the female protagonist which is responsible for the chief narrative movement of the film. The screenplay is economical in this respect, too much so perhaps in not allowing any sense of the effect of her wrongful imprisonment, but in general it maintains such a cracking speed that one scarcely cares about such motivation, which – it might well be argued – belongs to a different genre. The final two Stevenson–Lee collaborations were made at Ealing in 1939 after a year in which they both absented themselves from films (he to write a novel, she to have a baby)[22] and by which time Balcon was installed as chief of production at Ealing. These two films are in very different mode: *Young Man's Fancy* is a vivacious romantic comedy and *Return to Yesterday* is a gently sentimental romantic drama of provincial theatrical life.

The issue of class, so central to any consideration of British cinema, was rarely a matter for serious scrutiny in 1930s cinema, peopled as it so often was with madcap heiresses and noblemen disguised as butlers. It cannot be said that there is anything very profound about the way in which *Young Man's Fancy* deals with the theme of class, capital and marriage, but it is articulated with exuberance and charm. A young aristocrat, Alban (Griffith Jones), escapes from an arranged marriage with a capitalist's daughter with the help of Ada (Anna Lee), a music-hall performer who lands in his lap when she is fired out of a cannon. His only hope of getting out of the marriage is to alienate his fiancée, Miss Crowther (Meriel Forbes), and her father, Sir Caleb (Felix Aylmer), by some outrage of behaviour. To this end he takes Ada off to Paris (during the time of the Second Empire) where they are caught in a Prussian siege, find themselves performing on stage, and fall genuinely in love before returning to England to face his parents. In fact, his father, the Duke of Beaumont (Seymour Hicks), finally gives him the way out to pursue his young man's fancy and marry Ada, leaving the capitalist's daughter at the church.

In such a bald outline there seems little to distinguish the film from so many 1930s pieces of cross-class liaisons and misunderstandings, but the story by Stevenson himself[23] and the screenplay, in which credit is shared by Roland Pertwee ('Dialogue') and Rodney Ackland and E. V. H. Emmett ('Additional Dialogue'), fill out these contours with a firm sense of character and some touches of real wit. There is in effect a double action: while Alban and Ada are falling in love, she having initially joined his plans knowing that he wanted only 'to *seem* to be doing something shocking', his mother, the Duchess (Martita Hunt), is continuing with the marriage plans. This aspect of the film is conducted with wit and character. The marriage the Duchess is eager to advance is to unite an ancient name and a brewer's fortune. There is nothing conciliatory about the Duchess's approach as she makes the Crowthers' inferior social status clear: 'Don't let's have any humbug. You *are* a brewer', later adding as they discuss the wedding, 'Canterbury won't do it *because* you're a brewer'. While Crowther asks the Duke with middle-class prurience, 'Is your son a clean-living man?', his daughter, with amusing opportunism, talks of its being 'easier' to swoon in the heat of the conservatory.

Neither aristocrat nor capitalist emerges with credit; as Charles Barr has rightly said: 'Robert Stevenson's Ealing pictures [*The Ware Case*, 1938, is the third] offer a very bitter picture of the ruling classes.'[24] In a Gainsborough version of this story, Martita Hunt's Duchess would be unlikely to emerge as so implacably acquisitive and haughty; she would have been nearer to comic caricature. Here, she is very funny but in a much blacker mode, providing the real basis for the film's drama; that is, the son's need to stop saying 'Yes, Mama'. The Duke, too, about whom there are stereotypical qualities of stage-door Johnny, seeking solace in the warmth of the music hall, is not merely sentimentalised. He has a very good scene with Ada in which he talks about 'marriages of this kind' (that is, cross-class) and urges her to make Alban believe she has changed her mind, pretending that she has let the Duke buy her off. This is clearly against the Duke's own feelings in the matter as his next remark makes clear: 'I'm not sure I ever liked my wife and now I think I hate her.' The unusual toughness of such a line is matched by the Duchess's contempt for Miss Crowther, telling her on her wedding day: 'Your opinions don't interest me and they never will.' For the Duchess, the proposed marriage is a business arrangement and she refuses to dress it up with sentiment. As far as the brewer is concerned, he is devoid of feeling, giving vent to such philosophy as 'Personal safety must take a second place where British capital is at stake'. The characters of Ada and Alban, in the context of this hard-headed opportunism, come to symbolise a romantic ideal in which the film finds value. 'It's a far far better thing I do ... ', says the Duke, quoting Dickens at his most romantic, as he sends Alban away from the church and off to find Ada. 'Between the honest worker and the gilded plutocrat, there's no understanding', says Ada's puppet-making father (Edward Rigby) to the Duke. The film's romanticism lies in suggesting that strong-minded Ada and rebellious Alban have found a way, though there is, realistically, no other suggestion of rapprochement between the classes.

Anna Lee plays Carol, the ingenue in a small seaside repertory company, in her last role for Stevenson, in *Return to Yesterday*, a film which is about nostalgia without succumbing to it, and this time it is she who receives rather than delivers the fake renunciation. Based on Robert Morley's play, *Goodness, How Sad*, it is imbued with that affection for the provincial theatre that Morley makes clear in his autobiography.[25] Morley contrasts the rigours of those days with the time he spent in Hollywood, where he made his film debut in 1938 in MGM's *Marie Antoinette* and where he and the rest of the cast 'were treated like visiting maharajahs'.[26] In the film, Robert Maine (Clive Brook), Hollywood idol, returns to the seaside boarding-house of his youth (it is surprising that no one recognises so famous a film star), while 'Will Ye No Come Back Again?' is heard on the soundtrack. Given that both Stevenson and Lee were about to head for Hollywood and that, apart from very rare exceptions, all their future work would be there, the song has a resonance which extends beyond the narrative situation of Robert Maine. So, ironically, does the gentle anti-Hollywood attitude which the film embraces. Maine helps the struggling theatrical company out of its difficulties, falls in love with Carol, bows out at the suggestion of the old actress, Mrs Truscott (Dame May Whitty), and returns to Hollywood and a wife who refuses to divorce him. In the meantime, he has 'rediscovered the thrill of living contact with living audiences', which may be read as not merely another small anti-Hollywood shaft, but also as a gesture towards the traditionally closer film–theatre ties in Britain, where so many film actors retained their roots in and preference for the theatre. Certainly the stage is most affectionately represented in the Torracombe Pier Theatre, and one might see in Carol's staying there instead of going to Hollywood with Maine a precursor of the Ealing leaning towards the small and the innocent, a distrust for the large-scale and the flashy; in a word, for Hollywood.

The film is in fact built around a series of oppositions: not just Torracombe/Hollywood and all that that represents, but also past/present and age/youth, innocence/experience and idealism/ materialism. In almost every case the film opts for what will become the usual Ealing choice in such matters, but in the matter of past and present it notably eschews nostalgia. 'The wise man lives in the present and regards the past as a banking account from which he draws experience', says Maine, whose return to yesterday has renewed him in some ways but has not provided a key to the future. Of Carol and her playwriting fiancé Peter (David Tree), old Mrs Truscott tells Maine, 'They're both at the same end of the ladder', of which he is on the top rung. Carol has taken a bold romantic initiative in going out in a boat with Maine and spending the night, innocently enough, with him, but the film is firm about where her hopes for a future lie: in amassing the life experience represented by the ladder rungs which separate her from Maine. It is equally firm that he cannot and should not 'come back again', certainly not in the expectation of finding everything, himself included, as once it was. Released in January 1940 and therefore in the making around the outbreak of war, the film must have had a special poignancy – though not offering easy comfort – in its acceptance that the past is over and can never be recaptured.

Stevenson's other Ealing film, *The Ware Case*, described by Rachael Low as 'faultlessly directed',[27] has not been available for the purposes of this study of his work. Michael Balcon refers to it as 'a production where the various elements fell into place quite easily by virtue of existing relationships',[28] recalling Clive Brook's having appeared in his first film in 1922 and Stevenson's having started his career at Gainsborough. Based on a play by George Pleydell Bancroft and a screenplay by Stevenson, Roland Pertwee and E. V. H. Emmett, it appears to have been regarded as a compelling murder drama about a gambling baronet (Brook), who is saved from disgrace but commits suicide when he realises his wife is in love with the solicitor who has defended him. *Film Weekly* noted: 'After an absence from the studios [see above], Robert Stevenson returned to direct this film, which shows that he has lost none of the qualities which should soon make him one of this country's very best filmmakers.'[29] When it was reissued in 1955, *Kinematograph Weekly* recalled how it had reviewed the film at the time (December 1938): 'Comprehensiveness is its keynote and star and title values its open sesame to universal success.'[30] Balcon himself recorded that its 'results on the first week [at the Odeon Leicester Square] were more than encouraging', suggesting that 'Ealing had, perhaps, turned the corner in the making of films other than the Gracie Fields and George Formby "vehicles"'.[31]

The one remaining Stevenson film of the decade is *Owd Bob* (1937), a regional drama, based on Alfred Olivant's popular novel[32] and essentially a vehicle for the Scots character actor Will Fyffe. He plays McAdam, irascible owner of sheepdog Black Wul which has been accused of killing sheep, and the film moves through his progressive alienation from the rural community. New farmer David Moore (John Loder) comes into competition with McAdam, over the sheepdog trials which David's dog Owd Bob wins, and he also falls in love with McAdam's daughter Jenny (Margaret Lockwood). There is a final reconciliation as David offers McAdam a pup from Owd Bob, though McAdam knows its father to be Black Wul. In the film's most moving scene, he has taken Black Wul for 'a wee walk in the glen' to shoot him, though telling Wul, 'You couldna help killing that sheep'. Fyffe was a good enough actor to make this outcome genuinely moving.

Tales of canine love are often embarrassingly sentimental but Stevenson avoids this trap. For one thing, the film is most refreshingly set in rural locations, unlike a good deal of British film-making in the 1930s, and there is a real sense of care in re-creating the shepherd's life and its problems, a feeling for place and people. For another, it takes seriously the working of sheepdogs, and the sequence of the trials, seemingly unfaked, is a highlight of the film; it is important from a narrative point of view, certainly, that David's Bob should win, so that by the end McAdam will have lost his championship trophy, his dog and his

daughter (in marriage to David), but the film allows real time and
attention to the performance of the trials. In doing so, Stevenson exhibits
what may well be the sole evidence in his 1930s work of the influence
of the documentary movement: the sheepdog trials achieve their narrative significance *because* they are seen as interesting in their own right
and as important in the lives of the protagonists. Third, there are
passages of comedy which gave scope to Fyffe and to Gainsborough's
resident yokel comics, Graham Moffatt and Moore Marriott, without
doing violence to the film's rural drama. Fyffe, in particular, has a
funny scene in which he takes over the procedures of a court hearing
into the damages caused to the local pub, and Moffatt and Marriott are
given their moment as bellringers on Jenny's wedding day (the time
taken over this acknowledges the status of the pair as studio comics).
Characteristically the film also has a romantic action, leading to the
wedding of McAdam's daughter Jenny and David Moore, an occasion
McAdam witnesses as a solitary figure on a hillside overlooking the
church. One commentator considered that Margaret Lockwood 'even as
a conventional ingenue [in *Owd Bob*] ... brought a tart flavour to her
romantic skirmishes with the hero (John Loder)'.[33] Maybe, but she is in
truth given little to do except to be a further bone of contention between
her father and David. Further, Loder, who seems to have been Stevenson's (or Gainsborough's) favoured leading man of the 1930s, is not
really a very expressive actor, so that the romance never assumes a
major dramatic interest in the film. Nevertheless, Stevenson builds on
a sturdy framework of conflicts between generations, between Scots and
English and between newcomer and old hands, and the result is a
regional drama of some substance.

With a director of the kind Stevenson was in 1930s Britain, the
problem is to do justice to his achievement without making unsustainable
auteurist claims for him. His Hollywood films are ripe for reappraisal,
especially perhaps in the decade before Disney claimed him. On the
basis of his British work it is possible to determine certain recurring
characteristics. The unusual preponderance of female-driven narratives
has been noted; without making claims for feminist intentions, one can
discern a readiness on Stevenson's part to allow his woman protagonists
their share in instigating narrative developments. He is also often interested in the youth–age binarism, sympathetically addressed in such
diverse films as *Tudor Rose*, *Owd Bob*, *Young Man's Fancy* and *Return to
Yesterday*, sometimes a matter for pain (as in the drama of Lady Jane
Grey), sometimes for optimism (as in the last-named film). Class division,
which, for the most part, British cinema of the decade is simply prepared

to take for granted, receives in Stevenson's work some tart comment, as in *Young Man's Fancy*, and is made fun of by the seaside actors who unconvincingly play upper-class characters in *Return to Yesterday*. In *Owd Bob*, the local squire, Lord Meredale (Edmond Breon), will automatically present the Championship Cup – and will automatically confiscate McAdam's sheep in payment for back rent. In view of the sympathy allowed to McAdam here, one suspects that Stevenson was alert to the potential pains of class divisiveness without the need to be explicit.

In technical terms, his films are fast-moving; even in the more lavish ones, such as *Tudor Rose* and *King Solomon's Mines*, the spectacle is not allowed to get in the way of the action. They are visually fluent without being flashy; he makes sparing but effective uses of dissolves and superimpositions to reinforce meaning, as in the appearance of railway lines and English station names over a close-up of the faces of the returning lovers in *Young Man's Fancy*, suggesting the evanescence of youthful vision, and he is clearly a director at home with actors. His films are lavishly cast in the Gainsborough tradition, often using actors with stage backgrounds; as Desmond Tester recalls, Stevenson did not favour a great deal of rehearsal and was astute at 'pulling [him] back' to the demands of film acting,[34] and an often stagey actor such as Clive Brook is encouraged to give one of his warmest, most intimate film performances in *Return to Yesterday*.

What one wants in the end to note about Stevenson is a Curtiz-like versatility across the typical range of genres open to British film-makers in the 1930s, and a warmth in dealing with matters of human concern that distinguishes him from the artificialities of the decade's journeyman film-makers. The pacifism that led him out of England at the start of the war may well indicate a reflectiveness and sophistication of thought that finds its way into what might otherwise have been hack work. As it is, these films from Gainsborough and Ealing constitute a batch of work which holds up better than many of the more lauded productions of the period. We can only speculate on the place he might have found in the rejuvenated British film industry of the wartime and immediately post-war years.

9. Godfrey Tearle and Julian Mitchell in *The Last Journey*

## CHAPTER 9

# Money for Speed: The British Films of Bernard Vorhaus

## *Geoff Brown*

'PITY such admirable direction and superb casting should be wasted on so banal a story.'[1] Thus wrote the London film correspondent for *Variety*, reviewing *Night Club Queen* after a preview screening at the Prince Edward Theatre on 22 March 1934. Admirably directed though it might be, this drama about family sacrifice, speedily adapted from a recent West End play, does not stand now as one of Bernard Vorhaus's brightest achievements. The film, indeed, remains largely in the shadows, despite the revived interest in Vorhaus, first fanned by the National Film and Television Archive in the mid-1980s.[2] But the quotation usefully points up a major disparity between achievement and material in Vorhaus's work that looms even larger now in the minds of viewers than it probably did to observers in the 1930s.

During his eight years spent in the British film industry, from 1930 to 1937, the American-born director Bernard Vorhaus worked at a level where time and money were in short supply, but unpromising or trivial material was plentiful. He worked largely for Julius Hagen at Twickenham, turning out thrillers, musicals, dramas; anything his boss required to fill the exhibitors' need for sufficient British film footage to meet the quota regulations. He could exert some power over casting; after being bewitched by Margaret Rutherford on stage, he found a choice role for her eccentric gifts in his film of *Dusty Ermine*, made in 1936. But Vorhaus had no power to change the ground rules of 'quota quickie' film-making.

Rule number one: you had to shoot fast, and finish your feature in under two weeks. Rule number two: your costs had to be less than £1 per foot of finished celluloid, since quota films were sold to exhibitors at £1 a foot, and profits had to be made somewhere. The combined force of rules one and two produced a tendency to pack scripts with dialogue scenes that could be shot economically in long takes in the studio. Unfortunately, the films' dialogue would not be written by Noël Coward. It would be written, probably, by Harry Fowler Mear, Hagen's story editor, a man of old-fashioned tastes who kept special files of doctor jokes, marital jokes and other wheezes for insertion at what he deemed appropriate moments. And you might have to work with an immovable fixture like the singer John Garrick, heavy on smiles and oleaginous charm, regularly featured in Twickenham's productions.

But rules exist to be broken or subverted. Vorhaus did everything in his power to make the best use of his restrictions and breathe cinematic life into his material. He went on location wherever possible, sometimes operating his own camera, and came back to the studio's cramped spaces in St Margaret's, Twickenham, with evidence, however brief, that a real world with fresh air and trees existed outside. He also endeavoured to spruce up the scripts, wherever possible, with salty characters far removed from the stock supply of Mayfair cardboard cutouts.

Once moments of high drama were reached in the scripts, Vorhaus would speed up the cutting to the rate of a montage, hurling at the screen images often lasting for only a few seconds. Or he would enter the characters' eyes and blur or otherwise distort a shot to suggest subjective perception. Anything to make the script into a real piece of cinema, and not just a product dutifully manufactured for a set price to meet a legal requirement. Unusually among the film directors working in Britain at the time, Vorhaus even looked the dedicated artist. Publicity photographs taken on the sets show him sporting a goatee beard, symbol at the time of a true bohemian.

Vorhaus was not alone at Twickenham or the other outposts of quickie productions in his ability to make genuine cinema. Some distinguished names of silent days sheltered under the umbrella of low-budget productions, such as the directors George Pearson, Henry Edwards and Adrian Brunel; some less distinguished names too (such as George A. Cooper). But in many cases if their spirits were willing their scripts were too weak, or too numerous, for much good to result; Pearson shot six films, mostly thrillers, during 1935 alone. 'Remuneration was small,' Pearson wrote in his autobiography *Flashback*, 'but just enough for existence. All vaulting ideas of film as an art had to be abandoned; only as a capable and speedy craftsman could one survive in that feverish and restless environment.'[3]

Youngsters new to the game, with muscles to flex, had more success at surviving, and carving something from nothing. At Wembley and elsewhere, the young Michael Powell toiled away on murder mysteries, crook thrillers and other oddments, mostly for the American producer Jerry Jackson, wherever possible filtering into the images quirky camera angles or Soviet-style montages.

Quota productions provided launching pads for other distinguished careers. John Bryan, whose production designs contributed much to the Dickens adaptations of David Lean, started in the mid-1930s as art director on *The Small Man, Men of Yesterday* and other shoestring ventures by the Baxter and Barter team of John Baxter (director) and John Barter (producer). Lean himself was another graduate: he left the cutting rooms of Movietone newsreels to edit low-budget features, including two of Vorhaus's own, *Money for Speed* and *The Ghost Camera*. Vorhaus loved the fast cutting that Lean brought to his newsreels. Lean in turn appreciated the director's lively approach: 'Highly inventive,' he described Vorhaus later, 'with a real love for film and as clever as a wagonload of monkeys.'[4]

In an interview, Vorhaus later recalled the hard work and dedication of Twickenham's crews as 'quite remarkable':

> In those days, there were no special effects departments. The property man was expected to provide whatever was needed and he damn well did. If you had cobwebs in a scene he made them. If you needed icicles, if you needed glass that you could crash through without cutting yourself he provided it ... Some of the directors were just interested in grinding the stuff out; some certainly tried very hard. But the crews in general, considering how difficult their working conditions were, it's amazing that they really tried to make good films: the cameraman and their helpers, and the sound crews, the grips, everybody.[5]

The actors, too, were often no slouches. *Night Club Queen* and *Crime on the Hill* found a home for Lewis Casson, usually seen partnering his wife Sybil Thorndike in something worthy on the West End stage. Henry Kendall, popular stage purveyor of breezy men about town, lent his nonchalant presence to *The Ghost Camera*. Many other cast members came to Twickenham via Shaftesbury Avenue, lured by fees that may have been small by Hollywood standards, but were larger than the sums the theatres offered. Vorhaus, for one, felt 'extremely grateful for the wonderful acting talent in [Britain]'. Other films featured Ida Lupino, John Mills and Geraldine Fitzgerald, all young, bright and beady-eyed.

All the talent in the world, however, could still go to waste if the director calling the shots was asleep on the job. Vorhaus was not. Born in New York City on 25 December 1904, he retained an American's taste for speed, and displayed a natural ability to think cinematically.

Vorhaus grew up with cinema. His sister Amy, eleven years his senior, was a scenario writer for the movies, and young Bernard accompanied her on trips to her studio at Fort Lee, New Jersey. While Amy was busy with story conferences, Bernard watched films being shot on the studio floor. Workers would give him scraps of celluloid which, once back home, he would cut up, splice into new configurations and run through his toy projector; an early intimation, perhaps, of his adult love of rapid-fire editing and montage.

Vorhaus's father, born on the Austrian–Polish frontier, had come to America at the age of seven. After working hard to support the family, he now had a distinguished law practice in New York, and was anxious for his son to join the business. Bernard struck a bargain. He would go through Harvard in three years rather than four. During the fourth he would break into movies. If he did not, he would abandon dreams of the silver screen and enrol in Harvard's law school.

Enter Harry Cohn, rough-tongued president of Columbia Pictures, on a periodic trip to New York:

> When I met him, he said, 'So you wanna write for films?' I said yes. He said, 'Well, what the hell makes you think you can write?' I said I'd written a few short stories. 'Alright,' he said. 'Boy. Girl. Heavy. Got it?' I didn't even know what 'heavy' meant: I wasn't familiar with theatrical terms at all. 'Boy's a fireman. Fire breaks out. He goes up ladder, breaks through window, finds girl in room with heavy. Now. Finish the story.' So I ad-libbed some kind of a thing, and he said, 'OK. I'll give you a job as a junior writer. 50 bucks a week, and you gotta pay your own fare to Hollywood.' That's how I got started.

Ensconced in Hollywood at Columbia by 1924, he wrote assorted scripts, including a six-reel comedy, *Steppin' Out*, that was kindly received. He moved on to Paramount, and the new conglomerate of Metro-Goldwyn-Mayer, where he served as assistant to Carey Wilson. He also formed a writing partnership with another young writer starting out, Jessie Burns. They placed an advertisement in the *Film Year Book* of 1926; they collaborated on an MGM comedy, *Money Talks* (1926), and a Fox drama with Lou Tellegen and Dolores Del Rio, *No Other Woman* (1929).

But directing, not writing, was Vorhaus's aim. At Columbia, he had worked as assistant to B. Reeves Eason, whose speciality was the precise choreography of pell-mell action (Eason staged the chariot race for the 1925 *Ben Hur*). He observed Robert Z. Leonard, an efficient if none too imaginative talent, re-shooting sequences on MGM's *Time, the Comedian*. Then in 1928, Vorhaus and Burns leaped into the director's chair themselves, writing, directing, producing and funding a two-reeler called *Sunlight*, featuring ZaSu Pitts. Critical comment was favourable, but there were no commercial takers for a silent two-reeler when the industry was in the throes of the talkie revolution.

Trying to bounce back from the disappointment, Vorhaus decided on a holiday in England with his last few hundred dollars. He landed in Plymouth in a burst of spring sunshine in 1929. Entranced, he explored the country by motorcycle. Reaching London after a week's adventures (he had never driven a motorcycle before, nor did he know that American 'gas' equalled Britain's 'petrol'), he found the film industry undergoing talkie convulsions of its own. This time Vorhaus was a beneficiary of the revolution, and was offered a job as supervisor by British Sound Film Productions (BSFP), the production subsidiary of British Talking Pictures, formed in 1928 and housed at the new Wembley Studios, which had officially opened for business in September 1929.

The productions of BSFP or its sister company Associated Sound Film Industries (ASFI, formed in October 1929) mostly came in two categories. There were sound shorts featuring variety and radio performers like the cross-talk comedians Clapham and Dwyer, revue artiste Norah Blaney, the portly xylophonist Teddy Brown, and the self-explanatory Emile Grimshaw Banjo Quartette. Some of the shorts featured marionettes operated by the Italian Gorno family, made in the likenesses of popular Hollywood film stars. (The family's stock of traditional marionettes had been destroyed in a fire at the Wembley Studios in October, one month after opening.) Vorhaus wrote the script for a Tom Mix parody called *Tom Mix-Up*; John Grierson also lent a hand to the series.[6]

Wembley also generated a few over-ambitious features, fashioned in multi-lingual editions. Vorhaus worked as production supervisor on ASFI's *City of Song* (1930), directed by the Italian Carmine Gallone, an operetta-like story about a singing Neapolitan guide (Jan Kiepura) who eschews the bright lights of an international career for the pleasures of home. ASFI also pushed out the tri-lingual *The Bells* (1931), now a lost film, directed by Oscar Werndorff and Harcourt Templeman, a version of the stage melodrama made famous by Sir Henry Irving. Both BSFP and ASFI then faded away, leaving the Wembley Studios free to be hired by quota producers, particularly Fox.

For Vorhaus, Wembley marked an inauspicious beginning in film production, though he enjoyed the company of an extraordinary collection of continental talents. Any production company anxious to make a splash had its continental affiliations in the early sound period. They needed to draw on European sound equipment, such as Klangfilm-Tobis. To make a mark on the international market, they also needed the visual gloss that European technicians could provide. Aside from Gallone, Vorhaus could have found wandering around Wembley the German director Henrik Galeen, cameramen Arpad Viragh (from Hungary), Curt Courant (from Germany) and Günther Krampf (from Austria), and the Russian-born jack of all trades Sergei Nolbandov.

In *City of Song*, the dialogue writer, Miles Malleson, supplies a choice speech after Jan Kiepura's Neapolitan songbird is introduced to London by Betty Stockfeld, the socialite who captured him on her European tour. 'Why bring him home?' one dinner-jacketed fool complains, perched on the edge of a sofa; 'After all, foreigners are alright abroad, one expects them.' But if British films of the 1930s had reflected such xenophobia, the quality would have been severely impoverished. Craftsmen from across Europe would not have worked on the Korda spectaculars made at Denham. The smaller films, the forgotten films of the 1930s, would also have suffered. The Anglo-French Edmond T. Gréville brought a visual sweep and a love of mirror shots to romantic assignments like *Brief Ecstasy*. European film practice also informed the quota quickies of Michael Powell, and the early work of Anthony Asquith.

Vorhaus's British features also stand out partly because of their foreign élan. They move fast. They use camera angles and sophisticated editing to interpret the script in visual terms; and not simply to embalm reams of dialogue in a placid alternation of medium shots. Truffaut's famous gibe about the words Britain and cinema being incompatible is a wholly unfair generalisation; yet the acres of middle-ground British cinema, stifled by literary or theatrical tradition, can be barren territory. Excitement often enters mainstream British cinema from outside territories: from the documentary movement; from the kitchen sink school of drama and fiction; from Europe, or America. Of course there is nothing to stop dullness being exported too; witness the films of the Austrian director Paul Stein, which sit on the screen the way a Black Forest gateau sits on the stomach.

Vorhaus's months at Wembley brought one concrete result. Once British Talking Pictures' operations collapsed, the company was left with reel upon reel of its sound shorts, some of them still in negative form. Vorhaus acquired the material, launched his own company Hall Mark Films, and used his editing skills to cut the footage into a series of six shorts called *Camera Cocktales*, released through MGM. New material shot by Vorhaus was interspersed throughout the bizarre cavalcade. The Gorno marionettes raised their heads again, in an Al Jolson parody, *Dimples and Tears*; Medvedeff's Balalaika orchestra strummed away; while Dale Smith and the Salisbury Singers warbled through the English songbook.

The *Camera Cocktales* may have been hack work, but the money they generated helped Vorhaus to launch himself further into independent production at the end of 1932 with two short features, *On Thin Ice* and *Money for Speed*. *On Thin Ice*, trade shown in February 1933, remains a lost film; and considering some of the contemporary reviews we may not be losing too much, apart from an early performance by the stage actress Ursula Jeans. 'A production which does not add to the prestige of British pictures,' snorted the *Kinematograph Weekly*. Certainly Vorhaus's script could not have given him much chance to shine; reports indicate a film of society charades, of jealous love and blackmail, set in British cinema's usual artificial world of nightclubs and grandiose mansions.[7]

*Money for Speed*, which emerged one month after *On Thin Ice* in March 1933, appears a more tantalising proposition.[8] The title alone suits Vorhaus's career as a director who achieved high-quality work on the lowest of budgets at a breakneck pace. With several friends he prepared a script about a triangular romance (two motorcycle speedway champions, plus one girl), and shot some speedway sequences as a taster. United Artists swallowed the bait, and arranged for distribution. A blonde-haired Ida Lupino, aged 15, made her second film appearance as the girl; while John Loder appeared as the caddish boyfriend who persuades her to make such a pitch for Cyril McLaglen, his speedway rival, that McLaglen will lose concentration, and lose the race. According to Oswald Morris, employed on the film as a camera assistant, Vorhaus showed no interest in the dialogue sequences the story required; he just wanted to rush about shooting motorcycle crashes, to such an extent that he was known on the set as 'Mad Vorhaus'. But there was a method to his madness, and this time reviewers gave Vorhaus thumbs-up: 'Here we have that *rara avis*, a successful British action drama, and its producers are to be congratulated on bringing to the screen the thrills of a popular British sport – speedway racing – and linking them with a straightforward but convincing story.'[9]

Casting around for someone to play Alice in their forthcoming production of *Alice in Wonderland*, Paramount Pictures saw footage of Ida Lupino in *Money for Speed* and offered her a contract. The Alice role did not materialise, but a Hollywood career certainly did. For Vorhaus, too, *Money for Speed* served as a major stepping-stone. Audiences were enthusiastic; in 1986 Vorhaus recalled, without boasting, that many preferred his little speedway melodrama to the main feature on the double-bill, the Ronald Colman vehicle *Cynara*.

The release of *Money for Speed* also made Vorhaus realise the vulnerability of an independent film-maker, at the mercy of his distributor. He took shelter at Julius Hagen's Twickenham Studios, where British release contracts were arranged with several distributors, including American-owned companies like Universal or Radio Pictures. Over the next four years he made seven films for Hagen; some bore the Twickenham label, others were called Real Art Productions. His first task, in June 1933, was a crime story prepared by the playwright and novelist J. Jefferson Farjeon, author of *Number Seventeen* (filmed by Hitchcock the previous year), *The 5.18 Mystery*, *The Crooks' Shadow* and other titles too frightening to mention. Farjeon's new opus was *The Ghost Camera*, so-called from the camera found in a car, whose film, when developed, appeared to contain evidence of murder.

*The Ghost Camera* and its immediate successor, *Crime on the Hill*, shot in September at Welwyn for British International Pictures and based on a current West End play, marked Vorhaus's entry into a peculiarly English genre: the mystery thriller. These are tales of nefarious doings in rural surroundings and sleepy hamlets, of amateur sleuths and wronged innocents. Vorhaus brought an outsider's eye to the material, and an impish sense of irony; even, in Sally Blane's performance in *Crime on the Hill*, a suggestion of the erotic. At the start of the film the imported American actress is discovered hiding behind bushes, presumably naked, close to the stream where Lewis Casson's vicar is placidly fishing, pipe in mouth, and chatting with the village doctor (played by another stage luminary, Sir Nigel Playfair). Retrieving her garments, Casson toys with her slip, embarrassed. Elsewhere, when properly clothed, Blane's physical attributes are featured with unusual prominence for a British film of the period.

Yet in other ways, these two thrillers dutifully respect conventions in performance, substance and tone. Note Ida Lupino stepping back with alarm as she cries 'Police!' when George Merritt's detective introduces himself in *The Ghost Camera*. In the same film, listen to the debonair West End drawl of Henry Kendall, kitted out in bow tie and horn-rimmed glasses; the man who finds the 'ghost' camera whose contents implicate Lupino's brother, John Mills, in a murder. 'I find it excessively stimulating,' Kendall says, once the plot starts to thicken; though you would not know from his flat, laid-back voice, as much of a period relic as the rectory set in *Crime on the Hill* (panelled walls, formal portraits, suits of armour, swords).

For his part, Vorhaus strives to add tension and visual interest to the piffling mystery plots. In *The Ghost Camera* he does everything to avoid the commonplace courtroom shots of judge, defendant, accused and jury. John Mills staggers down the aisle into court to the lurchings of a subjective camera. The judge, Felix Aylmer, lays out the incriminating evidence in forcefully intercut close-ups that grow progressively closer. We hear the jury's verdict indirectly, only gauging it from the sight of the clerk covering his pencil drawing of Mills with prison bars.

In *Crime on the Hill* (the crime is the murder of the village squire, Sally Blane's guardian), Vorhaus delights in puncturing rural bliss with irony. Through characterisation and dialogue, Vorhaus suggests that this 'Garden of Eden' (the vicar's words in the opening scene) is not what it seems. The camera focuses ominously on a tombstone's phrase: 'Rest in Peace'. The village bazaar becomes the site of a corpse, dramatically discovered in the gloom of night pierced by lanterns.

The script, adapted from a play by two practised thriller writers, Jack de Leon and Jack Celestin, offers a late revelation that could have topped all others. The murdered squire, it turns out, was addicted to drugs, but since the character exists only as a piece of plot machinery – a body found slumped in a chair – his drug habit has little resonance.

Stage material was regularly acquired by Twickenham and the other low-budget suppliers for rapid screen transfer; when speed of production was essential, there was a natural attraction in buying ready-made plots and dialogue. *Crime on the Hill*, filmed in September 1933, had appeared on Shaftesbury Avenue in April. Anthony Kimmins's melodrama *Night Club Queen*, shot at Twickenham in February 1934, opened at the Playhouse Theatre the previous November. Anthony Armstrong's *Ten Minute Alibi*, one of the 1930s' most popular thrillers (there were 878 performances in London), took longer to reach the screen; after opening in the West End in February 1933, this ingenious tale of a playboy cad, the girl he seduces, the boyfriend who kills him, and the clock manipulated to provide an alibi, moved into production at Beaconsfield Studios in September 1934.

Vorhaus's film, made for the producer Paul Soskin, found its own measure of success. Phillips Holmes, on holiday from Hollywood, was the cast's most notable name; he played the boyfriend. The *Variety* reviewer went so far as to call the film 'one of the most absorbing bits of picture entertainment produced anywhere'.[10] Yet in interview Vorhaus remembered *Ten Minute Alibi* as one of his least interesting ventures, primarily because he could find no way of breaking out of the material's stage straitjacket.

Vorhaus's memory cannot be challenged; no print of the film is available for viewing. But in *Night Club Queen*, we can see the director snatching his chances whenever they surface. Anthony Kimmins's improbable plot tells of a lawyer's wife who secretly runs a nightclub to finance her son's Oxford education, and ends up accused of murder. Through careful placing of the camera, Vorhaus makes James A. Carter's nightclub set seem far bigger than it is, big enough to incorporate the dancing feet of the Sherman Fisher Girls and the spirited performance of Mary Clare as the doting mother brought low by fate. Lewis Casson spends most of his time being irascible in a wheelchair, casting aspersions on the nightclub queen – 'the old hag' – without realising that the old hag is his wife. The film cannot be claimed a great discovery; but Vorhaus certainly makes the material far more persuasive than it has any right to be.

Sometimes, however, Vorhaus had to retire defeated. In 1986 he bravely nominated *Street Song*, the last of his four Twickenham productions of 1934, as 'the worst thing I've done': 'I shouldn't have done it. A Quota film had to go on the floor at Twickenham that week, and I had an idea. I put a writer on it. But what emerged was just terrible, and I couldn't both rewrite and shoot it at the same time. It was awful.'

Vera Allinson's screenplay, developed from a story by Vorhaus and a fellow American, Paul Gangelin, offers a standard issue sentimental musical, built to house the actor-singer John Garrick. A street singer, he takes shelter from the police in the impoverished pet shop run by Rene Ray and her kid brother. A landlord on loan from a Victorian melodrama needs the rent quick, or else. Garrick lets his vocal cords rip; during the number 'In Our Little Noah's Ark', audience members in the shop include puppies, a bear cub and a cockatoo fluffing its feathers. Garrick also gatecrashes the radio broadcast of the BBC dance band director 'Roy Hall' (an obvious combination of Roy Fox and Henry Hall). En route to the finale, the kid gets run over. Some moments have a weird kind of charm, but the bulk is awful indeed.

Yet even in his darkest hour, Vorhaus can be seen trying to give the film a little pep. The camera ventures briefly on location; Garrick's feet are seen in close-up pounding the pavement as he seeks work. We see building sites, and signs declaring 'No Hands Wanted'. The glimpse of real life does not last, but the shots help us measure the amount of mawkish artifice elsewhere.

Vorhaus's earlier Garrick vehicle, *The Broken Melody*, shot in November 1933, is no happier an experience. The story is boldly preposterous. Garrick plays a French composer who is sent to Devil's Island for murdering his wife's lover, escapes, and writes an opera based on his experiences, which is duly heard on opening night by the prison governor, visiting Paris. The melodrama gives Vorhaus no room for quirks of characterisation or humour other than the unintentional kind. 'Where the deuce is that symphony in F?' Garrick cries, rifling through his papers. Merle Oberon, on loan from London Film Productions, digs out a single sheet – this is obviously the world's shortest symphony. But the trouble does not lie just in the script. Both films demonstrate the pitfalls of mounting any kind of musical at a studio whose musical director is W. L. Trytel, the man whose old-fashioned, mediocre, patchwork scores hang like a shroud over Twickenham's soundtracks.

Vorhaus's failure with the Garrick musicals came about partly because he was tackling an uncongenial genre. Throughout his career in England and America, he periodically avoided what he knew he could do best – the mystery thriller – in favour of difficult assignments. In Hollywood in the 1940s, he tried several westerns, even an ice-skating musical (*Ice-Capades Revue*); but his best work, as in England, came in well-crafted thrillers like *Affairs of Jimmy Valentine* and *The Spiritualist*.

After *Street Song*, Vorhaus must have plunged with relief into his next Twickenham assignment in May 1935, *The Last Journey*, one of the best 'quota quickies', and the sturdiest of all his surviving British films. It lasts just 66 minutes, or 6,000 feet's worth of celluloid; and into them Vorhaus has packed more excitement per inch than many of British cinema's prestige classics of the period can manage.

In some ways the film has to move fast; it concerns a runaway train that jumps red lights, roars through stations and turns passengers to quivering jellies as the train driver, tormented by inner demons, follows his route to destruction. The original story is another offspring from the fertile mind of J. Jefferson Farjeon, who had previously featured trains in his plays *Number Seventeen* and *The 5.18 Mystery*.

The basic plot is banal and melodramatic. Faced with retirement after a lifetime on the engine footplate, and fuelled by an erroneous conviction that his stoker is having an affair with his wife, train driver Bob Holt (played by Julien Mitchell) plans to make his last journey well and truly his last. 'I'm going straight to hell, and I'm not going alone; we're all going, we're all going together!'

Like *Friday the Thirteenth*, made two years before, and the myriad disaster movies made more recently, *The Last Journey* enlivens the drama by highlighting the individual stories of the disaster's innocent participants. Travelling on the 3.07 p.m. train from London we find a honey-voiced bigamist and his latest conquest (Hugh Williams and Judy Gunn), two escaping crooks, a detective in mufti (Frank Pettingell), and a brain specialist (Godfrey Tearle), duly summoned to the engine to soothe the disturbed driver's mind before the train crashes into the buffers at Mulchester's terminus station.

These are characters caught in extreme situations, often with dialogue to match. Yet Vorhaus, characteristically, does his best to humanise them. In between suffering bouts of what one might call Farjeonitis, Julien Mitchell's Bob Holt emerges as a sympathetic working man, proud of his 40 years' employment, so wedded to his job that his home looks out on to a marshalling yard. Michael Hogan's Charlie, his footplate mate, is equally no caricature. As the train hurtles forwards, Vorhaus cuts between characters, and finds room in the mêlée for the mail van workers, talking while they sort what appears to be fan mail for Hollywood stars.

Fast cutting and location shooting with the Great Western Railway's finest rolling stock add to the film's impact. Some shots last only one, two or three seconds. Vorhaus and his editor Jack Harris (later to work for Lean in the 1940s) make us breathless as we try to keep pace. Passengers cling to doors, screaming. As the train races through the crowded platform of Homechurch Station, a toupee is blown on to a woman's mouth. Up ahead on the same track, a goods train idly chuffs along; can it be shifted to a siding to avoid collision? Meanwhile, along country roads, Mickey Brantford's Tom, beloved of Judy Gunn's Diana, is racing along in fast pursuit; when the car proves too slow, he switches to a plane. Speed, speed, speed; always to the accompaniment of rattling wheels and billows of steam.

Some interiors were re-created at Twickenham, using back projection, wind machines and other devices to suggest a train in motion. Hagen's studios at Twickenham had never coped with back projection before; but Vorhaus's team coped admirably with surmounting technical challenges with little time and money. At no time do we experience that Hornby train-set feeling, engendered, for instance, by the copious model work in Hitchcock's film of *Number Seventeen*.

For a low-budget thriller, *The Last Journey* made a considerable impact on release, and received the incidental accolade of inclusion in one of Gallagher's cigarette card series, 'Film Episodes', alongside other new releases like *Top Hat* and *Bonnie Scotland*. Vorhaus himself was receiving recognition, at least within the British industry. When Anthony Havelock-Allan, the future producer of *Brief Encounter*, asked to learn how films were made, in his early days in the business (he joined British and Dominions Film Corporation in 1933), he was advised to observe the fastest and most efficient director working in Britain: Bernard Vorhaus. And when Vorhaus's next film, *Dark World*, made for Fox-British, went into production at Wembley, the studio correspondent for *Picturegoer* magazine, E. G. Cousins, pointedly noted: 'The thing that interests me most about this production is the fact that Bernard Vorhaus is directing it. He manages to get a slickness and a smoothness into most of his films that are reminiscent of Hollywood product. Very few of our directors achieve it.'[11]

Trade reviews indicate that *Dark World* was just as slick and smooth as Cousins expected. Since no print is known to have survived, we have to make do by imagining the distinguished stage actor Leon Quartermaine driven to such jealousy by Tamara Desni's dancer that he tries to electrocute his rival in love: his own younger brother.

Back at Twickenham, Vorhaus found himself embroiled in *Broken Blossoms*, the ambitious remake of D. W. Griffith's silent melodrama about the Limehouse waif (Dolly Haas), her vicious father (Arthur Margetson) and the Chinaman (Emlyn Williams, more Welsh than Chinese) who tries to save her. This moved into production at Twickenham in October 1935. Vorhaus served as technical supervisor – the film's producer on the floor – and watched with dismay as the appointed director Hans (later John) Brahm and his cameraman Curt Courant led the story further and further into a soft-focus wonderland with no connection to reality.

Brahm, who had served as supervisor on *The Last Journey* and other recent Twickenham productions, was a refugee from Nazi Germany; *Broken Blossoms* was to be his directing debut, though originally Griffith himself was proposed. Vorhaus's job was essentially to keep Brahm on track, which he did. But it was too late to change the film's artificial style and incorporate location work in Limehouse. 'This would have been such a godsend,' Vorhaus recalled in 1986

> because you would have seen the social, economic background of these characters, instead of having them exist in a void. You would have seen them literally under the debris of the decaying Limehouse of the Depression ... I would have shot the bulk of it on location in very sharp hard focus; this was the reality. And then let the love story, which was the fantasy of the young Chinaman with this little girl, be in even softer focus. As things were, it was all shot in the studio, and Twickenham was not even sufficiently sophisticated to give the resemblance of reality that you would have got with a big Elstree studio. So all I could do really was to keep the film on schedule, and see that it was cut alright.[12]

Hagen's ambitions continued to rise, and the size of the films moved in parallel. During 1935 he formed J. H. Productions, intended home for prestige ventures; he formed Twickenham Film Distributors; he acquired new studio spaces at Elstree and Hammersmith. Ultimately, Hagen's expansion plans were to wreak havoc on Vorhaus's British career. But for the moment Vorhaus could luxuriate in his next assignment, *Dusty Ermine*, a crime thriller about counterfeiters, mounted in January 1936 at Elstree, featuring extensive location work in the Alps.

The material was based on a play by Neil Grant, first performed in London the previous September at the Arts Theatre. Two of the actors transferred from stage to screen: Arthur Macrae as the languid Gilbert Kent, nephew of a veteran forger just released from Wormwood Scrubs; and Katie Johnson as the forger's sister-in-law, in love with the quiet domestic life. While the film was still in progress, a second stage production appeared at the Comedy Theatre.

Vorhaus gave Grant's thriller a vigorous shake, adding an eccentric role for Margaret Rutherford as the counterfeiter's handmaid Miss Butterby; and opening out the plot to take full advantage of location shooting in the Swiss Alps, where the counterfeit gang had their HQ. At times, when the characters chase each other on skis, or when Vorhaus superimposes a clockface on the wheel of a speeding car, we experience the thrill of genuine cinema. At other times, we remain locked in a Shaftesbury Avenue theatre. 'Who do you think you are?' asks Jane Baxter's heroine, the forger's niece, prettily adorned throughout much of the film in white jacket and beret, as Anthony Bushell presses his inquiries too closely. 'I have every reason to suppose I'm Inspector Forsyth of Scotland Yard,' he says pompously; a line that prompts a startled reaction in close-up.

*Dusty Ermine* is scattered with bright touches and directed with considerable assurance; yet the artifice of its plot and characters strangles some life from the film, which never happens with *The Last Journey*. In retrospect the most personal aspect of the film is its dramatic use of snow and skis. Winter sports became one of Vorhaus's main hobbies – he was still skiing in his eighties. Characters in other Vorhaus films periodically take to skis, most noticeably in *Winter Wonderland*, made at Republic in 1947 for *émigré* producer Henry Sokal, another skiing enthusiast who had helped to supervise *Dusty Ermine*. There is a memorable ski ballet, with ladies and gents dressed in different combinations of black and white; and a splendidly cut ski race, directly echoing *Dusty Ermine*. Vorhaus's final film, *Fanciulle di lusso* (*Luxury Girls*), an indifferent feature shot in Italy in 1952, comes to life only when a torchlight search for a missing girl unfolds on a snowy mountain, white smoke billowing against the darkness.

Vorhaus's next, and last, British film brought him back home from the Alps with a bump. Locations this time were the cotton mills of Manchester's Vantona Textiles Company, the city's Belle Vue amusement park, and all the sights of Blackpool. *Cotton Queen*, made in August 1936 for the American comedian-turned-producer Joe Rock at Elstree, concerned the rivalry between two Lancashire cotton manufacturers, played to broad effect by Stanley Holloway and Will Fyffe.

Though *Cotton Queen* was hardly congenial material for Vorhaus, there were pragmatic reasons for tackling North Country comedy. George Formby and Gracie Fields were currently riding high at the box office; Rock's backer J. H. Iles was a North Country entertainment financier. Louis Golding, a writer specialising in novels with northern settings, contributed additional dialogue. Vorhaus, for his part, did what he could to sustain visual interest. A crash between the rival firms' lorries generates lurching camerawork and quick cutting. The Cotton Queen competition at Blackpool Tower inspires a few fancy moments with the band conductor and the surrounding brass instruments. At other times there is not much Vorhaus can do other than watch Holloway parade his walrus moustache and Fyffe give a barrage of cross-eyed looks.

By the time *Cotton Queen* was released to cinemas in May 1937, Vorhaus's active career in British films was over. During 1936 Julius Hagen had been staving off disaster by applying for a new loan, engineering a flattering appraisal of his assets by moving cameras and sound equipment between his studios whenever the appraisers were due. But the loan delayed the end only by a few months. Receivers were appointed in January 1937 to the various corners of Julius Hagen's empire: Twickenham Studios, J. H. Productions, and Twickenham Film Distributors. Hagen's studios at Riverside and Elstree were relinquished, and by 1938 Twickenham was closed.

Vorhaus found himself out of work, and out of pocket; one of many victims of the British film industry's financial crisis, just as he had been one of its beneficiaries with the coming of sound. The mill owners of *Cotton Queen* had their financial problems too, but an American entrepreneur played by C. Denier Warren came to the rescue by offering them a lucrative contract providing they merge their mills. And America came to Vorhaus's aid, or so it seemed, in the shape of Herbert J. Yates, president of Republic Pictures. Yates had seen some of his British work, and offered him employment; the first of his ten Republic films was *King of the Newsboys*, a hectic drama set in New York, shot in January

1938. He also began working for producer Sol Lesser at RKO, making four films in 1939–40.

And so Vorhaus found himself directing western melodramas, hoodlum stories, saccharine vehicles for child star Bobby Breen (plus, in the case of *Fisherman's Wharf*, a performing seal), and a lumbering John Wayne. He had his flops; he had his triumphs, particularly once he struck a working relationship with the cameraman John Alton, which began at RKO in 1940 with *The Courageous Dr Christian*. He was still confined to B-movies and low budgets; and in some ways he found himself given less room to manoeuvre than he had directing 'quota quickies': 'I didn't know at the time what a treadmill Republic was, or I think maybe I would have taken more of a chance, and made more of an effort to go somewhere else. There was a tendency to overplay everything, to get the most out of everything. And the kind of thing they wanted to turn out was quite limited.'

Yet if the material in Hollywood was not always what Vorhaus may have wished, he kept congenial company, particularly with left-wing scriptwriters. Like many others of his generation, Vorhaus had become politicised by the Spanish Civil War, and the crushing of the legitimate government by Franco and the forces of fascism. Here was a real, burning issue; the films he worked on, by comparison, were twitterings from Cloud Cuckoo Land. Toiling away with him at Republic and RKO were two future members of the Hollywood Ten: writers Samuel Ornitz (involved in *King of the Newsboys* and the interesting *Three Faces West*) and Ring Lardner Jr (two *Dr Christian* films). Other colleagues were spared the Ten's jail terms, but still had their careers sabotaged by the blacklist in the 1950s, including writers Ian McLellan Hunter (the *Dr Christian* films and *The Spiritualist*), Gordon Kahn (*Tenth Avenue Kid*), Francis Edward Faragoh and Guy Endore (*Lady from Louisiana*).

Vorhaus, an active member of the Hollywood Anti-Nazi League, became caught up in the nightmare. After serving in the Air Force and Signal Corps film units during the war, supervising production of official films, he re-emerged in the commercial industry in 1947. Following *The Spiritualist*, a silly but seductive thriller about a fake medium made in 1948, Vorhaus ventured into independent production in New York, and found some success with *So Young So Bad* (1950), an earnest drama about delinquent girls.

Gathering storm clouds forced Vorhaus to return to Europe in 1951, where he made two inconsequential films in France and Italy with backing from United Artists: *Pardon My French* and *Fanciulle di lusso*. Pressure continued to mount. While in Europe he was named as a communist sympathiser during Edward Dmytryk's testimony to the House Un-American Activities Committee on 25 April 1951. The projectionists' union in America then threatened to block all United Artists' products if the company released any further Vorhaus film.

So there was no further Vorhaus film. His current European project, *Stranger on the Prowl*, was taken over by another blacklist victim, Joseph Losey. Vorhaus moved back to England with his wife and family, mulled over various minor offers, then decided to retreat for safety's sake to another business entirely: the flat conversion business. Stimulated by converting his own house in Primrose Hill, London, he took evening classes in architecture, and established his own company, Domar Properties, combing London for suitable large houses, organising the conversion into self-contained units, and selling them off to satisfied clients. This second career is not as incongruous as it may at first appear: Vorhaus only achieved his stylish effects on low-budget films through extensive planning and imaginative marshalling of available resources. The resources simply switched from scripts, actors and limited money to bricks, mortar and limited floor space. Vorhaus also put his creative energies into gardening, developing and designing an acre of land at Heron's Reach, near Pangbourne.

During the 1950s other blacklisted talents had found work under pseudonyms in British film or television (particularly the series *The Adventures of Robin Hood*); by 1957, Joseph Losey had come out of the shadows and was directing under his own name. But aside from two television documentaries on Russia, made in 1961 for Moscow television but never broadcast, Vorhaus stayed hidden until the 1980s, when he was rediscovered by the National Film and Television Archive and invited to watch his British films, films largely forgotten for 50 years.

He was pleased and flattered by the attention, but also found aspects of his rediscovery unnerving: at the time he said, 'My feeling is usually, "Jesus, I could have done that so much better".' Yet he admitted to finding *The Last Journey* 'very refreshing', and parts of *Dusty Ermine* 'quite fun'. In advance of screenings, he would say with wry modesty, 'I think you may find it mildly amusing'.

He would also emphasise the dedication of his colleagues in low-budget productions in England, working under often impossible circumstances. They showed more commitment, in his eyes, than their counterparts in America. But they might not have worked nearly so hard if the man at the helm had not shown such exuberant imagination, skill and pluck; if he had not, in short, been Bernard Vorhaus.

## The Films of Bernard Vorhaus

### America

1928    *Sunlight* (short; co-d. Jessie Burns)

### Britain

1932    *Camera Cocktales* (six shorts re-edited from existing material) (Hall Mark Films)
        *On Thin Ice* (Hall Mark Films; released 1933)
        *Money for Speed* (Hall Mark Films; released 1933)
1933    *The Ghost Camera* (Real Art Productions)
        *Crime on the Hill* (British International Pictures)
        *The Broken Melody* (Twickenham Film Studios; released 1934)
1934    *Night Club Queen* (Real Art Productions)
        *Blind Justice* (Real Art Productions)
        *Ten Minute Alibi* (British Lion Film Corporation; released 1935)
        *Street Song* (Real Art Productions)
1935    *The Last Journey* (Twickenham Film Studios)
        *Dark World* (Fox-British Pictures)
1936    *Dusty Ermine* (J. H. Productions)
        *Cotton Queen* (Joe Rock Productions; released 1937)

### America

1938    *King of the Newsboys* (Republic Pictures)
        *Tenth Avenue* (Republic Pictures)
1939    *Fisherman's Wharf* (Principal Productions/Bobby Breen Productions, for RKO)
        *Way Down South* (Principal Productions/Bobby Breen Productions, for RKO)
        *Meet Dr Christian* (Stephens-Lang Productions, for RKO)
1940    *The Courageous Dr Christian* (Stephens-Lang Productions, for RKO)
        *Three Faces West* (Republic Pictures)
1941    *Lady from Louisiana* (Republic Pictures)
        *Angels with Broken Wings* (Republic Pictures)
        *Hurricane Smith* (Republic Pictures; released 1942)
        *Mr District Attorney in the Carter Case* (Republic Pictures; released 1942)
1942    *Affairs of Jimmy Valentine* (Republic Pictures)
        *Ice-Capades Revue* (Republic Pictures)
1943    *Identification of a Japanese Zero* (short) (US Air Force)

1945 *Yalta and After* (US Signal Corps; never released)

1947 *Winter Wonderland* (Walter Colmes–Henry Sokal, for Republic Pictures)

   *Bury Me Dead* (Eagle-Lion Films)

1948 *The Spiritualist* (Eagle-Lion Films)

1950 *So Young So Bad* (Individual Pictures, for United Artists)

## *Europe*

1950 *Pardon My French* (Cusick International Films, for United Artists; released 1951. English-language version of *Dans la vie tout s'arrange*, directed by Marcel Cravenne, for Sagitta Film. Filmed in France)

1952 *Fanciulle di lusso/Luxury Girls* (Cines/Riviera Films. Filmed in Italy)

1961 *Searchlight on Russia: No.1, Space Travel*; *No.2, The Lively Arts* (Cavo Films/Moscow Television. Two programmes for television transmission, never broadcast)

10. Walter Huston in *Rhodes of Africa*

## CHAPTER 10

# Berthold Viertel at Gaumont-British

## Kevin Gough-Yates

B ERTHOLD Viertel directed three films in Britain between 1934 and 1936: *Little Friend, The Passing of the Third Floor Back* and *Rhodes of Africa*, all for Gaumont-British which, during the 1930s, was the largest film production company in Britain. They were the last films of his career, and have been totally neglected in the history of British cinema. Of British film historians, only Rachael Low makes a brief mention of his work in Britain.[1] If he is remembered at all in English-speaking circles, it is for his anti-Nazi activities in the 1930s and as the father of Peter Viertel, the scriptwriter and novelist, who paints an unflattering picture of him in his memoir, *Dangerous Friends*.[2]

Viertel, with a reputation as a poet and theatre director, had, for financial reasons, started writing and directing for the cinema in 1922. He collaborated with such luminaries as Fritz Kortner, Béla Balazs, Oscar Homolka, Karl Freund and Walter Reimann. His films – *Ein Puppenheim* (*A Puppet House*) (1922), *Nora* (1923), *Die Perücke* (*The Wig*) (1924), *Die Abenteuer eines Zehnmarkscheines* (*The Adventures of a Ten Mark Note*) (1926) – all influential in the history of German silent cinema, have all but disappeared, and at least one (*Die Abenteuer eines Zehnmarkscheines*) seems to be lost.

His second foray into film-making came four years later with the collapse of his theatre ensemble, *Die Truppe*. The debts incurred were taken, by Viertel, as personal liabilities and in order to pay them off he accepted an offer from Fox in Hollywood, arranged by Friedrich Murnau, the director of *Nosferatu* (1922) and *Der letzte Mann* (*The Last Laugh*) (1924). His family moved to Hollywood where his wife, the actress Salka Steuermann, eventually settled into a career as an MGM scriptwriter, contributing especially to a number of Garbo films, and became a renowned hostess to members of the Hollywood exile and *émigré* community.

Viertel directed eight films in Hollywood but found its philistinism and induced paranoia intolerable.[3] He was loaned out to Warner Brothers[4] and moved finally to Paramount.[5] His sensitivity to apparent slights, his general volatility and bursts of anger and his non-conformist temperament were inflamed by his being forced to direct a form of cinema that was entirely detached from the lives of the audiences for whom the films were supposedly being made. For a while he convinced himself that he could smuggle sense into dreadful subjects but, essentially, he wanted only to escape.

All his American films were plagued by studio interference and, by 1932, he had had enough. At the height of the depression, when there were twelve million unemployed in the United States and there was political upheaval in Europe, he was scheduled by Paramount to direct *The Cheat* with Tallulah Bankhead and Irving Pichel, then an actor, but he was unable to come to terms with the studio and a story that centred on the problems with sex and money as experienced by the Long Island rich. The film was taken over by George Abbott and, 'disturbed and shaken', Viertel looked elsewhere.

In July 1932, with nothing certain, he left his family in Hollywood and sailed for France to meet the now London-based producer and director Alexander Korda. Viertel wrote tormented letters to Salka which revealed his distress at the turn of events in Germany; he was aghast at 'the metamorphosis of George Grosz' from a '"Left-wing European" to Ku Klux Klan', and he came to recognise that he may have been foolhardy to have left Hollywood without a contract.[6] Indeed, other things may have drawn him to Europe: the recent death of his mother, a need to see his father who was now desperately ill, and a desire to be closer to the political events that were unfolding.[7]

If he had had great expectations of Korda he was soon disabused. In 1932, Korda had yet to make a significant mark on British film production and was struggling to raise production money. His first big success, *The Private Life of Henry VIII*, was still a year away. He and Viertel discussed a subject for Elisabeth Bergner, whom Korda had recently placed under contract (in 1934, Bergner appeared in the Korda film, *Catherine the Great*, directed by her husband, Paul Czinner), they contemplated making a film with Greta Garbo, and considered Thomas Mann's *Joseph and His Brothers*, only the first part of which had been published; it was a project that remained, unmade, on the Korda books throughout the 1930s.[8] Korda had no film for Viertel to direct, but we know from the London Films books that he did offer him some script work, almost certainly on *Joseph and His Brothers*.

London, Viertel thought, would be the best place to work but, as Korda could offer him nothing, he recklessly went to Berlin where he saw Nazis and communists campaigning, facing each other, on street corners. In letters home he optimistically exaggerated his opportunities (perhaps 'Brecht's *St Joan of the Stockyards* or Hauptmann's *Hannale*, the latter as a film for UFA. I was offered a marvellous play by a Hungarian dramatist ... ') but, as with all his apparent offers, it came to nothing.[9] Early in October, however, Korda, in London, recommended him to Gaumont-British who were 'interested', but not until the following year. He considered the Soviet Union where Erwin Piscator and John Heartfield, among others, were making German- and Russian-language versions of the communist writer Anna Segher's story, *Der Aufstand der Fisher St Barbara* (*The Revolt of the Fishermen*) (1929).[10] Viertel, however, sensed danger and rationalised away another 'opportunity'. 'After Hollywood', he wrote, 'I am not afraid of dictatorship, but the language! Having barely learned English I cannot face Russian.'[11] In late December, however, he went to Vienna to see his dying father and it was not until 31 January 1933, with Hitler already Chancellor, and after he himself had been ill, that he returned to Berlin. He had received an offer to write and direct a version of Hans Fallada's recently published novel about German unemployment after the First World War, *Kleiner Mann, was nun?*[12] (Ironically, although an American version, called *Little Man, What Now?*, was made by Universal the following year,[13] seemingly using the same set designs, Salka, who had recently written an original screen story about American unemployment, was told by the MGM story editor that 'nobody wanted to see such a film'.) He received a work permit which, as an Austrian working in Germany, he required but only after protests from the theatre critic Herbert Ihering, Eric Engel and others. In almost no time at all Europa responded to pressure and 'assigned the non-Jew Mr [Fritz] Wendhausen, as co-director and cut Berthold's salary'.[14] Wendhausen, who was not to remain in Nazi Germany, was embarrassed and Viertel 'made it very clear to the gentlemen of Europa Film that as an unredeemable Jew and Austrian, I am willing to step out, even after they have signed my contract. But, although I am sure my name won't appear on the film, they have no intention of letting me go.'[15]

Viertel was kept in Berlin by the refusal to pay him until the completion of the screenplay but, after the Reichstag fire, his account settled, he left for Prague where he met up with Heinrich and Thomas Mann,

Berthold Brecht, Arnold Zweig, Alfred Polger, Kurt Weill, and others on their way into exile ultimately in the United States.

He returned to Vienna, moved on to Paris and was soon in London, contracted for one film to Gaumont-British, which was in the middle of its ambitious and costly production of Lion Feuchtwanger's *Jew Süss* with Conrad Veidt. Viertel proposed a small subject, an adaptation of *Kleine Freundin* (*Little Friend*) by Ernst Lothar. Our image of Viertel at this time derives substantially from Christopher Isherwood's association with him as co-scriptwriter and assistant during its production, which culminated with his characterisation of Viertel as Dr Friedrich Bergmann in the novel *Prater Violet*.[16] Isherwood recognised Viertel immediately, his 'was the face of a political situation. The face of Central Europe'.

Later, Isherwood took pains to argue that Bergmann was a composite of Viertel and other iconoclasts he had met in Hollywood and that the novel had nothing in common with *Little Friend*.[17] He remembered Viertel as

> chronically lonely for his family ... He talked about them continually ... For hours, Viertel would talk of anything, everything but *Little Friend* – of the Reichstag Fire Trial ... of his productions for *Die Truppe* in Berlin in the nineteen-twenties ... of the poetry of Hoelderlin; of the awful future in store for the world; of the nature of woman ... Viertel's attitude towards [the film] varied continually. Sometimes he denounced it as prostitution ... Sometimes he saw Christopher and himself as heroic rebels against bourgeois culture ... Sometimes he discovered a deep significance in the story, decided that it was even perhaps some kind of masterpiece.[18]

'I am fighting to establish the value of this film', Viertel told Peter Witt during its making. 'I am sparing no effort for it. The more lyrical, the more psychological a manuscript is, the more does it attract me as a potential screenplay.'[19] For Viertel it was an opportunity for self-expression denied him in Hollywood but it was small fry. Michael Balcon took no direct interest in it and Robert Stevenson, who was later to become a director for Disney, became its associate producer. By Isherwood's account, Stevenson was sympathetic and pressurised Viertel only when it became essential for the film to be made. Viertel was completely surrounded by German speaking exiles. Heinrich Fraenkel, with whom he had co-adapted *Die heilige Flamme* for Warner Brothers in Hollywood, was now working at Gaumont-British and contributed to the scenario. His designer was Alfred Junge, who was becoming firmly established as the leading art director in Britain. The story is of a young girl, Felicity, played by Nova Pilbeam in her first film, who is distraught at the break-up of her parents' marriage.[20] Viertel, who was especially interested in psychoanalysis at this time, looked for a way to emphasise that *Little Friend* was a story of marital crisis imagined, more than seen, through the eyes of a child. Isherwood, in *Prater Violet*, captures how it monopolised Viertel's thinking; 'Christopher' tries to meet up with him for the first time only to discover that he has 'just popped out for some cigarettes. Didn't seem to fancy what we had'. He dashes round the corner to a little tobacconist's, but has just missed him. The girl assistant had thought Bergmann 'Quite a character', they had 'got to talking about dreams'.

> Bergmann had told her of a doctor, somewhere abroad, who said that your dreams don't mean what you think they mean. He had seemed to regard this as a great scientific discovery, which had amused the girl and made her feel somewhat superior, because she'd always known that. She has a book at home which used to belong to her aunt. It was called *The Queen of Sheba's Dream Dictionary*, and it had been written long before this doctor was born.[21]

Although reviewers, with the exception of C. A. Lejeune in the *Observer*, who nevertheless questioned 'its psychology', seem not to have recognised it, Viertel planned the film to have the form and logic of a dream.[22] It opens with Felicity asleep in bed, bombarded by 'parental' voices issuing instructions. She awakens to hear her parents arguing loudly about an affair her mother appears to be having. Felicity is haunted by the likely consequences of her mother's infidelity, she confronts the man concerned, who has always referred to her as his 'little friend', she finds support and protection from Leonard (Jimmy Hanley), a delivery boy a little older than herself, she runs away, and finally, after a struggle to defend her mother in court, she tries to kill herself. The parents, at her bedside, aghast at the consequences of their self-centredness answer her plea and come together again.

The story, which originally took place in Vienna, was reset in London. The first and last sequences, in which Felicity lies in bed, are intended as a framing device; all that is inside it is part of her dream, which has transformed a domestic quarrel into a life-threatening event. The cold, unsympathetic acting and the visual distortions all emphasise the single intention. Viertel does not attempt to adopt a naturalistic approach, rather he exploits theatrical conventions for effect and risks audiences perceiving it as over-acting. To achieve the sense of dream visually, Viertel used the design of the film and the photography in combination. He was fortunate to have as his photographer Günther Krampf, one of Europe's leading lighting cameramen, who had worked with Friedrich Murnau, Ludwig Berger and G. W. Pabst in Germany. He had been intended for *Jew Süss* but was, instead, delegated to *Little Friend*, perhaps because he was a German speaker and could communicate directly with Viertel.[23] The camera is extremely mobile, emphasising a single viewpoint, and there are little pools of light to illuminate key objects. The rest is allowed to fall into darkness, so that there are planes of light. Objects were cross-lit with tiny 500-watt 'pups' and people and artefacts stand isolated, separated by patches in which the light is low or non-existent. The total effect is stereoscopic. This is clearest in the birthday party sequence where Viertel makes demands on Krampf that no English photographer of the time could have achieved.[24] His designer Alfred Junge responded to the overall theme of imagination and dream; buildings stand isolated or in curious spatial relationships. Sound and music, too, complement the images, rising in volume and emphasis whenever Felicity is distressed.

The most remarkable episode is when her father (Matheson Lang) takes her to the pantomime *Jack and the Beanstalk*, and the Giant, played by Fritz Kortner in a non-speaking role, storms on looking for the Englishman to devour.[25] We see the Giant through her eyes as he fills the stage, Jack becoming a miniature special effect. She is terrified as he appears to be abnormally huge. It is a remarkable idea, spoilt only by the failure to confirm her point of view by showing her face for a second time.[26] For Viertel it was, he later recalled, 'one of my keenest experiences, this seeing things through the serious eyes of a child'.[27]

In spite of his loneliness, his anxieties about Salka and his children and about the political situation, Viertel, after his experiences in Hollywood, felt more at ease in Britain. In an article in *Cinema Quarterly* he shows himself to be a director unusually committed to combining and controlling the disparate elements of the film-making process:

> [B]etween the director and the completed film, there is a vast and complicated machinery. First he has to translate everything he sees ... onto a two-dimentional screen ... This ... is further complicated ... by the machinery of sound. A second mechanical world has sprung to life ... and opening up endless possibilities which have yet to be explored ... a director must be able to divide his future picture ... into little particles of a kaleidoscope ... always bearing in mind the final unity.[28]

This article, one of the clearest ever written about the role of the film director, explains why he preferred London to Hollywood.

> To augment these difficulties pictures are produced by an industry ... unlike the legitimate stage [which] lives on the messages of people who

have carried their subjects in their hearts, maturing them perhaps through-out many years. The moving picture industry gives the orders. The moving picture industry collects subjects and makes writers work on them, within a rigid time limit. There is little space left for organic growth from within, the work must be done rather under the conditions of enforced labour, and all progress is watched and supervised by special experts. The industry is in a growing process of mechanization and division of labour. For every part of the picture a department is responsible ... America, as the most industrial country of the world, as the country of mechanization and rationalization of labour, goes on mechanizing picture work. No longer is the director supposed to cut his own film ... An enormously complicated system of departments ... reaches without inter-ruption into the creative process, each in his own field destroying every unity of mood.

Hence, Viertel argues, 'original messages' are seldom seen on the screen. The American industry

is at its best when using robust themes in those matter-of-fact stories on which it pours sentimentality as a pastry cook pours icing on a cake ... Directors who are able to deliver ... messages ... after all those instances of obstruction ... have to be built like heavyweight champions ... Things are in this respect a good deal easier in Britain ... Although it is technically more difficult, and the organization is not so highly developed it is easier to deliver a personal message here. What I should like to fight for is that this chance should be used to a greater extent, then more and more pictures should be done which have something to say.

He found London a very different working experience to that of Hollywood. It was slower, there were long weekends, he was encouraged to propose ideas and suggestions and was not simply assigned a script. In London, he made friends with other film-makers. His association with Murnau, his poetry, and his work in the theatre were not lost on Paul Rotha, the British documentary film-maker, then determinedly battling to break into feature films. On 3 February 1935, Rotha assembled a team, all exiles from Europe and working at Gaumont-British, to see a silent version of one of his own sound projects, a story by Tolstoy directed by Fedor Ozep, *Zhivoi Trup* (*The Living Corpse*) (1928). Rotha's version was to feature Conrad Veidt and the English actress Madeleine Carroll. Rotha was to direct it, Viertel was to write it, Alfred Junge was to design it, Mutz Greenbaum was to photograph it, and a Russian called Schlanoff was to be its technical adviser.[29] Gaumont-British was not interested.

Viertel's bitterness at Hollywood frequently spilled into interviews. To Murray Boltinoff, for example, he confirmed his view of it as isolated and ignorant. New York or London would be more 'advantageous to the industry, for then it would be closer to its subjects instead of isolating itself from the masses'.[30] Two days later *Variety* reported him in similar vein: 'The future of pictures lies in doing themes you burn to do, that you're interested in, that have something you want to say, that you feel you've got to say.' In Hollywood he had found the necessity of feeding stars with material so demanding that it was almost futile to propose stories to producers. Straightaway the producers want to know 'who it's for. Who can we fit it to? ... In America material is purchased for a star ... Always it is the star who is of prime consideration, not the story, not the idea.'[31]

Gaumont-British, on the other hand, satisfied with *Little Friend*, contracted him for three more films. He prepared a life of Byron, *The Chained Eagle*, not as the figure of scandal, but as the fighter for freedom. According to the film producer Robert Dunbar, who had been an assistant on *Little Friend* and was working on the Byron script with Viertel, the Foreign Office disapproved of its apparent allusions to Hitler and Balcon rejected it, offering him instead a play by Jerome K. Jerome, originally published as a short story in 1907, *The Passing of the Third Floor Back*.[32] The setting is a small boarding house, the Hotel Belle Vue, in Bloomsbury, London, run by Mrs Sharpe, a greedy and spiteful landlady, an unmerciful bully of the maid who has been rescued from a reformatory. The boarders are a group of bitterly disappointed people and include a young failed architect, a retired army officer and his wife, their daughter Vivian, the unpleasant Mr Wright, a builder of slum developments, an Irish woman, Mrs de Hooley, with grandiose social aspirations and snobbish claims of links to the aristocracy, and a secretary, 'on the wrong side of thirty'. Viertel recognised the difficulties of adapting it to the screen, but saw great possibilities if he could achieve successful psychological motivation for the characters. Although the opening images of London could be anywhere, a city, as the title announces, 'of countless streets, roofs upon roofs, wildernesses of houses of which but few are homes'. The first closer shot is reminiscent of Alfred Hitchcock's silent film *The Lodger*, a notice 'Room to Let' in the window above the door of the hotel, and we should remember that the script's co-writer was Hitchcock's wife, Alma Reville. In the basement scullery, Stasia, a young skivvy, works at the sink. A flower she has found, planted and delights in, is thrown to the floor by the landlady, who begrudges her any pleasures. Stasia whines about the unfairness of the world and pleads, 'If only there were one decent person in the world, but there isn't.' Her prayer is soon answered for, just as she is rushing despairingly out of the house, a stranger (Conrad Veidt) appears at the door wanting to rent the tiny back room on the third floor. There is a glow around his face, a church archway immediately behind him on the other side of the road. At the end of the film, Christ-like, the figure vanishes through the same door as mysteriously as he appeared, his last words to Stasia being, 'I came because you needed me.'

Viertel, in a review of *Prater Violet* in 1946, describes how Isherwood recognised differences between himself and Bergmann. Isherwood had 'added hastily' to an interviewer that Viertel had not argued with his bosses, the way that Bergmann does in his novel. 'No doubt,' he adds with some irony, 'Isherwood wanted ... to protect his model in the reality of professional life against the eventual consequences of bygone rows with bosses.'[33] Feuding, scheming and arguing are the *sine qua non* of film-making and, on *The Passing of the Third Floor Back*, Viertel's producer, nominally the associate producer, was Ivor Montagu, a friend and associate of Eisenstein and Hitchcock's associate producer. He spoke Russian and German fluently and, like Heinrich Frankel, was a valuable link between the frequently foreign technical staff at Gaumont-British and management.

The constraints at Gaumont-British, however, were growing; it was already in long-term decline, unable to generate a profit and trying to cut costs. Feeling the strain, Montagu wrote to S. C. Balcon: 'Apparently, a starting date had been given Viertel for Wednesday, 10 April, 1935, rather than the originally agreed 11th April ... Having regard to the character of the man, the effect to the picture of his feeling at ease ... it would in practice have better results for the picture to start Thursday.' Montagu was instructed that the Wednesday must be kept to and advised Viertel who went over his head to Maurice Ostrer, one of the brothers whose company it was: 'Without consultation with mee [*sic*] – [Viertel] was permitted to start Thursday.' The original schedule of six weeks and four days was technically possible but, 'having regard to the limitations (and qualities) of the director it was quite out of the question that, with this director, it would be done faster'. The studio, nevertheless, wanted to cut the shooting schedule by a week. Montagu thought 'that, having regard to his character, better practical results could be obtained from placing before him a schedule which he thought practicable or attainable, than [by] putting him under the shadow of a schedule he knew quite well to be – for him at least – impracticable.'

It made no difference and Montagu found the situation humiliating. He was instructed to cut back and Viertel was complaining not to him, but going over his head. Viertel 'was working as hard as he possibly

could', and 'work was proceeding at a normal rate'. Pressurising him to
reduce the number of shots 'was quite impossible ... because he is
unable to visualise their unnecessaryness before he sees them on the
screen'. Forcing him into a 'discussion of them would, having regard to
his character a) make him so nervous as undoubtedly to affect the
quality of the picture b) not necessarily achieve the desired objective.'

Montagu was putting forward the best case he could. S. C. Balcon,
who found Viertel irritating, slapped Montagu down but Viertel found
a way round them both. In every case, Montagu argued, 'I have been
placed in a false position to the director and made to appear as one
who in servile enthusiasm to reduce the company's expenses, urges him
to impossible feats, the impossibility of which is admitted as soon as he
discusses alone with the executive.' How could Montagu expect to keep
Viertel in line when 'the director had definitely been petted into feeling
that he can rely on protection against me'.[34]

In preparation for *The Passing of the Third Floor Back*, Viertel studied
the film *The Barretts of Wimpole Street* which had recently been adapted
for the screen by MGM. It had similar restricted action with everything
taking place in and around a London house. He was to have few sets,
fewer than on any film Viertel had previously directed. There would be
only one sequence shot outside the studio, when the whole household
takes a bank holiday at Margate.[35] 'In Barretts,' Viertel noted,

> the restricted action of the story was overcome by the skilful use of the
> camera ... and if I may say so – of the dog, 'Flush'. By following the
> movements of the various players, the cameras virtually 'acted' a part in
> the film. It created the correct atmosphere, and laid symbolic emphasis on
> the right people at the right time. In *Passing of the Third Floor Back*, we shall
> use our cameras in the same way ... and, in this connection I must say
> how fortunate I am in having as my chief cameraman, young Curt
> Courant, who is certainly one of the most brilliant creative photographers
> to graduate from the famous UFA studios.[36]

Typically, he utilised music to unite the apparently separate stories in
the film. In one episode he used source music, played on the piano in
the lounge, to link five important confrontational scenes in different
parts of the hotel. He made a distinction between the surface story of
the mysterious stranger played by Conrad Veidt, who quietly overcomes
the quarrelsome, jealous, bickering temperaments of the lodgers, and
the deeper theme or message 'which has inspired the innumerable
sermons by eminent churchmen – about the play: the eternal struggle
of good against evil – as represented by the evil-minded Mr. Wright and
the other inhabitants of the household'.

Veidt was to be more of a presence than a character. While remaining believable in character, he should be felt rather than seen. And the message 'must be conveyed to the audience as a subsidiary of the actual drama'. His problem, Viertel argued, was 'to convey this without the audience ever thinking they are watching anything ethereal or unrelated to the stark realities of life.' Adopting the same approach as he had with *Little Friend*, Viertel took advantage of the lighting skills of his photographer to emphasise the theme that would otherwise have to be carried by the dialogue. Veidt, as the mysterious, saintly figure confronts avarice and meanness throughout the film. His face is contrasted with the other lodgers: that of Vivian (Anna Lee) in love with the young architect, but unable to marry him because of the pressure of her parents, the Major and his wife, determined to marry her off for money to the evil Mr Wright and so retain their social status. In the obligatory scene in which goodness directly confronts evil, the stranger goes to Mr Wright's room. Wright, as exploitative in personal relationships as he is in business, dismisses the stranger's sanctimonious sentiments. For him, everyone has a price. He has risen from poverty and is now in a position to buy what he wants, the young Vivian or the maid. Courant, a specialist in filters and gauzes, uses his lighting to emphasise Wright's sense of power but, as the stranger rises from his chair, enhanced by carefully graded lighting and the photographic angles, he begins to dominate the monstrous Wright. 'All that happens is that the stranger rises from his chair,' Veidt told a *Film Weekly* interviewer, 'but the expression on his face and the angles from which he is photographed, combine in helping to convey to the audience the real symbolism behind his words.'[37] Veidt's performance, the most relaxed in the film, is interesting on another count. All of the other characters are presented as caricatures. As Mrs de Hooley (Sarah Allgood) walks across the lounge she is a parody of elegance, a child dressed in her mother's clothes; when Mr Wright (Frank Cellier) flourishes his over-size chequebook to pay for his board, he is a grotesque image of the successful man; Mrs Sharpe, the landlady (Mary Clare) hovers over him, her fingers poised like the beak of a bird waiting to pounce on a worm. Veidt is at once more natural, but there is a trace of expressionism in his performance. In the stranger's confrontation with Mr Wright, Veidt restrains his rage, the veins standing out on his neck, his hands held rigid like claws. Viertel is meticulous in allowing variations in character. Although no one is entirely untouched by the sense of evil that Mr Wright personifies, everyone is redeemable. When Stasia, on a day-trip to Margate, falls into the river, it is the otherwise cruel Mrs Sharpe that calls out for her, as if it is her own child in danger of drowning. The Major and Mrs Tomkins have a similar sense of identification and recognise their cruel selfishness. In the end, everyone is rescued from Wright's perverse hands; he is destroyed by his own depravity and dies suddenly of a heart attack.

Viertel, like the stranger in *The Passing of the Third Floor Back*, was well aware of his status in England as a wanderer, a foreigner and a Jew. The *Jewish Chronicle*, while writing of his 'profound belief in the film as a means of expression' reminded its readers that 'He is a Jew, vigorously conscious that he, as all of us, is a product of Jewish history, of Jewish culture, of Jewish inheritance.'[38] He was sensitive to anti-Semitism in England. During 1936, the British Union of Fascists had become virulently active in East London. François Lafitte shows how, in 1940, 'some newspapers systematically fostered anti-foreign feeling by inflammatory articles and misleading news items, and ... this was done in many cases by men with uneasy consciences. Both in the Press and in public speeches certain gentlemen whose pro-Nazi views were notorious in peacetime were among the loudest to clamour to "intern the lot".'[39] 'Here in England,' Viertel wrote to Salka in California, some 'papers are openly anti-Semitic. Only the Quakers perform miracles of helpfulness.'[40]

Viertel's final subject for Gaumont-British was surprising, a film on the life of the British colonialist Cecil Rhodes, part of a programme of imperial subjects and one of three made at Gaumont-British that combined, in Jeffrey Richards's phrase, 'patriotism with profit'.[41] Rhodes, as a film subject, had been in the air for a couple of years and, in October 1934, John Corfield, the managing director of British National Films, had approached Winston Churchill, an admirer of Rhodes and his work, to write it, but Churchill was already contracted to Korda and couldn't oblige. General Smuts expressed concern that it might stir racial prejudice and it was abandoned until, with the help of its chairman, Viscount Lee of Fareham, a figure acceptable to government circles, Gaumont-British took it up. Rhodes was to be played by George Arliss, an actor noted for playing distinguished figures – Disraeli, Voltaire and Meyer Rothschild among them. Michael Balcon travelled to Hollywood where Arliss was completing *Cardinal Richelieu* to 'make definite arrangements' for him to co-write and star in it. Suddenly, and at the point when it was ready to go, it was realised that Arliss did not in the least resemble Cecil Rhodes and the part went to Walter Huston, a friend of Mark Ostrer, one of the major shareholders in Gaumont-British. Oscar Homolka came in by virtue of having worked with Viertel in *Die Truppe*, and sharing the same agent, Eric Glass.

Viertel, it should already be clear, had less control over *Rhodes* and much of the character's relentless pursuit of power in Africa was not to be seen on the screen. Viertel retained Oscar Werndorff and Derek Twist, the designer and editor respectively, from his previous film, but was given the run-of-the-mill British photographer, Bernard Knowles.[42] The second unit work, filmed on African location, was directed by Geoffrey Barkas, but much of it appears vaguely conceived and undirected.[43] There was no Ernst Toch working on this film, only the same routine composer, Hubert Bath, this time uncredited, that he had been given for *The Passing of The Third Floor Back*. It is barely conceivable that Viertel was happy with a hero who treats black Africans as children deserving biblical punishment when they misbehave. The king, Lobengula (Ndanisa Kumalo), is shown as bloated, as if through drink or drugs, as well as vain and foolish, an easy victim of Rhodes's negotiating techniques. The opening titles, though, do recognise an ambiguity of character: 'By some he was hailed as an inspired leader. By others he was reviled as an ambitious adventurer.' Viertel's conception of Rhodes is a development of the persuasive stranger of *The Passing of the Third Floor Back*. He turns an argument by the quietness of his tone and the appropriateness of his reasoning, only now the film's hero justifies British imperialism.

The brutality with which black mining labour was treated is not hidden but, in this celebration of white colonialism, neither is it emphasised. A labourer accused of swallowing a diamond is dragged, in fear of his life, in front of a mine-owner, Barney Barnato (Frank Cellier), who appears to be reaching for his gun to shoot him. Instead he drags from his pocket his standard treatment for such transgressions, a bottle of castor oil. Rhodes watches amused and without comment, his obsession is only with controlling the Kimberley mines. The savagery with which native tribes are suppressed is little more than suggested. When a young professional writer, Anna Carpenter (Peggy Ashcroft), takes Rhodes to task, her comments are interrupted by a turn in the drama, an urgent need for Rhodes to take political action.

Visually, there are few of the distinctive touches that contribute to the effectiveness of Viertel's other films at Gaumont-British. As neither Rhodes nor his associates appear to have a personal life, much of the action is that of boardroom drama. Although ten years is covered in the space of a dissolve, the personalities do not develop or change. 'The whole film lacks intimacy', wrote *Picturegoer* which, ironically considering the grounds that were used for replacing George Arliss as the lead, also pointed out that Walter Huston looked nothing like Rhodes.[44]

Constrained on all sides, Viertel was unable to bind the elements into a cohesive whole. There is no delineation of personality by lighting. The supporting actors are mostly stereotypes with no depth of character. The exception to this is Oscar Homolka, whose relatively small but towering performance, as Paul Kruger, is the most memorable of the film. Kruger is constantly fussed over by an adoring wife (René de Vaux) but, even here, there is nothing but perfunctory conversations between them. Homolka's pacing and his sense of rhythm provide the only occasions for reflection. In an American review which poured extravagant praise on the film, Homolka was described as 'an actor of superior ability whose performance has never been surpassed by that of any Hollywood star ... a cinematic masterpiece'.[45]

In one scene only, early in the film, does Viertel reveal some directorial panache. Rhodes, intent on buying out the mining competition, enters a gambling hall and attracts the attention of Barney Barnato. It begins on a close-up of the two, the camera moves backwards as they move into the scene, and widens to reveal two doctors gambling their practices on the fall of the cards; dance music continues in the background throughout. In a single shot Viertel incorporates the essence of South Africa as it was when Rhodes found it: alcoholism, gambling and whoring.

Criticism of the film emphasised its lack of accuracy and its presentation of Rhodes. It was, naturally, something that Viertel and Gaumont-British had anticipated. Viertel skilfully replied to one grievance, avoiding any suggestion as to Rhodes's greatness:

> [A]s the director ... I should like to state what was in my mind when I made the picture ... In history the fact rules, in drama it is the imagination. The dramatist is concerned with his own necessity – the events must build up a dramatic idea ... Our ideas about hero-worship have changed. A man is worth as much as the ideas for which he stands ... I saw Rhodes and his main opponents, Lobengula and Kruger, each representing the land in a different stage of development; the primitive man, the patriarchal farmer, and the representative of progressive capitalism spreading modern civilization ... Of course the screen must make them meet, personally and more dramatically than they really did ... To represent the truth of the ideas, not the similarity of faces and the exact order of events was the object.[46]

Even Michael Balcon joined in the fray. To an objection to the omission of the famous Indaba in the Matopo Hills, he wrote:

> My ... view was that Mr Viertel had made an impressive film character study of Cecil Rhodes. That was what he set out to make: a biographical

study – not a biography ... We did not take this decision to omit the
Indaba incident from the film without deep and prolonged consideration
... not only was the scene in the original script but it was actually shot
... Professor Hernshaw has mentioned the inaccuracies of the famous
Disraeli film. There were equally serious inaccuracies in *The House of
Rothschild*. Again *Clive of India* failed to portray the final phase of Clive's
life ... Shakespeare did not hesitate to introduce inaccuracies to heighten
the dramatic effects of his plays, and the liberties taken by Scott in his
historical novels are astounding ... perhaps ... I may reasonably claim
that what is good enough for Shakespeare should be good enough for
Gaumont-British![47]

Balcon was deeply patriotic and wanted, as acceptable propaganda,
to help create a favourable national image abroad. Richards reminds us
that 'the key to understanding these films is their exaltation of British
Character ... which set the British ... apart ... and justified their ruling
a quarter of the globe.'[48] In Rhodes's case, his Oxford education distinguishes him from the worst exploiters of Africa. His dream, to unite
it, to carry the white man's burden on his own shoulders while sacrificing
his life to his dream, makes him into a romantic hero, the 'Great White
Father'.

Although he thought *Rhodes* a better subject than many that had been
imposed on him in Hollywood, Viertel had become the victim of the
system he so much deplored, just one person on a production line. Yet
he had nowhere else to turn. He had burnt his boats in Hollywood, he
was cut off from Germany, and Korda could not offer him work. Above
all, he was constrained by a financial crisis within the British film
industry which had over-expanded, steamed up by protectionism and
Korda's early success in America. Government legislation had been
designed to allow the fledgling British film industry to develop and to
provide conditions for training. Studio space had multiplied and more
films were being made than the domestic market could absorb. Only
Korda had, in any systematic way, managed to penetrate the American
market. In the mid-1930s other financial interest groups, convinced that
Korda's apparent success pointed to easy money, entered the game.
Korda's backer, the Prudential Assurance, was only the first of many
and no others had its sense of responsibility. Early in 1937, film companies began to collapse. The earlier mistakes and over-expansion of
Gaumont-British began to catch up with it, and in June it was announced
that the company had lost close to £98,000 on the previous year's
trading.[49] '"Cease Work" Ordered at Big British Studio', announced the
front page of the *Daily Express* on 24 February 1937: 'the effect is likely

to shake the whole industry.'[50] It stopped production completely and when it started again Ivor Montagu had left and Michael and S. C. Balcon, deeply resentful at the manner in which the Ostrer brothers had interfered with their production programme, were no longer with it. There was a change of tone in the company's output and Viertel was not offered a fourth film to direct.

In London, his anti-Nazi activities, his involvement with the communist-dominated Free German League of Culture (*Freier deutscher Kulturbund*), of which, along with a host of other luminaries, he was an honorary president, and his contributions to *émigré* newspapers such as *Die neue Weltbühne* and *Das neue Tage-Buch* made him unpopular with the Home Office and, in May 1939, his British residency permit was not renewed.[51] His attempts to realize fresh film projects had come to nothing and he spent the war years in America, active but earning very little.[52] Isherwood, ensconced in California in mid-1939, wrote: 'Here I am living very quietly, seeing hardly anyone, and hoping vaguely that when Berthold arrives he will get me a movie job.'[53] But Viertel was unable to find one for himself. Instead the family house became the centre of *émigré* social and cultural life, while he dreamt of a post-war Europe where films and theatre would 'become part of the reconstruction, of the building up of the new realities of peace'.[54] Viertel had explored cinema, much as he had theatre and literature. He was opposed to realism in the cinema, as he had been in the theatre, and constantly urged a return to imagination; making a film, as far as Viertel was concerned, was not simply a question of production.[55] Although he never directed a film in colour, he was 'pro-colour film'. 'Elimination should be the first axiom of colour photography,' he argued. 'One will learn by-and-by not to spread colour out as in a patchwork quilt ... This is only partly a technical question. It is a question of vision, composition of form ... what technicians won't do, artists will.'[56] Artistic expression, less than realism, was his primary concern. Integrity was more important than commercial success.

When he died in 1953, he was barely remembered as a film-maker at all and none of his obituaries recalled his contribution to British films. Even his years in England were all but forgotten. Hilde Spiel, in a letter to the *New Statesman and Nation*, described him as 'inspired poet, talented producer, raconteur and wit ... one of the last great men of the *fin-de-siècle* central European twilight'. She recalled his poetry, his novella, his 'superb productions in Dresden' and his post-war triumphs at the Burg Theatre in Vienna.[57] Her sense of him is curiously close to that of Isherwood's 'dynamic portrait' of Bergmann, continually discussing, debating and revising his work; she describes him as 'a great writer, though he left most of his novels unfinished'. She mentions his films but seems to have overlooked that he worked at Gaumont-British. 'He failed in Hollywood,' she wrote. He was 'a man of genius though there is nothing to prove it except the conviction of his friends that he was one.'[58]

11. Portrait photographs of Miles Mander and Adrianne Allen

## CHAPTER 11

# Loose Ends, Hidden Gems and the Moment of 'Melodramatic Emotionality'

### Tony Aldgate

To judge from standard accounts of British cinema during the 1930s, Adrianne Allen, Marjorie Gaffney, V. Gareth Gundrey and Miles Mander are hardly names to conjure with. They do not evoke instant reaction or ready recognition and, indeed, one would be hard pressed immediately to identify their principal roles as, respectively, actor, writer–assistant director, writer–director, and actor–writer–director. Even Rachael Low's usually dependable and informative 'official' history, *Film Making in 1930s Britain*, affords them little more than fleeting attention. Though all four are cited intermittently during her extensive lists of mainstream feature film credits for the period, only Gundrey and Mander merit mention in the main body of her text. The former as the scriptwriter first assigned to the production of R. C. Sherriff's *Journey's End* (1930) whose screenplay was rejected by producer Michael Balcon; the latter, merely as an aside in the context of reference to his better-known brother, the Liberal MP for East Wolverhampton, Geoffrey Mander, whose parliamentary activities on behalf of the film industry generally or against censorship, in particular, are more fully represented.

As if to exacerbate matters, however, Low's listings singularly fail to include Gundrey's 1931 film, *The Stronger Sex*, despite it being a Gainsborough picture with scenario by Angus MacPhail, while she also noticeably gives the directorial credit for one of Miles Mander's few films granted any wider critical recognition, *The Morals of Marcus* (1935), to a certain 'Miss Mander'. Low's evident error in transcription might just be excused as an isolated incident had her mistake not been repeated, even compounded, when Patricia Warren's otherwise equally admirable account, *British Film Studios*, elevated this non-existent person to neat mythic status in stating that *The Morals of Marcus* 'seems to have been a family affair, the scenario by Miles Mander and directed by Miss Mander'.

These shortcomings and aberrations apart, however, Low and Warren make some mention of Mander. Another commentator to do so was Paul Rotha who clearly formed a warm friendship with Mander and singled out *The First Born* (1928), starring Madeleine Carroll, for special praise in his history of *The Film Till Now*. Directed by Mander and based upon his own play, *Those Common People*, Rotha thought it provided 'evidence of his wit and intelligence in filmic expression' and applauded its 'light commentary on married life, flavoured with an environment of semi-political domestication ... Mander has obviously a shrewd knowledge of feminine mentality', Rotha maintained, 'and succeeded in transferring this into his handling of Madeleine Carroll'. Had the film also been cut along the lines intended by Mander's original 'sophisticated and clever' treatment and not blighted in the hands of an editor imposed by errant distributors, Rotha felt certain it would have proved 'a unique instance of an English domestic tragi-comedy in the cinema'.[1]

Despite the paucity of writing on Gundrey and Mander, they fared better at least than either Adrianne Allen or Marjorie Gaffney whose careers and achievements in British cinema during the 1930s remain completely uncharted territory. Yet Allen, for a start, received considerable personal acclaim from then contemporary critics for her first film role in Norman Walker's *Loose Ends* (1930), sufficient to overshadow its major stars, Edna Best and Owen Nares, and to lead after just three more performances in British films – including Gundrey's *The Stronger Sex* and Mander's *The Woman Between* (both 1930) – to a lucrative American contract at £800 a week with the Paramount studios. In the States, Allen worked first for Hollywood's sole female director of note, Dorothy Arzner, on *Merrily We Go to Hell* (1932) which was based upon the book by Cleo Lucas, *I, Gerry, Take Thee, Joan*; and then on Stephen Roberts's *The Night of June 13* (1932), written by one of Paramount's women scriptwriters, Agnes Brand Leahy, from a story by Vera Caspary (whose novel *Laura* was later turned into the 1944 film noir classic). On her return from America, Adrianne Allen starred in Mander's *The Morals of Marcus* before virtually retiring from the screen (just five films between 1935 and 1954) in order to concentrate on a successful transatlantic stage career.[2]

Marjorie Gaffney's contribution to 1930s British cinema was made solely off-screen, essentially as a scriptwriter though she appears to have started in the film industry as assistant director to Victor Saville on *Kitty* (1929), *The W Plan* (1930) and *Hindle Wakes* (1931). Clearly, Gaffney enjoyed a fruitful working relationship with Saville, especially since some of her principal screenwriting credits (whether solo or collaborative ventures) were also done for him (and producer Michael Balcon), including starring vehicles for both Jessie Matthews – *Evergreen* (1934), *First a Girl* (1935) – and Cicely Courtneidge: *Me and Marlborough* (1935). Gaffney also scripted Jessie Matthews's first film directed by her husband Sonnie Hale, *Head Over Heels* (1937). And for the producer–director team of Herbert Wilcox and Jack Raymond she wrote *Night of the Garter* (1933) and *The Rat* (1937), as well as scripts for Wilcox and Raymond individually, such as *The Gang Show* and *Sunset in Vienna* (both 1937), and *The Mind of Mr Reeder* (1939). In addition, she shared the scriptwriting credit on *My Old Dutch* (1934) for producer Ivor Montagu and director Sinclair Hill.

Though Gaffney's prowess was most evident in her scripting abilities, Miles Mander was one director who plainly felt her skills as assistant director should not go unrecognised and he employed her as such on several of his films, including *The Woman Between* (1931). In a 1934 article for *Film Weekly*, moreover, Mander cited Gaffney as prospective 'directorial talent'. After acknowledging that women had contributed substantially to 'the business of scenario writing' and surveying a list of successful screenwriters to bear out his point – Frances Marion, Doris Anderson, Bess Meredyth, Sonya Levien, Karen de Wolf and Kay Strueby in the United States, Lydia Hayward, Billie Bristow and Gaffney in Britain – Mander lamented the lack of opportunities for women to try their hand as directors. Dorothy Arzner, he believed, had shown what could be achieved in America. 'Starting as an assistant in the cutting room', he stated, 'this brilliant woman served her apprenticeship in every department of the film factory until she has now established herself as one of the best directors in any country.' And Marjorie Gaffney, he felt, might well follow suit in Britain. 'She has, like Dorothy Arzner, been through every department of film production', he maintained, and, 'She has that rare gift – a picture mind'.[3]

In the event, despite Mander's plea to British film producers that 'women should be allowed a chance' to direct, his proselytising fell on deaf ears. The openings for women directors in British cinema throughout the 1930s remained non-existent, which can hardly have surprised Mander, after all, in view of his jaundiced if strongly held conviction that 'This is England and, of course, we must not try anything new here'. He decamped to America in 1936.[4] What is perhaps most interesting about Mander's plea that women be afforded greater opportunities to direct films, however, is the way in which he equated it as leading quite naturally to a concomitant increase in the 'emotion' and 'sentiment' likely to be forthcoming in their films. This, he felt, was something which was sorely lacking in British cinema of the day, born of its generally male-orientated direction and the fact that, in particular, 'nine out ten English directors are frightened to touch it [emotion]'. Avoiding the subject was part of a larger male malaise, in Mander's opinion, since 'The Englishman is so notoriously afraid of showing that he, too, has feelings'. Although it is couched in what would now be recognised as crudely paternalistic and patriarchal terms – he was seeking an injection, as he put it, of 'The feminine touch' into films – Mander sheds fascinating light on a trait discernible in one genre of British cinema, at least, by the outset of the 1930s.

This triple association of 'woman's film' resulting in films with greater 'emotional' force and supposedly manifested in an altogether 'un-British' fashion has also surfaced again more recently. It is, of course, inevitably beset by problems, not least the difficulty of defining its notoriously vague and elusive terms of reference. As Justine King argued in 1996:

> There is, though, another more insidious problem attendant upon any discussion of the British woman's film. As Richard Dyer has perceptively pointed out, the 'official' characterisation of British cinema almost precludes the recognition of its propensity for melodramatic emotionality. The conceptualisation of the 'typically English film' consistently seems to attract the ideologically loaded epithet 'restrained' (which reflects not only a middle-class bias but, I would argue, a masculinist bias too) whereby demonstrative displays of 'excessive' emotionality – worst of all, tears – are regarded as inappropriate, both on and off screen. It is, then, an easy enough matter to see why the woman's film might be regarded as something of an unwelcome cuckoo-in-the-nest here. For, despite twenty years or more of sustained critical attention which has repeatedly demonstrated the aesthetic and ideological complexities of the genre, the woman's film still carries the taint of triviality, emotional excessiveness and brash Hollywood populism. In short, it might well be considered as rather 'un-British'.[5]

Though King's researches are essentially concerned with pitting this 'peculiarly skewed and selective characterisation' against an analysis of woman's film in British cinema of the 1980s in order to highlight the inadequacies of its conceptualisation, she notes first and foremost that it singularly 'fails to take account of British cinema's sustained investment in melodramatic emotionality'. To this end, she traces a legacy of films stretching from the 1980s back to the 1940s – such as *Room with a View* (1985), *Jane Eyre* (1970), *The L-Shaped Room* (1962), *A Taste of Honey* (1961), *Two Thousand Women* (1944) and *Millions Like Us* (1943) – which have been traditionally 'swept under the umbrella of other film movements or genres (the wartime morale film, the New Wave film, the "quality" literary cinema)'. But they still adhere to 'the fundamental tenets of the woman's film', in King's opinion, because this 'generic eclipse' crucially fails to take account of the considerable investment all the films have in 'melodramatic emotionality', her key characteristic of woman's film throughout British cinema history.

It is a compelling idea and not unrelated, arguably, to the kind of issues raised in Mander's 1934 article for *Film Weekly* where, however baldly put, he championed greater investment in emotionality as part and parcel of more women's input to British cinema. In addition, it is possible to push the lineage that King identifies further back in time to the outset of the 1930s when the genre of 'society drama' in particular appears to have served the function as a conduit for the sort of 'melodramatic emotionality' she identifies. The genre was much in evidence in British cinema at the beginning of the 1930s for obvious reasons. It was the 'changeover period' from silent to sound films, and as a result the British film industry drew more than ever upon stage productions for its inspiration. After all the theatre provided a ready-made source of drama with spoken dialogue for easy and immediate transposition to cinema. Stage actors, furthermore, were carefully trained in 'voice production' and greatly experienced at projecting the 'clarity' and 'purity' initially much sought by the film industry. Society drama, finally, was already a well proven and highly popular stage genre. Thus, film producers happily plundered the genre at will for speedy translation to the screen.

By no means everybody was pleased with the move. Several commentators felt it inevitably stifled development of native scriptwriting talent, lent substance to the charge that British cinema was needlessly over-dependent on theatrical productions for its sources, and, in all, thereby contributed to the poor cinematic quality of British films. Sidney Gilliat spoke for many, then and now, when he said: 'Talkies only came in for the ordinary person around 1930–1931 in England and it took an awfully long time to change from this horrible drawing-room conception of British theatre which impinged itself on the British film.'[6]

Perhaps this judgment, however generally sound, is in need of nuance or revision. Certainly, there is good reason to suggest that the society drama genre, albeit lifted wholesale from stage to screen, offers greater riches than has hitherto been acknowledged. Its vital moment proved somewhat short-lived, to be sure, and confined to the period around 1930. It seems to have depended not just upon the vogue among film producers for importing stage properties and the impetus afforded by directors like Miles Mander but also, significantly, on a sudden if temporary hiatus in the degree of authority exercised over the film industry by the British Board of Film Censors. There were key personnel changes at the BBFC (a new president in November 1929 and a new chief censor in March 1930) which, combined with teething problems over the censorship process to be adopted in dealing with the advent of sound to films, resulted in a lapse in the BBFC's otherwise stringent control. And it was only with the introduction in November 1930 of pre-production scrutiny of scripts, scenarios or synopses to overcome the difficulties that the situation was slowly restored to normal. Sound films which went into production between late 1929 and late 1930, in short, escaped the worst strictures of the BBFC. *Loose Ends, The Stronger Sex* and *The Woman Between* were three such films which embarked upon production in February, June and October 1930 respectively. They were beneficiaries of the hiatus in the censorship process but shared a good deal more in common besides.[7]

*Loose Ends* (1930), directed by Norman Walker, was made at Elstree Studios for British International Pictures and was adapted from Dion Titheradge's successful stage play by both Walker and Titheradge.[8] The credits roll against a rousing chorus-line backdrop of dancing girls but soon give way to the opening scenes set in the St Martin's in the Field refuge for the destitute and homeless. Here, Malcolm Forres (Owen Nares), a graduate of Trinity College, Cambridge, now fallen on hard times, laments life's misfortunes in the midst of his fellow 'doss house' residents. 'It's the rich that always brings trouble,' says one; 'Give and you shall receive tenfold,' the vicar counsels. 'How can you give anything to the world when you haven't any place in it?' is the harsh retort from Forres who desperately hopes that 'Tomorrow brings a new life'.

Forres's prayers are answered when a chance car accident lands him in the company of Nina Grant (Edna Best), a successful up-and-coming young actress, and her 'fast set' of smart society friends. They include Nina's confidante, Brenda Fallon (Adrianne Allen), the lothario Raymond Carteret (Miles Mander), Sally Britt (Sybil Arundale), a journalist and society gossip-monger, and the pianist-songwriter, Cyril Gayling (Gerard Lyley), another Cambridge graduate. Nina falls for Malcolm and marries him in haste on a whim ('I believe you'd be good for me') much to the chagrin of her 'loose friends' who greatly resent the introduction of 'a man of sane and healthy ideas' into their charmed circle. Carteret, especially, has long desired Nina and continues to make advances to her in public. He taunts Forres and advises: 'Don't be so sensitive.' 'Has nobody got any feelings nowadays?' Malcolm pleads. 'Everybody,' replies Carteret, 'but we don't let them get the better of us.'

Finding his position intolerable, Malcolm prevails upon Nina to alter her mode of life ('This sort of life, it just rots all your senses') and to conform to his ideas about seeking a quieter, more stable existence in the country. Initially very reluctant ('What about my work? Why should I bury myself in the country?'), Nina finally agrees to the proposal. No sooner has she relented, however, than another member of her circle, the newspaper editor Winton Pinner (Donald Calthrop), reveals he is going to publish an exposé on her new husband. Pinner has suspected Forres from the outset ('There's something about Malcolm that belongs to the front page') and, after piecing together occasional clues, discovers that Forres is a convicted murderer who has just served a 15-year sentence in prison. Nina is aghast and affronted by her husband's audacity in condemning her way of living while he was guilty of murder, as well as his duplicity in keeping it well hidden. When the scandal breaks in the press, she fears for her career and reputation.

Forres confides in her devoted friend, Brenda, that his crime was merely the revenge killing of a man who had seduced his sister and driven her to suicide, but he is determined now to do the honourable thing by Nina and set her free. He contemplates giving her grounds for divorce by committing an arranged adultery but is repelled by the sordid necessity of being found with 'one of those women'. 'That won't be necessary,' says Brenda, who has secretly loved Malcolm all along and offers herself as 'the other woman'. Mistaking her genuine affection for more of the fast set's loose and immoral ways, Forres resolves to disappear abroad thereby departing Nina's life completely. 'He came for sympathy and advice,' Brenda tells Nina who sees him leaving her flat. 'He got both,' she continues, 'but the sympathy made him cry and he didn't understand the advice.' Once Brenda has explained the truth about Malcolm's conviction and disclosed her own feelings for him, Nina is led to realise that she still loves her husband. They both note the irony of their situation: 'The only decent man we two have ever met, the only upright moral clean-thinking man in all our set, should be what the world calls a murderer.' But how to find him?

By chance, Malcolm has visited the St Martin's refuge one last time before going off to join a merchant ship bound for South America. 'It's a world of sorrow that young man carries away,' observes the vicar. And 'a stranger' (J. Fisher White), prompted by compassion and learning of Forres's plight, calls on Nina to tell her where he is destined. She seeks her husband out at a dockside inn and, despite his protestation that 'Love doesn't come to men who are not worthy', she assures him of her deep and abiding affection. Nina is confident now, even bold, whereas Malcolm is weak and weary. 'I can't fight any more,' he says, 'I'm tired.' 'Come here and rest,' Nine replies, as she cradles him in her arms.

The film ends as it began, then, replete with melodramatic devices and excessive emotionality – its defining characteristics throughout. Much was owed here to Dion Titheradge's former stage script and the *Bioscope*'s critic warmly praised the screen adaptation of *Loose Ends* for its 'very effective rendering' of the original play. Titheradge's wider theatrical expertise as writer of innumerable revue sketches clearly accounted for the many aphorisms scattered throughout the script ('Theatre managers are divided into two classes – those who've seen better days and those who expect to be knighted'; 'It takes one man to write a song and four German-American names to make it a hit'), which was commended for its 'keen social satire'. Although, overall, *Bioscope* considered that Norman Walker's *Loose Ends* painted a 'rather depressing picture of decadent modern society', it was nevertheless deemed to be 'a British film of outstanding interest' and 'a conspicuous success ... with dramatic qualities which will appeal to the general public, while the critical will appreciate the wit and satire shown in the presentation of an unpleasant lot of people'.[9]

In the critical parlance of the *Bioscope*, of course, terms such as 'decadent' and 'unpleasant' were intended to identify the film's more disturbing features and to convey the morally reprehensible nature of its characters. In this particular regard, although not considered sufficient to mar its redeeming qualities, *Loose Ends* was plainly found to be transgressive for its time. Yet it is precisely its totality of transgressive aspects – in theme and language as well as characterisation – that is most striking about the film when viewed today. The language is often forthright, and such that it could hardly have survived pre-production script scrutiny which the BBFC, as we have seen, instituted in the autumn of 1930. The Board would undoubtedly have demanded excision of lines such as: 'You are a cow', 'Pitiful Christ', 'You dirty swine', and 'You were both suffering from too much sex'. The fact that these lines also avoided being cut despite the post-production review process which was invariably required anyway for award of a BBFC certificate and subsequent cinema release (in the event, *Loose Ends* was given an 'A' certificate), says much about the new-found organisational problems which afflicted the Board in the spring and summer of 1930. *Loose Ends*, in short, 'got away with' a great deal of excessive language that would hardly have been countenanced a year or so later.[10]

The depiction of the various characters who constitute Nina's circle of 'smart society friends', moreover, is melodramatically accentuated and heightened to a considerable degree. The role of the pianist-lyricist Cyril Gayling, noticeably, is presented as overtly camp. Given to composing songs with dubious titles ('Two Loose Ends'), and inclined to engage in conversations full of meaningful double-entendres about his homosexuality ('I know him intimately' – 'Is there a man you don't know?'), it is perhaps no surprise it was considered 'an objectionable part' in the eyes of the *Bioscope* though it was conceded the role was well acted by Gerard Lyley. Miles Mander, too, was credited with playing his equally objectionable character with 'easy cynicism'. And while Edna Best was criticised somewhat for failing to bring the requisite amount of 'feeling or emotion' to the lead role of Nina, Adrianne Allen was applauded for stealing the show, in effect, as her friend, not least for the 'difficult' scene with Owen Nares where she 'rises brilliantly to the occasion' and 'secures the entire sympathy of the audience', when offering herself as 'the other woman' in adultery. Although, for the *Bioscope*, the acting in *Loose Ends* was merely another factor contributing to the satirical portrayal of a transgressive 'decadent' clique, it is the sheer excess of emotive force in the playing of the principal characters that renders the film all the more fascinating in retrospect.

Much the same might be said, finally, for the treatment of the film's major themes, where an excess of melodramatic emotionality and the representation of transgression are the key constituents in evidence, once again, nowhere more so than with regard to women. Women are the protagonists and their concerns are signalled as paramount throughout, constantly testing the bounds of social and moral conventions. Nina is visibly mortified at Malcolm's initial proposal of marriage, for instance, preferring 'just to live' with him instead. 'Why should I bury myself in the country?' she asks, when Malcolm suggests leaving their hectic London social scene and abandoning her successful career, thereby prompting his doleful reply: 'You're very independent. I've heard things in this flat that would make a navvy blush.' 'What have I done to deserve this?' is Nina's lament on learning of her husband's scandalous background and his deceit in hiding it from her. Brenda, moreover, is the one who recommends that Malcolm 'be unfaithful' as a way out of the couple's dilemma and advises an arranged adultery, with herself, as the means to divorce: 'It's only a matter of form.'

Malcolm declines the offer, of course, convinced it is not necessary to 'degrade' himself and certain in the knowledge that 'This place is crushing me'. His moral probity and steadfast rectitude win his wife and the day. Once again, though, despite being always locked into a stolid sanctimonious persona, Nares's rendition is emotionally charged throughout (and was commended for its 'strong emotional power' by the *Bioscope*). As presented, it is a constantly tear-jerking performance and he does, quite simply, cry at the appropriate and telling moments. If in the final analysis, moreover, the film resolves all its narrative tensions by the typical expedient of a highly moral closure, then this is probably very much in keeping with Norman Walker's preferred inclination as director. The film does, after all, restore the moral order and reinscribes prevailing conventions. The noticeable failure to explore further the issues it raises, and the ever-present resort to satire in dealing with its characters' contradictions, were doubtless a result of Walker's own evolution as a distinctly moralising, even evangelising, director, a career trajectory which his subsequent films (not least for J. Arthur Rank) showed to increasing effect and which culminated in his directing religious films. Such easy recourse was less evident in the work of other directors.[11]

*The Stronger Sex* (1931) was scripted and directed by Gareth Gundrey for Gainsborough Pictures from a scenario by Angus MacPhail based upon the original stage play by John Valentine.[12] The film opens on the morning of a grand society wedding between Mary Thorpe (Adrianne Allen), a rich woman and Staffordshire colliery-owner, and Warren Barrington (Colin Clive), a wastrel intent on making the best marriage he can to ease his considerable debts. John Brent (Martin Lewis), Mary's business partner and long-standing if secret admirer, presents her with a string of pearls which when placed beside Warren's photograph knocks it to the floor. 'My present seems to be causing trouble,' says John. Mary is deeply in love with Warren but by chance overhears an intimate conversation between him and Joan Merrivale (Renee Clama), soon revealed as his mistress, to whom he confides that Mary is 'the trusting sort', easily deceived, and hardly likely to prevent their continued affair. 'You may find out how quickly one can change,' Mary says to herself. Albeit greatly disillusioned, she decides to continue with the wedding. But the lucky mascot falls off their car and the omens bode ill for the future.

On honeymoon in France, accompanied by his valet, Parker (Gordon Harker), and her maid, Thompson (Elsa Lanchester), things go from bad to worse. Though Mary ensures she and her husband are in separate rooms and locks the adjoining door, Parker acquires the key and gives it to Warren. Warren slips into Mary's bedroom and wants to make love to his wife. Mary repels his advances and reveals she knows his true motive for marriage. 'I'm not so weak or trusting as you might think,' she declares, and is not convinced by his claim that 'Perhaps it's you I want'. For the marriage to continue or Warren to get his hands on any of the money, she states, it must be on her terms – 'If you leave my room now and for good'. Goaded by her new-found will and resolve ('The weaker sex becomes strong, eh?'), Warren advances towards Mary. Despite her heartfelt appeal – 'Please don't make me hate you' – Warren is determined to have his way, even if it means forcing himself upon her. Mary puts out the light as he moves closer to her bed.

Returning to England, it soon becomes clear Mary and Warren have finally settled upon leading separate lives. But when Warren's lover, Joan, rings him immediately in an attempt to arrange a tryst, she is surprised to learn he has terminated their affair. On reflection, he bitterly regrets his 'madness' in France and very much wants to make amends to his wife in the best way he thinks fit. To start, he wants to take up a desk job at the mine. Mary consults her partner, John, who happily agrees. John knows that things are amiss between the couple and he reassures Mary that he will always be there if she needs him. By the time of the miners' concert, some four months later, Warren is even more contrite and has proved a conscientious worker in the interim. Despite his best efforts and now genuine declaration of love, however, Mary has decided to get a divorce. Mary confides as much to John ('I don't love him any more. He killed all that'), and hints that she realises she has always loved him, just as she recognises he has always loved her in turn.

Sensing that his wife and her business partner are growing closer, Warren starts to lose interest in his work and fails to order a new load of pit props. No sooner does he summon up the courage to confront John about the blossoming relationship than there is a cave-in down the mine. The women, elders and children of the local village gather fearfully at the pit head as the emergency services are rushed into action and descend to retrieve the dead or injured as well as rescue survivors, if possible. It is the first accident at that mine in twenty years and Warren, who feels responsible for the tragedy, joins the rescue team. Although all the miners are eventually accounted for, Warren becomes lost in a shaft. Not only is there the danger of gas but a new fall soon traps him. John goes to the rescue and breaks through to make contact. Further falls entomb them both. 'What colossal irony,' Warren says, 'you and I buried in the same grave.'

With just one respirator between the two men, a hard decision must be made. John offers it to Warren. 'Most touching,' he states, 'but Mary would never forgive me.' Yet John won't take it. They toss a coin for the respirator and Warren deceives John about the winning call. 'Let's reason this out,' John argues adamantly, still refusing to grasp the sole remaining life-line, 'There's Mary to think of.' 'I am thinking of Mary,' replies Warren, who proceeds to knock John out, put the respirator over his comrade's face, and nobly sacrifices his own life by deliberately descending deeper into the shaft to face certain death from poisonous gas. At the mine head, expectant crowds gather while Mary is alone in the office. As the last cage comes up, she emerges to see John arrive at the surface safe and sound. 'Warren, is he safe?' she asks. John's downcast look is sufficient by way of response. 'Poor Warren,' says Mary, as she clasps John's hand and he takes hers in return.

Though opened up briefly to allow some evocative location shooting and crowd scenes which serve as prelude to the mining disaster that climaxes the film – praised by *Picturegoer Weekly* for providing 'authentic colliery background', and which compare favourably with mining films later in the decade such as *The Stars Look Down* and *The Proud Valley* – Gareth's Gundrey's *The Stronger Sex* showed all the hallmarks of its origins in John Valentine's stage play and society drama.[13] It is, essentially, a proscenium-bound theatrical property for three principal characters, with incidental walk-on parts for token representation of 'the lower orders' (done largely to comic effect in the case of the servant figures but with greater care and attention when dealing with the miners' community). While Gundrey appeared to have little genuine interest in lending much by way of visual import to the piece, he was acutely intent on exploiting its emotive potential to the full for the screen. He was well served, anyway, by a storyline which contrived many moments of melodramatic excess highlighting both love scorned and long re-pressed, deceit and infidelity, marital rape, heartfelt contrition, just retribution, sacrificial death and final restitution. But in his handling of the actors, especially, Gundrey sought to extract performances that would match the level of emotionality required by the narrative themes and characterisation. If he was less successful than expected with Colin Clive – prompting the criticism from *Picturegoer Weekly* that Clive did not 'live up to his *Journey's End* reputation' – Gundrey was more than compensated by Adrianne Allen who demonstrated in her playing, once again, the talents for which she was increasingly recognised and would put to even greater effect in her next film, for Miles Mander.

*The Woman Between* (1931) was directed for British International Pictures by Miles Mander from a script by himself and Frank Launder

which was based upon Miles Malleson's 1925 stage play, *Conflict*.[14] The
film opens at an all-night coffee stall on the Thames embankment where
Tom Smith (Owen Nares), a down-and-out, seeks warmth from the
freezing cold. A Rolls-Royce coupé pulls up and out steps Major Sir
Clive Marlow (David Hawthorne) to get coffee for himself and his
fiancée Lady Pamela Bellingdon (Adrianne Allen), who nestles into her
furs in the car. Smith, recognising Marlow as a former fellow under-
graduate at Cambridge University, deceitfully pockets his change and
slinks off into the dark.

It is gone three in the morning by the time Marlow and Lady Pamela
return to the splendour of Bellingdon House whereupon he presses her,
once again, about getting married. Pamela is content just to continue
their love affair but Marlow hates the subterfuge and thinks it 'dishonourable' to his friend, Lord Bellingdon (C. M. Hallard). 'If I don't
feel dishonourable I don't see why you should – he's my father,' says
the lord's 'modernistic' daughter. Then Marlow sees a man on the
terrace steps and fears a burglary is about to happen. Bellingdon appears
and Pamela goes off to bed. The two men catch the 'burglar' in the
main living room but it turns out to be Smith who is really quite casual
and unconcerned, in the circumstances, and only popped in for 'a chat'
with his old university chum. Over a drink and with Bellingdon now
more at ease, Marlow and Smith reminisce about their days at Cambridge. Smith, it transpires, was a good speaker in debates and had the
'best rooms' in college. Sandwiches and more whisky soon produce an
air of good-humoured camaraderie as Smith tells how life turned sour
for him thereafter. Tearfully, Smith recounts that his father's business
went bust so he took to composing songs then writing for a living. But
'my stuff began to get too serious' and met with only modest success.
Finally, when he was 'at the bottom' he tried his hand as an actor
though again to little avail. 'I'm sorry, this begging,' he sobs, 'it's rotten
when you're not used to it.'

On hearing Smith's confession that he also stole Marlow's change at
the coffee stall and followed the couple home, Lord Bellingdon stiffens:

> I don't want to seem hard or inhuman and I'm sorry for all the mis-
> fortunes you've detailed to us. But to put it quite bluntly I can't pretend
> to be overburdened with sympathy for you. You've told us a pretty pitiful
> story but you've had plenty of time to rehearse it. And, of course, you
> are an actor … I don't want to mock and sneer, I'm not bad-hearted but
> I'm hard-headed. I look at this as a practical man of the world and,
> frankly, I don't believe a man falls through society to the bottom as you've
> done without something in himself to drag him down.

Smith is incensed and retaliates:

> That's a fine thing for a man to say who's at the top. You must be damn
> pleased with yourself ... I've been through too much to hear such rot. If
> you think that because you're rich you're a tremendously fine deserving
> human being, you're all wrong. If you're rich these days, you may be a
> rogue or you may be just lucky. I'll give you the benefit of the doubt.

Although Bellingdon continues to doubt Smith's motives and feels 'If
he's got any manliness in him, he doesn't end up by begging', both
Marlow and Bellingdon finally give him money to be rid of an embar-
rassing and uninvited guest. Six months later, however, Tom Smith
reappears in the vicinity, this time as a prospective parliamentary
candidate for the constituency in the forthcoming general election. Clive
Marlow is standing as the Conservative Party candidate and Pamela is
discussing his chances and their love affair with her friend, Helen
Tremayne (Barbara Hoffe). 'Which party?' asks Helen. 'Don't be funny,'
scoffs Pamela, 'I suppose you think he'd be Labour.' 'Well, you never
know these days,' Helen muses. 'Yes, but Clive's not eccentric,' Pamela
says, 'and he's quite clever at times.' Pamela really has little interest in
politics, however, and prefers to talk about the pressure exerted by
Marlow and her father to settle down and get married. 'What's the
matter with you, my dear,' chides Helen, 'is that you have never been
in love.' 'It's not loving him I'm bothering about – it's marrying him,'
Pamela retorts; 'I don't want my marriage to be a sort of brown paper
parcel in which I wrap up my romance and seal it and say "that's that".
I want my marriage to be something more.'

Tom Smith, it transpires, is the surprise Labour candidate. On visiting
Marlow and Lord Bellingdon, he seeks an assurance they will not use
his past against him and it will be 'a straight fight, without personalities'.
Though Bellingdon has reservations on the matter, Marlow readily
agrees. Pamela is introduced to Smith and is immediately interested in
him. 'There didn't look anything wrong with him. Why do people
belong to his party?' she asks her father, later. 'Envy. A lot of thieves
and robbers,' Bellingdon replies. 'Don't you think you may be a little
bit prejudiced?' she presses. 'I dare say, I hope so,' he counters, but, 'If
a man's got an open mind he can't keep anything in it.' Yet, 'He had
quite nice manners, a nice voice, and he was quite nicely dressed,'
Pamela persists; 'Seriously, is there any reason at all why an intelligent
person should belong to them?' Bellingdon finishes the conversation
sharply and emphatically:

Do you believe all women are equal? I know very well men aren't and it's nonsense to pretend they are. I expect my butler to touch his hat to me, not because I'm a better man but because I know that I'm different. I don't resent saluting the King, so why should Daniel resent touching his hat to me. He doesn't. In any properly ordered society, people have got to have their places, and know 'em. Without that you'd have chaos. Give that lot power for a few years and we'd all starve.

Pamela, though, is fascinated by Tom and wants to learn more about his ideas. She invites him to tea. Warned by Helen that she is 'playing with fire', Pamela retorts: 'For months I have been praying for the tiniest bit of fire to play with, but I was afraid it had all gone out in me.' Initially intent on provoking Tom, she is the one increasingly provoked when he points out that she and her father enjoy two residences, with some 60 rooms and 20 servants at their disposal, and all for the benefit of just two people. 'If there were 100 people in a room representing the population of this country – your country, my country, our country,' he continues, 'two would be very rich, eight comfortable, 60 poor, and 30 more or less starving.' 'You're young and vigorous and vital, and the world's in such a mess,' Tom admonishes her; 'It ought to be the job of the young and vigorous to do something about it.'

Pamela's dawning interest in politics prompts her to tackle Clive about his campaign. Though somewhat mollified by his claim that 'The progress we're making is astounding and we're going as fast as we can', she bursts into tears when Clive mistakenly prides himself on sparking this sudden interest. She knows, deep inside, it was Tom who was responsible for doing that, and generating other feelings besides. So, after attending one of his meetings, she follows him back to his lodgings. Given that she is evidently 'a real lady' and Tom, after all, is 'a bit of a gentleman himself', his landlady feels confident about leaving them alone together in his bedroom at night. Pamela has not yet been 'converted' to his cause but she has felt 'disturbed' by his words. What Tom fears most, of course, is that she has learned about his past from Clive or her father. Not so. Still, Tom proceeds to reveal much, though not all, about himself ('Somehow or other I don't want you to despise me') and of his conversion to Labour politics as a result of an idyllic country sojourn enjoyed with the money given him by Clive and Lord Bellingdon. Most of all, he found 'a purpose without which for me life would be a senseless thing'. Pamela is visibly moved. As she goes, they kiss.

On the eve of the election, Clive is outraged to learn she went back to Smith's rooms and that she wishes to end their affair. When

Bellingdon is told of the matter, he confronts his daughter: 'You couldn't have done more if you were in love with him.' She is, plainly, and Clive realises as much. So, too, does her father who now exposes Tom as a petty thief. When Tom arrives suddenly at the house and is accused of the crime, he outlines the circumstances surrounding the coffee-stall incident. 'Is that all?' she asks; 'What a fuss to make about a thing like that.' 'My God. I'd rather be ruled by Bolsheviks than women,' fumes her father, 'absolutely no standards.' But Pamela feels increasingly in control of the situation and is gaining in self-confidence. So when her father starts 'harping on' about her being alone with Smith in his room, she tells him in no uncertain terms to 'get off to bed'. She knows where she stands and who she wants. She wants Tom.

Tom is forced to explain matters further but does so, simply and honestly, including mention of their kiss. Bellingdon, determined upon 'protecting my daughter from herself', threatens Tom with a 'declaration of war' and 'to make it publicly known how utterly unfit you are to take part in public life' unless he agrees never to see Pamela again. Pamela, for her part, is amused by all this and despairs of talk about how 'abominably' she has treated Clive. But she is still interested in Tom's reaction. For Tom, clearly, it is a moment of crisis and a test of his love. 'If I refuse to make this promise never to see you again, will you see me?' he asks Pamela. 'If you want to see me, I shall be glad,' she replies. The bolder for her response, Tom will not be blackmailed and answers Bellingdon, 'You can do your worst.' Once assured that her love for Tom is truly reciprocated, Pamela finally declares she will even marry him if he so wishes.

Lord Bellingdon will have none of it, however, and threatens yet again to make public what he knows about Smith to the crowd now gathering in the grounds of the house. But two can play at that game and his daughter deals what she thinks will prove a winning card. She is quite prepared to reveal everything about her relationship with Clive Marlow and to cast it in such a dark light, moreover, that it will tear both his and her family's reputation to shreds. 'It's a nice thing for the candidate who stands for all that's respectable,' as Pamela tauntingly puts it, 'to have seduced the daughter of his best friend, under his own roof.' 'Under whose roof?' asks her father, utterly bewildered by now. 'Oh, under all sorts of roofs,' Pamela replies, confident and nonchalant; 'If it comes to telling tales, this seduction business is going to be worse for Clive than the coffee-stall incident for my man.'[15]

This revelation clinches matters as far as Lord Bellingdon is concerned and reduces Clive to silence. It serves only to complicate things in

Tom's mind, however, since he is plainly hurt and now less certain that he wants to be 'her man'. Although suddenly frightened by what she has unleashed, Pamela is hardly inclined to take back her words or apologise for past actions ('I'm not sorry about what's happened with Clive, or ashamed'), but she does want to know what Tom thinks. And she is mightily relieved as well as genuinely happy to hear him say, 'It makes no difference ... It's now that matters.' As all agree 'to end this decently', Pamela paves the path to resolution. 'You believe your party is the one bulwark of civilisation don't you?' she asks Clive; 'And you believe yours is the hope of the world?' she asks Tom. 'Yes,' they answer. 'Then go out and say so,' says Pamela, taking each by the arm and leading them to address the large crowd assembled outside.

Left alone with her father, Pamela is a source of comfort and consolation, albeit in her own special way, as ever: 'Never mind. It can't be helped. You go to the club and find someone else who's got insubordinate children and who believes the world's going to the dogs. There are lots of them. And have a good dinner. You'll feel ever so much better.' Outside, a section of the crowd starts singing 'The Red Flag', only to be joined after a few bars by a hearty rendition of 'God Save The King'. As hats are doffed, Lord Bellingdon is revitalised and reconciled with Pamela. The camera withdraws from the proceedings as the doors close finally on the image of father and daughter together.

Having witnessed, at first hand, Adrianne Allen and Owen Nares working together so effectively on *Loose Ends*, Miles Mander clearly sought to reunite them for *The Woman Between* in order to capitalise upon their successful partnership. If the result, according to the critic on *Picturegoer Weekly*, was a 'cleverly directed' piece 'in which the dialogue and not the action is the mainspring', it was none the less also considered to be 'unnecessarily "sexy"'. This was the recurrent phrase of reproach adopted by the reviewer and found most appropriate for a film whose 'theme is not too savoury' and which 'concerns the mating of an Earl's modernistic daughter with a Labour candidate, after she has lived with a friend of her father's'. And although it was recognised that the film was somewhat 'political in theme as well', since there was evidently 'no political bias' to be detected, it was therefore felt from 'that angle, at any rate, it will offend no-one ... There is no doubt that the characters are interesting and very well portrayed,' the reviewer continued, and Mander 'has used his camera with artistic effect which helps the continuity and saves us from many of the more wordy sequences'. But in spite of the film's redeeming qualities, the *Picturegoer Weekly* critic could not help returning finally to the major point of concern: 'There is so much cleverness in this picture that it makes me wish all the more that British producers would avoid such unnecessarily "sexy" subjects.'[16]

Quite where *Picturegoer Weekly* drew the line between 'sexy' and 'unnecessarily sexy' is difficult to fathom, but one thing is clear: this aspect was considered to be the film's most questionable feature and here, above all, it was deemed transgressive. Yet what was it exactly that so rankled? Clearly, the presentation of Pamela, the principal and, virtually, the only female character. She is the source of sexuality and, increasingly, the motivating force which advances the film's themes and narrative thrust. Adrianne Allen's performance, moreover, was exceptional in its characterisation and brilliantly rendered. What she represented and the way she represented it, of course, were doubtless the factors that perturbed the critic on *Picturegoer Weekly*. It was in its depiction of woman, in short, that the film gave offence. But it is precisely in this respect and in its investment in melodramatic emotionality – the characteristic of the society drama genre – that the film is most of interest today.

# Notes

## 1. Cinema-going preferences in Britain in the 1930s

I would like to thank John Armstrong, Ben Fine, Ian Jarvie, Bernard Hrusa Marlow and Jeffrey Richards for their detailed reading of, and comments on, this chapter at various stages in its development. This applies also to the respective audiences of the Business History Unit at the LSE in October 1993 and the Quantitative Economic History Conference at Peterhouse College, Cambridge, in September 1994.

1. Rachael Low, *Film Making in 1930s Britain* (London, 1985), Table 1, appendix, p. 275, based upon the films registered by film renters. The 1927 and 1938 Film Acts defined the renters' year as 1 April to 31 March.

2. I. C. Jarvie, *Hollywood's Overseas Campaign: the North Atlantic Movie Trade, 1920–50* (Cambridge, 1922), Introduction and Ch. 5.

3. Low, *Film Making*, p. xiv.

4. This dismal reading of the effects of the 1927 legislation is found commonly in texts: see Simon Hartog, 'State Protection of a Beleaguered Industry', in J. Curran and V. Porter (eds), *British Cinema History* (London, 1983), p. 64; Robert Murphy, 'Under the Shadow of Hollywood', in Charles Barr (ed.), *All Our Yesterdays: 90 Years of British Cinema* (London, 1986), pp. 52–3; James Park, *British Cinema: the Lights That Failed* (London, 1990), pp. 41–2; Julian Petley, 'Cinema and State', in Barr (ed.), *All Our Yesterdays*, pp. 32–3. For a detailed social analysis of the reasons behind the alleged superiority of Hollywood films shown in Britain, see Peter Stead, 'Hollywood's Message for the World: the British response in the 1930s', *Historical Journal of Film, Radio, and Television*, vol. 1, no. 1 (1981), pp. 19–32; and Peter Stead, 'People and the Pictures: the British Working Class and Film in the 1930s', in N. Pronay and D. Spring (eds), *Propaganda, Politics and Film* (London, 1982).

5. Implicit in this research is the principle that the most sensible method of establishing film popularity is through the box office. POPSTAT represents in effect an approximation of relative box-office returns.

6. R. Stone and D. A. Rowe (*The Measurement of Consumers' Expenditure in the UK, 1920–38* [Cambridge, 1966], p. 81) adopt Browning and Sorrell's earlier estimates of cinema attendance; see H. E. Browning and A. A. Sorrell, 'Cinema and Cinema-Going in Great Britain', *Journal of the Royal Statistical Society*, vol. 117 (1954), pp. 133–65. These are based upon Entertainment Tax returns. Using the same methods to estimate expenditure in other entertainment sectors in Britain for the 1937/38 financial year, Stone and Rowe found that as much as 64.4 per cent of expenditure was accounted for by cinema admissions, with theatres taking 12.8 per cent, racing 5 per cent, football 4.3 per cent, cricket 0.2 per cent and other categories 13.3 per cent.

7. For a more detailed presentation of pertinent statistical data see John Sedgwick, 'The British Film Industry's Production Sector Difficulties in the Late 1930s', *Historical Journal of Film, Radio, and Television*, vol. 17, no. 1 (1997), pp. 49–66, Table v.

8. George Orwell, *The Road to Wigan Pier* (Harmondsworth, 1962), p. 72. For a detailed account of cinema-going in 1930s Britain see Jeffrey Richards, *The Age of the Dream Palace: Cinema and Society in Britain 1930–1939* (London, 1984), Ch. 1; Richards, 'Cinemagoing in Worktown: Regional Film Audiences in 1930s Britain', *Historical Journal of Film, Radio, and Television*, vol. 14, no. 2, (1994), pp. 147–66; and Richards and Dorothy Sheridan (eds), *Mass-Observation at the Movies* (London, 1987), Chs 1–3.

9. Douglas Gomery, *Shared Pleasures: a History of Movie Presentation in the United States* (London, 1992); W. I. Greenwald, *The Motion Picture Industry: an Economic Study of the History and Practices of a Business*, unpublished PhD thesis (New York University, 1950); M. D. Huettig, 'Economic Control of the Motion Picture Industry', abridged from a publication of the same title published by University of Pennsylvania Press (1944) and found in T. Balio (ed.), *The American Film Industry* (Wisconsin, 1985); John Izod, *Hollywood and the Box-Office, 1895–1986* (Basingstoke, 1988); Richard Maltby, 'The Political Economy of Hollywood: the Studio System', in P. Davies and B. Neve (eds), *Cinema, Politics and Society in America* (Manchester, 1981); Richard Maltby, *Hollywood Cinema* (Oxford, 1995).

10. Greenwald, *Motion Picture Industry*, p. 107.

11. *Minutes of Evidence taken before the Departmental Committee appointed by the Board of Trade to consider the position of British films*, chairman: Lord Moyne, HMSO (London, 1936), p. 9, para. 57.

12. Low, *Film Making*, pp. 3–4, maintains that the commercial odds were firmly stacked in favour of the distributor who received a minimum flat rate plus a percentage of the variable box-office takings, depending on the renters' assessment of the film's popularity.

13. See Simon Rowson, 'Statistical Survey of the Cinema Industry in Great Britain in 1934', *Journal of the Royal Statistical Society*, vol. 99 (1936), pp. 67–129, p. 77: and Browning and Sorrell, 'Cinema and Cinema-Going', p. 135. Leslie Halliwell, *Seats in All Parts* (London, 1986) gives a contemporary account of cinema-going in Bolton. See also Richards, *Age of the Dream Palace*, pp. 25–6; and Richards, 'Cinemagoing', p. 153, for further evidence on audience preferences in 1930s' Bolton. The argument being developed appears to fit comfortably within an interesting new approach to consumption developed by Ben Fine, and Ellen Leopold in *The World of Consumption* (London, 1993), in which the authors analyse 'the way in which production and consumption are united together and the ways in which each is moderated by the connections between them' (p. 4).

14. A full set of cinemas used to generate these results can be found in John Sedgwick, *The British Film Industry and the Market for Films, 1932–37*, unpublished PhD thesis (London Guildhall University, 1995), appendix 4.1.

15. The mid-range price has been calculated by taking the mid-point of the price range for each cinema, found in the *Kine Year Books* of 1932–39. Allen Eyles was able to fill in a small number of gaps from his personal records.

16. Rowson, 'Statistical Survey', p. 76; Linda Wood (ed.), *British Films, 1927–1939* (London, 1986), p. 120. Note these figures are exclusive of cinemas in the Irish Free State and Northern Ireland.

17. Rowson, 'Statistical Survey', p. 78; *Kine Year Books*, 1932–39.

18. Rowson, 'Statistical Survey', p. 70. From the *Kine Year Books*, I have calculated that there were only six cinemas in Britain which had mid-range prices significantly in excess of one shilling for the provincial cities and three shillings for the London West End and not included in the sample – one in London, one in Newcastle and four in Liverpool. The addition of these cinemas would have completed this tier of exhibition and thus strengthened the sample set.

19. For a detailed account of the diffusion of these 119 'hit' films, see Sedgwick, *British Film Industry*, Chs 5–6.

20. Rowson, 'Statistical Survey', p. 83. Rowson estimates that there were 3,872,000 cinema seats in Britain during 1934 (Table 4, p. 76). For that same year the sample cinemas listed 146,000 seats of which there were 25,500 ABC seats and 49,000 Gaumont-British seats. See also Wood (ed.), *British Films*, p. 119, for the size of cinema circuits in Britain.

21. This is likely to be an under-estimation, since films scoring less than the arithmetic mean POPSTAT score were likely to have been rented at a small flat-rate tariff, while main features took up to a 60 per cent share of the box-office ticket sales.

22. See H. M. Glancy, 'MGM Film Grosses, 1924–1948: the Eddie Mannix Ledger', *Historical Journal of Film, Radio, and Television*, vol. 12, no. 2 (1992), pp. 127–44; Glancy, 'Warner Bros Film Grosses, 1921–1951: the William Schaefer Ledger', *Historical Journal of Film, Radio, and Television*, vol. 15, no. 1 (1995), pp. 55–73; R. B. Jewell, 'RKO Film Grosses, 1929–1951: the C. J. Tevlin Ledger', *Historical Journal of Film, Radio, and Television*, vol. 14, no. 1 (1994), pp. 37–50; John Sedgwick, 'Richard B. Jewell's RKO Film Grosses, 1929–51: the C. J. Tevlin Ledger: a Comment', *Historical Journal of Film, Radio, and Television*, vol. 14, no. 1, (1994), pp. 51–8; Sedgwick, 'The Warners' Ledger 1921–22 to 1941–42: a Comment', *Historical Journal of Film, Radio, and Television*, vol. 15, no. 1 (1955), pp. 75–82, for detailed analyses of the film budgets and revenues of three principal Hollywood studios, during the 'classical' period.

23. Barry King, 'Stardom as Occupation', in P. Kerr (ed.), *The Hollywood Film Industry* (London, 1986), p. 162.

24. King, 'Stardom', p. 162.

25. Sedgwick, 'British Film Industry's Difficulties'.

26. For the accounts of Korda's management of Denham see Karol Kulik, *Alexander Korda: the Man Who Could Work Miracles* (London, 1975), Chs 11–12; Low, *Film Making*, pp. 218–29. The importance of *The Private Life of Henry VIII* to the financial fortunes of London Films is discussed at length by Kulik, pp. 94, 95, Ch. 10; and Sarah Street, 'Alexander Korda, Prudential Assurance and British Film Finance in the 1930s', *Historical Journal of Film, Radio, and Television*, vol. 6, no. 2 (1986), pp. 161–79.

27. During 1932 a number of films from Germany as well as films made by occasional independent American production companies, e. g. Harold Lloyd and Caddo, were successful, causing the USA(A) market share calculation to be lower than at any other time during the investigation. This coincides with the downturn in Hollywood budget and output schedules during the most severe period of the American depression.

28. Marcia Landy, *British Genres: Cinema and Society, 1930–1960* (Princeton, 1991), p. 485.

29. Sedgwick, *The British Film Industry and the Market for Films*, pp. 25–8; *Minutes of Evidence*, p. 27.

30. Rowson, 'Statistical Survey', p. 115.

31. For Korda, see Kulik, *Alexander Korda*, pp. 127–30; for Balcon, see John Sedgwick, 'Michael Balcon's Close Encounter with the American Market, 1934–36', *Historical Journal of Film, Radio, and Television*, vol. 16, no. 3 (1996), pp. 333–48 as well as Michael Balcon, *Michael Balcon Presents … a Lifetime of Films* (London, 1969), Chs 4–5; and for Basil Dean, *Mind's Eye* (London, 1973).

32. Richards, *Age of the Dream Palace*, p. 160.

33. Ibid., Ch. 1.

34. Richards, 'Cinemagoing'; and Richards and Sheridan (eds), *Mass-Observation*, Chs 1–3.

35. I. C. Jarvie, *Hollywood's Overseas Campaign*, p. 8.

36. The year 1936 saw a spectacular increase in film industry investment: the capital

value of new companies doubled from the 1935 level of £1. 07m to £2. 10m and then tailed away so that levels in 1938 were ten times lower. See *Kine Weekly*, 6 January 1938 and 12 January 1939.

37. Street, 'Alexander Korda'.

38. Low, *Film Making*, pp. 199–208; F. D. Klingender and S. Legg, *Money Behind the Screen* (London, 1937).

39. Izod, *Hollywood and the Box Office*, Ch. 9.

40. Kulik, *Alexander Korda*, Ch. 12; Low, *Film Making*, pp. 142–3. Low intriguingly suggests that the internal distribution arrangements of Gaumont-British were far from satisfactory and may have led to the production wing of the organisation cross-subsidising the exhibition wing.

41. Sedgwick, 'British Film Industry's Difficulties'; Low, *Film Making*, pp. 115–16, 270. Warners generated approximately one-third of film revenues from foreign markets of which Britain was the most important. See Sedgwick, 'Warners' Ledger', Table 1.

42. Sedgwick, 'Michael Balcon's Close Encounter'.

43. Under the 1938 legislation films could be registered for quota purposes where domestic labour costs included in production budgets were at least £7,500. This in effect restricted quota film budgets to a minimum of 15,000 feet. Films with domestic labour costs three times (£22,500) and five times (£37,500) greater than that were allowed to count for double and triple quota length purposes respectively. Accordingly, the American producers were encouraged to make expensive films in Britain in order to reduce the number of domestic films carried by the distribution wings of their organisation in the domestic market. See Low, *Film Making*, p. 50; and Margaret Dickinson and Sarah Street, *Cinema and State: the Film Industry and the British Government, 1927–84* (London, 1985), p. 98.

44. Jarvie, *Hollywood's Overseas Campaign*, p. 8. See also, Sarah Street, 'The Hays Office and the Defence of the British Market in the 30s', *Historical Journal of Film, Radio, and Television*, vol. 5, no. 1 (1985), pp. 37–55.

## 2. Julius Hagen and Twickenham Film Studios

1. Jeffrey Richards, *The Age of the Dream Palace: Cinema and Society in Britain 1930–1939* (London, 1984), p. 6.

2. A. Jympson Harmon, *Star*, 2 December 1935 (BFI Library Services, microfiche).

3. *Bioscope*, 5 January 1928.

4. *Bioscope*, 5 November 1928.

5. Jympson Harmon, *Star*, 2 December 1935 (BFI Library Services, microfiche).

6. *Daily Telegraph*, 9 January 1937.

7. *Kine Weekly*, 6 January 1932.

8. *Kine Weekly*, 26 May 1932.

9. BECTU History Project, 19 November 1988.

10. A. Jympson Harmon, *Star*, 2 December 1935 (BFI Library Services, microfiche).

11. Bernard Vorhaus, interview with author, 23 October 1986.

12. BECTU History Project, 19 November 1988.

13. For further information on working at Twickenham Studios, see Linda Wood, *Low Budget Production and the British Film Industry, with Particular Reference to Julius Hagen and Twickenham Studios 1927–38*, unpublished MPhil thesis (Polytechnic of Central London, 1989).

14. *Kine Weekly*, 22 June 1933.

15. *Kine Weekly*, 11 January 1934.

16. *Kine Weekly*, 21 June 1934.

17. *Kine Weekly*, 26 September 1934.

18. *Kine Weekly*, 10 January 1935.

19. *Kine Weekly*, 9 January 1936.

20. *Kine Weekly*, 2 May 1935.

21. *Kine Weekly*, 5 December 1935.

22. *Kine Weekly*, 2 May 1935.

23. A. Jympson Harmon, *Star*, 2 December 1935 (BFI Library Services, microfiche).

24. *Dusty Ermine* (£39,111); *Spy of Napoleon* (£45,449); *Man in the Mirror* (£33,379); *Clothes and the Woman* (£30,278); *Silver Blaze* (£30,777); and *Vicar of Bray* (£20,398); unattributed newspaper cutting, 27 February 1937 (BFI Library Services, microfiche).

25. *Kine Weekly*, 9 January 1936.

26. Ibid.

27. *Kine Weekly*, 17 December 1936.

28. *Kine Weekly*, 14 January 1937.

29. *Daily Telegraph*, 9 January 1937.

30. *Evening News*, 14 January 1937.

31. *Kine Weekly*, 2 September 1937.

32. Rachael Low, *Film-Making in 1930s Britain* (London, 1985), p. 175. Low also comments on the size of Hagen's salary which, she points out, was far higher than Michael Balcon's when he was in charge of Britain's most important studio, Gaumont-British at Shepherd's Bush.

33. *Daily Mail*, 18 January 1937.

34. *Kine Weekly*, 4 March 1937.

35. *Daily Mail*, 18 January 1937.

## 3. Hollywood and Britain

1. Rachael Low, *Film Making in 1930s Britain* (London, 1985), p. 195.

2. Sidney Gilliat is quoted in Geoff Brown (ed.), *Launder and Gilliat* (London, 1977), p. 82.

3. Kristin Thompson, *Exporting Entertainment: America in the World Film Market, 1907–34* (London, 1985), p. 125.

4. The attempts made to curb 'block-booking' were largely unsuccessful. 'Gentleman's agreements' simply replaced the agreements that were once made on paper. The quota itself, however, ensured that British films received playing dates. Margaret Dickinson and Sarah Street, *Cinema and State: the Film Industry and the British Government, 1927–84* (London, 1985), pp. 72–3.

5. Thompson, *Exporting Entertainment*, pp. 127–8.

6. Ibid., p. 127.

7. The importance of British earnings for the Hollywood studios during this period is the subject of the first chapter of the author's PhD thesis. Mark Glancy, *Hollywood and Britain: the Hollywood 'British' Film, 1939–45*, unpublished PhD thesis (University of East Anglia, 1993), pp. 15–64.

8. Dickinson and Street, *Cinema and State*, p. 69.

9. Michael Balcon, *Michael Balcon Presents ... a Lifetime in Films* (London, 1969), pp. 92–3.

10. Michael Powell, *A Life in Movies: an Autobiography* (London, 1986), p. 216.

11. Ibid., pp. 220–1.

12. Low, *Film Making*, p. 33.

13. Ibid., pp. 186–97.

14. Ibid., p. 195.

15. Ibid., p. 187 and pp. 262–4.

16. Ibid., p. 187.

17. For a mathematical demonstration of this, see John Sedgwick, 'Richard B. Jewell's RKO Film Grosses, 1929–51: the C. J. Tevlin Ledger: a Comment', *Historical Journal of Film, Radio, and Television*, vol. 14, no. 1 (1994), pp. 51–8.

18. In August 1996, the National Film Theatre in London held a short season of British 'B' films made during the 1930s, and this provided an opportunity to witness the admirable qualities of a selection of these films. Ian Christie's introduction to the season makes the parallel between 'quota quickies' and Hollywood's 'poverty row'. Ian Christie, 'Typically British: British Bs of the Thirties', National Film Theatre Programme Notes (August 1996), p. 16.

19. The least expensive of these studios' 'B' films cost between $28,000 and $50,000 in the early 1930s. With the exchange rate of $4.90 to £1 sterling, this means that they were also made at costs of approximately £1 per foot. See Mark Glancy, 'MGM Film Grosses, 1924–1948: the Eddie Mannix Ledger', *Historical Journal of Film, Radio, and Television*, vol. 12, no. 2 (1992), pp. 127–43; Glancy, 'Warner Bros Film Grosses, 1921–1951: the William Schaefer Ledger', *Historical Journal of Film, Radio, and Television*, vol. 15, no. 1 (1995), pp. 55–73; and R. B. Jewell, 'RKO Film Grosses, 1929–1951: the C. J. Tevlin Ledger', *Historical Journal of Film, Radio, and Television*, vol. 14, no. 1 (1994), pp. 37–50.

20. Robert Murphy, 'Under the Shadow of Hollywood', in C. Barr (ed.), *All Our Yesterdays: 90 Years of British Cinema* (London, 1986), p. 56.

21. Low, *Film Making*, pp. 39, 196.

22. The critic for the *Monthly Film Bulletin* found that 'the direction and dialogue are clumsy and the acting is definitely poor' in *The King's Plate*, while *Under Cover* was considered to be 'naive' and 'barely competent'. See *Monthly Film Bulletin*, 31 January 1936.

23. Rachael Low refers to 'long, long silent Indian films' that were registered for quota purposes by MGM, but probably were not booked for exhibition. As she points out, such films probably served to fill a shortfall in footage requirements. Low, *Film Making*, p. 195.

24. For example, critics for the *Monthly Film Bulletin* described Hagen's *Make it Three* as 'shoddy' and 'obviously deficient', and supposed that it was made 'in the minimum time' (28 February 1938). In King's 'unconvincing' *Reasonable Doubt*, 'coincidence and credibility are both strained' (31 December 1936). And although Fitzpatrick's *The Captain's Table* 'moves apace without digression', it was said to lack 'ingenuity' (30 November 1936).

25. *Monthly Film Bulletin*, 30 November 1936.

26. Marion Meade, *Buster Keaton: Cut to the Chase* (London, 1995), p. 221.

27. *Monthly Film Bulletin*, 7 October 1934.

28. *Monthly Film Bulletin*, 13 February 1935.

29. *Monthly Film Bulletin*, 30 April 1936.

30. Critics for the *Monthly Bulletin* gave reluctant praise to *Sweeney Todd* (31 March 1936), *The Crimes of Stephen Hawke* (30 May 1936) and *Sexton Blake and the Hooded Terror* (28 February 1938).

31. Eckman's comments are discussed in Dickinson and Street, *Cinema and State*, p. 68; and in Low, *Film Making*, pp. 38–9.

32. Thompson, *Exporting Entertainment*, p. 125.

33. *Film Weekly*, 30 May 1931.

34. Simon Hartog, 'State Protection of a Beleaguered Industry', in J. Curran and V. Porter (eds), *British Cinema History* (London, 1983), p. 68.

35. Low, *Film Making*, p. 42.

36. Ibid., p. 52.

37. 'Memo from Mr. Somervell', 23 April 1938 (Public Record Office, London: BT 64/103).

38. Brown, *Launder and Gilliat*, p. 82.

39. Glancy, *Hollywood and Britain*, p. 41.

40. The eight British films were: *The Ghost Goes West, First a Girl, It's Love Again, The Secret Agent, Queen of Hearts, Come Out of the Pantry, Boys Will be Boys* and *Ourselves Alone*. See *Kine Weekly*, 11 January 1937.

41. Leonard J. Leff, *Hitchcock and Selznick: the Rich and Strange Collaboration of Alfred Hitchcock and David O. Selznick in Hollywood* (New York, 1987), pp. 23–4.

42. Kenneth Barrow, *Mr. Chips: The Life of Robert Donat* (New York, 1985), p. 102.

43. Brown, *Launder and Gilliat*, p. 86.

44. Balcon's opinion was expressed in a telegram to Ben Goetz. I am grateful to the Turner Entertainment Corporation for allowing me to see the legal files of all the MGM-British films. Michael Balcon to Ben Goetz, 19 April 1937, *A Yank at Oxford* legal file, Turner Entertainment Corporation, Los Angeles, California (hereafter Turner Entertainment). *Rage in Heaven* was eventually made in Hollywood in 1941 with Robert Montgomery and Ingrid Bergman.

45. MGM did film *Soldiers Three* in 1951, but *Finishing School* never emerged. Brown, *Launder and Gilliat*, pp. 86–7.

46. Ben Goetz to Louis B. Mayer, 16 December 1936, *A Yank at Oxford* legal file, Turner Entertainment.

47. Ben Goetz to Michael Balcon, 27 May 1937, *A Yank at Oxford* legal file, Turner Entertainment; and Ben Goetz to Louis B. Mayer, 9 August 1938, *Goodbye, Mr Chips* legal file, Turner Entertainment.

48. Balcon, *Michael Balcon Presents*, p. 100.

49. Brown, *Launder and Gilliat*, p. 82.

50. Balcon, *Michael Balcon Presents*, pp. 110–11.

51. Ibid., p. 101.

52. Franklin was originally assigned to direct the film, but was replaced by Sam Wood just before filming began. MGM thought it would save £25,000 by having Wood direct rather than Franklin, who was known as a slow and costly director, Franklin nonetheless maintained a keen interest in the story, which he referred to as his 'favourite child'. Plans for Sidney Franklin to direct *Goodbye, Mr Chips* at Denham are discussed in Victor Saville to Robert Ritchie, 21 January 1938, *Goodbye, Mr Chips* legal file, Turner Entertainment. Franklin recounts his involvement in his unpublished autobiography. I am grateful to Kevin Brownlow for allowing me to read this manuscript, which he owns. Sidney Franklin, *We Laughed and We Cried*, p. 262.

53. John Monk Saunders wrote the original treatment for *A Yank at Oxford* in 1934. Between 1934 and 1937, 34 other writers worked on the script. Saunders received screen credit along with six of the others: Malcolm Stuart Boylan, Walter Ferris, Sidney Gilliat, Leon Gordon, Michael Hogan and George Oppenheimer. The other 28 writers were: Chandos Balcon, R. V. C. Bodley, David Boehm, J. P. Carstairs, Lenore Coffee, John Considine, Frank Davis, Virginia Faulkner, F. Scott Fitzgerald, K. Kirkpatrick, Harold Goldman, John Higgins, Monckton Hoffe, Samuel Hoffenstein, Arthur Hyman, Bradley King, Sidney Kingsley, Charles Lederer, Joseph Mankiewicz, Elliot Morgan, Roland Pertwee, Gottfried Reinhardt, H. E. Rogers, Ben Travers, Catherine Turney, Hugh Walpole, Maurine Watkins and Frank Wead. *A Yank at Oxford* script files, MGM Script Collection, University of Southern California, Los Angeles (hereafter MGM/USC).

54. *A Yank at Oxford* earned a worldwide gross of $2,736,000 and profit of $513,000. Glancy, *Hollywood and Britain*, p. 157.

55. Thalberg was working on the script at the time of his death in 1936, with Charles Laughton and Myrna Loy set to play the leading roles. 'Notes from Mr. Thalberg', 16 July 1936, *Goodbye, Mr Chips* script files, MGM/USC.

56. *Goodbye, Mr Chips* earned a worldwide gross of $3,252,000 and a profit of $1,305,000. Glancy, *Hollywood and Britain*, p. 157.

57. Low, *Film Making*, p. 268.

58. *The Citadel* earned a worldwide gross of $2,598,000. Unusually, though, the foreign earnings ($1,611,000) were far higher than the North American earnings ($987,000). The profit was $938,000. Glancy, *Hollywood and Britain*, p. 157.

59. These are mentioned as 'properties being worked on' in a telegram from Denham to California. Ben Thau to Louis B. Mayer, 9 August 1938, *The Citadel* legal file, Turner Entertainment.

60. The script files reveal that MGM screenwriter George Oppenheimer worked on the *A Yank at Eton* screenplay between November 1938 and July 1939. The casting decisions and the location shooting are also indicated. *Eton Story* by George Oppenheimer, 14 November 1938; Memo from Victor Saville, 31 May 1939; and *A Yank at Eton* by George Oppenheimer, 1 July 1939; *A Yank at Eton* script files, MGM/USC.

61. Barrow, *Mr Chips*, pp. 128–41.

62. Murphy, 'Under the Shadow of Hollywood', p. 58.

63. 'Memo from Mr. Somervell', Public Record Office, Kew, BT 64/103.

# 4. Celluloid shockers

1. In arriving at the (approximate) figure of 350, I have relied on the synopses in Denis Gifford's *The British Film Catalogue 1895–1970: a Guide to Entertainment Films* (Newton Abbot, 1973). One of the first problems which arises in counting the number of thrillers is that of terminology. Gifford does not actually use 'thriller' as one of his generic categories but rather 'crime', which he defines thus: 'Dramatic plot turning on any aspect of crime, including mystery, murder, detection, violence' (p. 13). The number of feature-length films which he categorises as 'crime' during the years 1930–39 totals 364. On a year-by-year basis the totals are: 20 crime films in 1930, 39 in 1931, 33 in 1932, 31 in 1933, 43 in 1934, 38 in 1935, 45 in 1936, 45 in 1937, 36 in 1938 and 34 in 1939. There was also, in addition, one British-made crime serial during the decade, *Lloyd of the CID* (Mutual, 1932), which comprised 12 episodes of around 15 minutes each.

Gifford's definition of 'crime' includes detective-mystery narratives (for example, films based on the work of writers such as Agatha Christie and Dorothy L. Sayers) which have not usually been described as thrillers or shockers (the difference is discussed in the main text). However, relatively few films of this sort were made during the 1930s. There are, though, a number of films which Gifford places in other categories which could be described as shockers, such as the six films which he labels 'horror': *Castle Sinister* (1932), *The Ghoul* (1933), *The Tell-Tale Heart* (1934), *The Unholy Quest* (1934), *The Man Who Changed His Mind* (1936) and *Dark Eyes of London* (1939). Furthermore, some of Gifford's 'war' films – *I Was A Spy* (1933), *Brown on Resolution* (1935) and *Dark Journey* (1937) – could also be described as thrillers. It is likely, therefore, that the number of films which could be classed as thrillers is actually even higher than 350.

2. See, for example, Clive Bloom (ed.), *Suspense Fiction in the Twentieth Century* (Basingstoke, 1989); Michael Denning, *Cover Stories: Narrative and Ideology in the British Spy Thriller* (London, 1987); Stephen Knight, *Form and Ideology in Crime Fiction* (London, 1980); Jerry Palmer, *Thrillers: Genesis and Structure of a Popular Genre* (London, 1978); and Colin Watson, *Snobbery With Violence: English Crime Stories and Their Audience* (London, 1971; rev. edn, 1987).

3. Dorothy L. Sayers, 'Introduction', *Great Short Stories of Detection, Mystery and Horror* (London, 2nd edn, 1948), p. 19.

4. Tzvetan Todorov, *The Poetics of Prose*, trans. R. Howard (Oxford, 1977), p. 44.

5. W. H. Auden, 'The Guilty Vicarage', in *The Dyer's Hand* (London, 1948), p. 93.

6. David Glover, 'Introduction' to Edgar Wallace, *The Four Just Men* (1905) (Oxford Popular Fiction edn, 1995), p. xii.

7. The phrase is attributed to Peter Dunn in an article for the *Independent* in 1987 and is quoted by Alison Light, *Forever England: Femininity, Literature and Conservatism Between the Wars* (London, 1991), p. 65. Light argues that Christie's fiction can be best understood in relation to the hegemony of the middle classes which it furthered by constructing a modern but still essentially conservative ideology of Englishness.

8. While it may have been true that the classic detective story was popular with the middle classes, the assumption that readership of the more full-blooded thriller was confined to the working classes is contradicted even by contemporary commentators. Edgar Wallace in particular seems to have had an appeal which transcended class boundaries. Wallace's obituary in *The Times* testified that his novels 'were sold in their thousands and read by bishops and professors and Cabinet Ministers, and by errand-boys and tweeny-maids, and all grades of culture in between'. *The Times*, 11 February 1932, p. 17.

9. Denning, *Cover Stories*, p. 18.

10. Palmer, *Thrillers*, p. 115.

11. Ibid., p. 128.

12. John Buchan, *The Thirty-Nine Steps* (1915) (Oxford, World Classics edn, 1993), p. 3.

13. Jeffrey Richards, *The Age of the Dream Palace: Cinema and Society in Britain 1930–1939* (London, 1984), p. 254.

14. Rachael Low, *Film Making in 1930s Britain* (London, 1985), p. 115.

15. Leslie Halliwell, *Seats in All Parts: Half a Lifetime at the Movies* (London, 1985), p. 42.

16. For the purposes of this article, where I am concerned with the thriller genre as a whole rather than individual auteurs, I am deliberately avoiding any extended discussion of the films of Alfred Hitchcock, which have been analysed extensively elsewhere. Hitchcock's 'classic thriller sextet' of the mid-1930s is placed in relation to the spy thriller genre by Tom Ryall in *Alfred Hitchcock and the British Cinema* (London, 1986), Ch. 6, pp. 115–40. The more traditional auteurist type of criticism can be found in both Maurice Yacowar, *Hitchcock's British Films* (Connecticut, 1977) and Robin Wood, *Hitchcock's Films Revisited* (London, 1991).

17. Forsyth Hardy (ed.), *Grierson in the Movies* (London, 1981), p. 118. Grierson was writing in *Everyman* and was reviewing the films *The Ghost Train* (based on the play by Arnold Ridley), *The Outsider* (from a play by Dorothy Brandon), *The Skin Game* (Hitchcock's adaptation of the play by John Galsworthy), *The Calendar* (based on an Edgar Wallace play) and *Chance of a Night Time* (a Ben Travers farce).

18. Russell Ferguson, 'Armaments Rings, Assassins and Political Madmen', *World Film News*, vol. 2, no. 5 (August, 1937), p. 4.

19. Jeffrey Richards and Dorothy Sheridan (eds), *Mass-Observation at the Movies* (London, 1987), p. 121. The respondent is a Mrs Skellen, a young woman who attended Bolton's Odeon Cinema on a regular basis. In general the Mass-Observation survey found that 'crime' films were the third favourite category among Bolton's cinema-goers, behind 'musical romance' and 'drama and tragedy' and equal with 'history'. Crime films were on the whole rather more popular with men than with women.

20. Peter John Dyer, 'Young and Innocent', *Sight and Sound*, vol. 30, no.1 (Spring 1961), p. 81.

21. Ryall, *Alfred Hitchcock and the British Cinema*, pp. 82–3. The comparison between the thriller and the music-hall films is a relevant one in that both were rooted in indigenous

strands of British popular culture which had their origins in the Victorian period. Both were considered culturally low-brow and both have suffered from critical neglect. For a consideration of music-hall films see Andy Medhurst, 'Music Hall and British Cinema', in C. Barr (ed.), *All Our Yesterdays: 90 Years of British Cinema* (London, 1986), pp. 168–88.

22. Richards, *The Age of the Dream Palace*, p. 254.

23. *The Times*, 11 February 1932, p. 13.

24. *The Clue of the New Pin*, directed by Arthur Maude, and featuring among its supporting cast a young John Gielgud, was made on an early sound-on-disc recording system called British Phototone. However, technical difficulties meant that when it was trade shown in March 1929 it was shown as a silent. Hitchcock's *Blackmail* (1929), made at British International Pictures using the superior RCA Photophone sound-on-film recording system, is recognised as the first British 'full-talking' feature film, though a silent version of the film was also shot at the same time.

25. *Film Weekly*, 28 January 1929, p. 13.

26. *Film Weekly*, 11 February 1929, p. 11.

27. Margaret Lane, *Edgar Wallace: the Biography of a Phenomenon* (London, 1964), p. 284.

28. *Film Weekly*, 8 March 1929, p. 12.

29. Lane, *Edgar Wallace*, p. 285.

30. Quoted in Geoff Brown (ed.), *Walter Forde* (London, 1978), p. 26.

31. Although Wallace's name appears on the credits of *King Kong* and was used extensively in the advertising for the film, according to the producer Merian C. Cooper, 'Edgar Wallace didn't write one word of *King Kong*, not one bloody word ... [But] I'd promised him credit and so I gave it to him'. Quoted in Orville Goldner and George E Turner, *The Making of King Kong* (New York, 1975), p. 59.

32. Low, *Film Making*, pp. 178–9.

33. Geoff Brown (ed.), *Launder and Gilliat* (London, 1977), p. 91.

34. Jeffrey Richards and Anthony Aldgate, *Best of British: Cinema and Society 1930–1970* (Oxford, 1983), p. 39.

35. *The Times*, 19 August 1940, p. 6.

36. James C. Robertson, *The British Board of Film Censors: Film Censorship in Britain, 1896–1950* (London, 1985), pp. 56–9.

37. Peter Hutchings, *Hammer and Beyond: the British Horror Film* (Manchester, 1993), p. 25.

38. Denis Gifford, *A Pictorial History of Horror Movies* (London, rev. edn, 1983), p. 200.

39. Michael Balcon does not mention the film in his memoirs, *Michael Balcon Presents ... a Lifetime of Films* (London, 1969). Nor does he mention any of the other films which were produced at Gaumont-British which might be described as 'supernatural', such as Maurice Elvey's *The Clairvoyant* (1935) and Robert Stevenson's *The Man Who Changed His Mind* (1936), which also starred Boris Karloff. Lawrence Kardish points out that 'This omission is curious considering Balcon would produce Ealing's *Dead of Night* (1945), one of the great supernatural films of all time'. 'The Idea of a National Cinema', in G. Brown and L. Kardish, *Michael Balcon: the Pursuit of British Cinema* (New York, 1984), p. 50. It might be that the omission is due to the fact that films about the supernatural did not fit the ideal of sober realism that was Balcon's main contribution to an indigenous British national cinema. Another possible reason for the neglect of *The Ghoul* is that, although it has never been a 'lost' film as such, there has been a misconception among some writers that it was never shown in Britain. This mistaken assumption seems to have started with David Pirie's book *A Heritage of Horror: The English Gothic Cinema 1946–1972* (London, 1973). When usually authoritative sources falter, others tend to follow suit: thus Marcia Landy in *British Genres: Cinema and Society, 1930–1960* (Princeton, 1991) writes that 'Boris Karloff starred in *The Ghoul* (1933), but the film was never distributed in

England' (p. 390). In fact, *The Ghoul* was one of the first films to receive the BBFC's new advisory 'H' rating (not yet a formal certificate) and was shown quite widely in Britain. (My thanks to Mr Ian Conrich for clarifying this point.)

40. *The Cinema*, 26 October 1939.

41. 'Sapper', *Bulldog Drummond* (1920) (London, Classic Thrillers edn, 1983), p. 122.

42. Denning, *Cover Stories*, p. 56.

43. Jeffrey Richards, *Visions of Yesterday* (London, 1973), p. 35.

44. Dyer, 'Young and Innocent', p. 81.

45. Ibid., p. 82.

46. *Film Weekly*, 12 July 1935.

47. Landy, *British Genres*, p. 347.

48. See the chapter on 'Tod Slaughter and the Cinema of Excess' by Jeffrey Richards in this volume.

49. Although there had been British series films based on Rohmer's character during the 1920s – the Stoll Film Company's episodic *The Mystery of Dr Fu Manchu* (1923, 15 episodes) and *Further Mysteries of Dr Fu Manchu* (1924, 8 episodes) – the 'devil doctor' was noticeably absent from the British cinema of the 1930s. The probable reason for this was that the British Board of Film Censors was sensitive about films which might portray Chinese characters in a bad light. Fu Manchu appeared only in American films during the 1930s, being impersonated by Warner Oland in three early talkies and by Boris Karloff in MGM's glossy production *The Mask of Fu Manchu* (1932). Henry Brandon also starred in the Republic serial *The Drums of Fu Manchu* (1940). It was not until the 1960s that Fu Manchu returned to the British cinema in a series of five films starring Christopher Lee and produced by Harry Alan Towers.

50. Richards and Sheridan (eds), *Mass-Observation*, p. 151.

51. Landy, *British Genres*, p. 129.

52. Patrick Macnee later said that Ralph Richardson's performance in *Q Planes* was one of the influences upon his characterisation of secret agent John Steed in the popular 1960s television series *The Avengers*. See Dave Rogers, *The Ultimate Avengers* (London, 1995), p. 18. Furthermore, with its plot device of a spy ship disguised as a salvage vessel capturing the aircraft by radio control, *Q Planes* can be seen as a forerunner of the James Bond spectacular *The Spy Who Loved Me* (1977), wherein a supertanker 'swallows' nuclear submarines having located them by using a secret tracking system.

53. Glover, 'Introduction', *The Four Just Men*, p. xviii.

54. Richards, *Visions of Yesterday*, p. 35.

55. Information on the British Film Institute Library Services microfiche on the film.

56. Charles Barr, *Ealing Studios* (London, 1977; 2nd edn, 1993), p. 190.

57. *Motion Picture Herald*, 8 July 1939.

58. Brown (ed.), *Walter Forde*, p. 39.

59. Dyer, 'Young and Innocent', p. 81.

60. Julian Petley, 'The Lost Continent', in Barr (ed.), *All Our Yesterdays*, p. 98.

# 5. Calling all stars

1. I am indebted to the NFT which had a season (in July 1996) of British musicals as part of its 'Typically British' series. Suitably subtitled 'Cheer Up' (a reference to one of the films), it provided much of the viewing material for this chapter. Thanks also to the NFTVA's Luke McKernan for explaining the criteria behind the choice of films shown.

2. Of the studies written, most are themed around the big stars of the interwar years, notably Matthews, Formby and Fields. As they and their films have had their histories,

they are not dwelled on here. See, for example, Jeffrey Richards, *The Age of the Dream Palace: Cinema and Society in Britain 1930–1939* (London, 1984); Andrew Higson, *Waving the Flag: Constructing a National Cinema in Britain* (Oxford, 1995).

3. Andy Medhurst, 'Music Hall and British Cinema', in C. Barr (ed.), *All Our Yesterdays: 90 Years of British Cinema* (London, 1986), p. 174.

4. Medhurst, 'Music Hall and British Cinema', p. 174.

5. The mixing of acts from the West End musical comedy tradition with those of variety led Marcia Landy to the conclusion that the film calls 'attention to the contrasts between live entertainment and cinema'. This is over-stated; music hall had always featured performers from other traditions, and in any case there was much border crossing between the traditions. Furthermore, vaudeville was found on the stage at the time. The Coliseum, for example, had 'vaudeville' shows, which were described as a 'compound of spectacular ballets, dance ensembles, and Variety' (*The Performer*, Xmas number, 1933, p. 46). Marcia Landy, *British Genres: Cinema and Society, 1930–1960* (Princeton, 1991), p. 330.

6. For a full discussion of the film see Richards, *Age of the Dream Palace*, and Higson, *Waving the Flag*.

7. *Kinematograph Weekly*, 29 April 1937.

8. *Monthly Film Bulletin*, vol. 3 (December 1936), p. 214.

9. *Bioscope*, 12 February 1930, quoted in John Montgomery, *Comedy Films* (London, 2nd edn, 1968), p. 172.

10. *Kinematograph Weekly*, 9 January 1936.

11. *McCarthy Ratings*, 1937.

12. *Monthly Film Bulletin*, vol. 6 (June 1939), p. 112.

13. *Monthly Film Bulletin*, vol. 4 (July 1937), p. 142.

14. Richards, *Age of the Dream Palace*, p. 44.

15. Rachael Low, *Film Making in 1930s Britain* (London, 1985), p. 145.

16. Low, *Film Making* p. 146.

17. Rick Altman, *The American Film Musical* (Bloomington/London, 1989), p. 140.

18. Herbert Wilcox, *25,000 Sunsets* (London, 1967), p. 140.

19. *Film Pictorial*, 10 September 1932.

20. *Film Weekly*, 5 September 1931.

21. *Film Weekly*, 14 December 1935.

22. Low, *Film Making*, p. 123.

23. *Film Weekly*, 29 December 1933.

24. George Rowell, *The Victorian Theatre* (Oxford, 1956), p. 143.

25. Presumed lost, a copy turned up recently in France, replete with French subtitles. Befitting a book about unknown aspects of 1930s film culture, it receives an extended review here.

26. *Play Pictorial*, April 1938.

27. *Sunday Times*, 19 December 1937 (clippings file, Theatre Museum).

28. Uncredited newspaper, 23 March 1939 (clippings file, Theatre Museum).

29. James Dillon White, *Born to Star* (London, 1957), p. 280.

30. Lynton Hudson, *The English Stage* (London, 1951), p. 194.

31. *Film Pictorial*, 13 May 1939.

32. Roy Armes, *A Critical History of British Cinema* (London, 1978), p. 103.

33. *Observer*, 19 December 1937 (clippings file, Theatre Museum).

34. *Daily Mail*, 2 May 1939 (clippings file, Theatre Museum).

35. Richards, *Age of the Dream Palace*, p. 256.

36. *Monthly Film Bulletin*, vol. 6 (May 1939), p. 93.

37. *Kinematograph Weekly*, 13 April 1939.

38. *Film Pictorial*, 13 May 1939.

39. Ernest Betts, *The Film Business* (London, 1973), p. 395.
40. *Monthly Film Bulletin*, vol. 3 (November 1936), p. 194.
41. *Film Weekly*, 14 January 1939.
42. John Stevenson, *British Society 1914–45* (London, 1990), p. 395.
43. *The Performer*, 20 September 1933.
44. *Variety, Cabaret and Film News*, 20 December 1933.
45. *Film Weekly*, 11 July 1931.
46. *The Performer*, 13 September 1933.
47. Rowell, *Victorian Theatre*, p. 148.
48. See Altman, *American Film Musical*, for an extensive discussion of the origins of the American musical.
49. George Nobbs, *The Wireless Stars* (Norwich, 1972), p. 15.
50. Ibid., p. 21.
51. A. J. P. Taylor, *English History 1914–45* (Harmondsworth, 1976), p. 384.
52. White, *Born to Star*, pp. 273–4.
53. Ted Kavanagh, *Tommy Handley* (London, 1950), p. 86.
54. *Monthly Film Bulletin*, vol. 1 (December 1934). p. 103.
55. Stephen Jones, *The British Labour Movement and Film, 1918–1939* (London, 1987), p. 140.
56. Stevenson, *British Society*, pp. 419, 420.
57. Ibid., p. 397.
58. Percy Scholes, *The Oxford Companion to Music* (Oxford, 1991), p. 421.
59. *Radio Times*, 6 January 1939.
60. *Monthly Film Bulletin*, vol. 3 (August 1936), p. 129.
61. *Film Pictorial*, 20 August 1932.
62. *Popular Music and Film Song Weekly*, 30 October 1937.

# 6. 'Thinking forward and up'

I should like to acknowledge the help given to me in this chapter by my Portsmouth colleague Laurie Ede. He generously provided me with some material on early Veidt films. I am also indebted to Tim Bergfelder of the University of Southampton for information and stimulating discussion.

1. See Sue Harper, *Picturing the Past: the Rise and Fall of the British Costume Film* (London, 1994), pp. 56–63. See also Jackie Stacey, *Star Gazing: Hollywood Cinema and Female Spectatorship* (London, 1994); and Annette Kuhn, 'Cinema Culture and Femininity in the 1930s', in C. Gledhill (ed.), *Nationalising Femininity: Culture, Sexuality and British Cinema in the Second World War* (Manchester, 1996), pp. 177–92.
2. Michel Mourlet, 'Apologie de la Violence', *Cahiers du Cinema*, 107, p. 24, reprinted in C. Gledhill (ed.), *Stardom: Industry of Desire* (London, 1991), p. 234.
3. Jeffrey Richards, *The Age of the Dream Palace: Cinema and Society in Britain 1930–1939* (London, 1984), p. 161.
4. See Ibid., pp. 155–224; and Kuhn, 'Cinema Culture and Femininity', pp. 181–6.
5. The Conrad Veidt Society in California still has a twice-yearly international newsletter full of arcane and fascinating material: it can be contacted via James H. Rathlesburger, 2757 Eleventh Avenue, Sacramento, California 95818.
6. Michael Powell, *A Life in Movies* (London, 1986), p. 306.
7. Fritz Sharf, 'Crescendo und Decrescendo', *Film und Brettl*, 1, January 1922, quoted in Wolfgang Jacobsen, *Conrad Veidt: Lebensbilder* (Berlin, 1993), p. 43.
8. See Michael Balcon, *Michael Balcon Presents … a Lifetime of Films* (London, 1969), pp.

74–6; and J. Allen, *Conrad Veidt: from Caligari to Casablanca* (Pacific Grove, California, 1987), pp. 133–40.

9. Public Record Office, Kew, BT 64/1000. Here the Home Office notes in a memo dated 13 April 1937 that Veidt 'is said to have established a permanent home in England and earnestly to desire naturalisation as soon as may be'.

10. In PRO HO 334/153, Veidt's naturalisation certificate can be found (no. AZ13570), together with his Oath of Allegiance. According to the Home Office, the detailed file on Veidt is no longer in existence.

11. These are release dates taken from Denis Gifford, *The British Film Catalogue 1895–1985* (London, 1986).

12. In the yearly poll of 'Ten Best Performances' in *Film Weekly*, Veidt came second in 1933 for his role in *I Was a Spy* (Madeleine Carroll came first for her role in the same film). In 1934 he came second for his role in *The Wandering Jew*, and in 1935 came sixth for his role in *Jew Süss*. In the *Picturegoer* poll for 1933, he came fourth for *I Was a Spy*; in its 1934 poll he came eighth and ninth for his roles in *The Wandering Jew* and *Jew Süss* respectively.

13. *Kinematograph Weekly*, 13 January 1938, 11 January 1940, 9 January 1941, 8 January 1942.

14. *Kinematograph Weekly*, 25 October 1934. It comments that Gaumont experienced a 'dislocation in finding stories for Conrad Veidt'.

15. Michael Balcon Papers, BFI Library, MEB C/30, material on *Karenina* project: 'there is no question of the international value of Conrad Veidt.'

16. *Film Weekly*, 12 March 1938; and Karol Kulik, *Alexander Korda: the Man Who Could Work Miracles* (London, 1975), p. 208.

17. This was 'There's a Lighthouse Shines Across the Bay', which was a song from the multi-lingual UFA science-fiction film called *FPI*. It was released in recordings by Veidt, Hans Albers and Charles Boyer. There is interesting material on the song on the sleeve of the CD *Why Ever Did They? Hollywood Stars at the Microphone* (Flapper, PAST CD 9735).

18. For full filmographies, see *Focus on Film*, 21, Summer 1975; *Movie*, 114, 1982; Allen, *Conrad Veidt*; and *Films in Review*, April, June and August 1993. There is some very useful reprinted material in Jacobsen, *Conrad Veidt: Lebensbilder*.

19. See Lotte Eisner, *The Haunted Screen* (London, 1973), pp. 137–49, on acting style and expressionism.

20. S. Freud, 'Psychopathic Stage Characters', in Penguin Freud Library Vol. 14, *Art and Literature* (Harmondsworth, 1990), p. 125: 'psychological drama turns into psychopathological drama when the source of the suffering in which we take part and from which we are meant to derive pleasure is no longer a conflict between two almost equally conscious impulses but between a conscious impulse and a repressed one.' See also Otto Fenichel, 'Neurotic Acting Out', *Psychoanalytic Review*, no. 32, 1945, pp. 197–206.

21. Jean-Marc Campagne, *Clovis Trouille* (Paris, 1965), pp. 27, 129. Trouille planned to give Veidt the paintings, but the actor's premature death prevented it. For other significant responses by artists and intellectuals to Veidt's performances in silent film, see Jacobsen, *Conrad Veidt: Lebensbilder*.

22. Christopher Isherwood, *Christopher and His Kind* (London, 1976), pp. 32–3.

23. Quoted in Wilfred Barlow, *More Talk of Alexander* (London, 1978), p. 300.

24. Wilfred Barlow, *The Alexander Technique* (London, 1973), p. 17. See also Barlow, *More Talk*; F. M. Alexander, *The Uses of the Self* (London, 1932); Aldous Huxley, *Ends and Means* (London, 1937). Of course, the Alexander technique had been in vogue in Weimar culture in the 1920s, and had informed many of the 1920s modern dance movements and performances on Berlin stages.

25. There are no extant papers about pupils from the 1930s at the Society for Teachers of the Alexander technique.

26. See Balcon, *Michael Balcon Presents*, pp. 55–99; and Sue Harper, 'Nothing to Beat the Hay Diet: Comedy at Gaumont-British and Gainsborough', in Pam Cook (ed.), *Gainsborough Studios* (London, 1997).

27. Besides offering employment to all the foreign nationals mentioned above, Balcon was negotiating to employ Max Reinhardt in 1934; see Balcon Papers (BFI Library), MEB C/30, exchange of letters between Balcon and C. M. Woolf.

28. PRO FO 395/487, FO memo, 16 September 1933.

29. Press Book of *Rome Express*, in BFI Library.

30. BBFC Scenario Notes (BFI Library), 9 May 1932. Normally, of course, the Board was extremely punctilious in this regard.

31. *Rome Express*, shooting script, S.4372, BFI Library.

32. Geoff Brown (ed.), *Walter Forde* (London, 1977), pp. 29–31.

33. See Balcon, *Michael Balcon Presents*, p. 63. See also a telegram in the Balcon Papers (BFI Library), C4 MEB C14: 'no time should be lost for Veidt subject irrespective of who directs.'

34. Daniela Sannwald, 'Continental Stranger; Conrad Veidt und Seine Britischen Filme', in Jorg Schoning (ed.), *London Calling: Deutsche im Britischen Film der 30er Jahre* (Munich, 1993), p. 89.

35. Pre-production script of *I Was a Spy*, S7670, BFI Library.

36. *Picturegoer*, 20 May 1933. Several other journals felt that the film signalled a new British realism which was anti-Hollywood: see *Daily Mail*, 4 September 1933; *News Chronicle*, 2 September 1933; and *Star*, 4 September 1933.

37. Balcon, *Michael Balcon Presents*, pp. 74–5. Prince Youssupoff and his wife brought a successful (and expensive) libel suit against MGM for suggesting, in *Rasputin and the Empress*, that the Princess had had a liaison with Rasputin.

38. Press Book of *I Was a Spy* in BFI Library.

39. *Film Weekly*, 22 April 1933.

40. Balcon, *Michael Balcon Presents*, p. 75.

41. Balcon Papers (BFI Library), E1, rough notes by Balcon dated 4 March 1937.

42. See *British Film Reporter*, January 1934, for general material on Hagen. See an unpublished MPhil thesis by Linda Wood, *Low Budget Production and the British Film Industry, with Particular Reference to Julius Hagen and Twickenham Film Studios 1927–38* (Polytechnic of Central London, 1989).

43. See H. Fowler Mear, *Power Behind the Throne* (London, 1931), and *Dangerous Love* (London, 1933) which, in terms of literary resources and competence, are at least 25 years out of date.

44. There is an interesting account of the theatrical version of *The Wandering Jew* in David Farrar, *No Royal Road* (Eastbourne, 1947), pp. 78–86. See BBFC scenario report of the film on 16 February 1933 (BFI Library).

45. *Picturegoer*, 19 August 1933.

46. See *Picturegoer*, 12 May 1934.

47. The BBFC scenario notes (6 February 1933, in BFI Library) are interesting; it is 'strong' material, but permitted because the woman in punished.

48. The book is structured so as to represent the class interests of five groups: the Princes, the People, the Jews, the Duke and the Others: see Edwin and Willa Muir's translation of Lion Feuchtwanger's *Jew Süss* (London, 1927).

49. See Dorothy Farnum and A. R. Rawlinson, *Jew Süss: Scenario of a Film* (London, 1935). This contains much useful information on the production history of the film. See also *Film Weekly*, 5 October 1934 for more details.

50. Balcon, *Michael Balcon Presents*, pp. 85–6.

51. Balcon Papers (BFI Library), MEB C/30, telegram from Balcon to Somlo: 'It would be a great stunt to have the three first cities of the world show this picture simultaneously.' See also ibid., E1, rough notes by Balcon dated 4 March 1937: 'We knew certain costume pictures had been successful and we were looking for a costume picture which was fictional rather than biographical or historical.'

52. Conrad Veidt, 'My Conception of the Jew', *Film Weekly*, 5 October 1934.

53. See Bryan Cheyette, *Construction of 'the Jew' in English Literature and Society: Racial Representations 1875–1945* (Cambridge, 1993).

54. *Picturegoer*, 28 April 1934.

55. Isherwood, *Christopher and His Kind*, p. 129.

56. *Picturegoer*, 12 May 1934; *Film Weekly*, 4 May 1934. American journals dealt differently, and in a less nuanced way, with Veidt's technique and charisma: see *Modern Screen*, June 1941.

57. *Film Weekly*, 5 April 1935. See also *Film Weekly*, 4 May 1934.

58. *Film Weekly*, 4 May 1934. He uses the same wireless metaphor in *Picturegoer*, 29 June 1939.

59. *Film Weekly*, 5 April 1935. See also *Film Weekly*, 2 August 1935.

60. BBFC scenario notes (in BFI library), 22 December 1932. This was a version first submitted by Fox. Gaumont-British had to take account of that when they submitted their scenario on 5 September 1933.

61. *The Times*, 13 April 1936. For Viertel's obituary, see *The Times*, 26 September 1953. See also Salka Viertel, *The Kindness of Strangers* (New York, 1969). In *Film Weekly*, 3 May 1935, Viertel insists that his work should be seen within the context of a European non-naturalist perspective. Viertel was, of course, the model for the *émigré* director in Isherwood's *Prater Violet*. (See Chapter 10 of this book for further details on Viertel.)

62. *Passing of the Third Floor Back*, shooting script, S.4372, BFI Library.

63. *Picturegoer*, 29 June 1935.

64. BBFC Scenario Notes (BFI Library), 27 March 1934, and resubmitted story 20 May 1935.

65. Balcon Papers (BFI Library), E1, rough notes by Balcon dated 4 March 1937. There is some material on the film in Brown (ed.), *Walter Forde*, pp. 35–6.

66. *King of the Damned*, final draft screenplay, S.7499, BFI library.

67. *Film Weekly*, 1 January 1938.

68. *Dark Journey*, Screenplay, S.7687, BFI Library.

69. Harper, *Picturing the Past*, pp. 20–30.

70. PRO BT 64/100. The whole file is invaluable since it shows the labyrinthine corporate structures (and often scams) involved in American-owned subsidiaries.

71. Ibid., the director received only £3,000.

72. *Film Weekly*, 29 December 1936.

73. *Film Weekly*, 12 March 1938.

74. Powell, *A Life in Movies*, pp. 302, 306.

75. Ibid., p. 305.

76. Ibid.

77. *The Spy in Black*, script dated 20 October, S.6804, BFI Library.

78. *Film Weekly*, September 1939.

79. Powell, *A Life in Movies*, p. 339.

80. *Picturegoer*, 13 April 1940.

81. *Picturegoer*, 25 February 1939.

82. PRO BT 64/114. The Board suspected all the personnel (Corfield the producer,

Powell, Junge and Veidt) of all being in a conspiracy together: a memo from Somervell on 15 July 1940 suggested 'one can only hope that if they are cheating they will sooner or later fall out'. Veidt's fee was said to be £7,000, Powell's was £2,000.

## 7. Tod Slaughter and the cinema of excess

1. John Ellis, 'Art, Culture and Quality', *Screen*, 19, Autumn 1978, pp. 9–49.

2. *The Cruel Sea*, *The Dambusters* and *Reach for the Sky* were the top box-office money-makers of 1953, 1955 and 1956.

3. Jeffrey Richards, *The Age of the Dream Palace: Cinema and Society in Britain 1930–1939* (London, 1984).

4. *The Times*, 22 May 1939.

5. Slaughter gets no mention at all in such standard histories of the British cinema as Charles Oakley, *Where We Came in* (London, 1964); George Perry, *The Great British Picture Show* (London, 1975); Roy Armes, *A Critical History of British Cinema* (London, 1978); Charles Barr (ed.), *All Our Yesterdays: 90 Years of British Cinema* (London, 1986); and Marcia Landy, *British Genres: Cinema and Society, 1930–1960* (Princeton, 1991). He gets a single mention in Rachael Low, *Film Making in 1930s Britain* (London, 1985), p. 187 ('old fashioned melodramas ... that were almost burlesques').

6. David Pirie, *A Heritage of Horror: The English Gothic Cinema 1946–1972* (London, 1973) and Peter Hutchings, *Hammer and Beyond: the British Horror Film* (Manchester, 1993) on Hammer; Sue Aspinall and Robert Murphy (eds), *Gainsborough Melodrama* (London, 1983) and Sue Harper, *Picturing the Past: the Rise and Fall of the British Costume Film* (London, 1994) on Gainsborough.

7. *World Film News*, 2, no. 7, October, 1937, pp. 3–4.

8. *The Spectator*, 6 October 1939, reprinted in David Parkinson (ed.), *The Graham Greene Film Reader: Mornings in the Dark* (Manchester, 1993), p. 333.

9. Michael Booth, *English Melodrama* (London, 1965), p. 14.

10. See for instance Jacky Bratton, Jim Cook and Christine Gledhill (eds), *Melodrama: Stage Picture Screen* (London, 1994); and David Mayer, *Playing Out the Empire* (Oxford, 1994).

11. Peter Brooks, *The Melodramatic Imagination* (New Haven and London, 1976), p. 4.

12. Ibid., p. 15.

13. Ibid., p. 41.

14. A. Nicholas Vardac, *Stage to Screen* (Cambridge, MA., 1949).

15. Bratton et al. (eds), *Melodrama*, p. 96.

16. Allen Eyles and David Meeker (eds), *Missing Believed Lost* (London, 1992), p. 35.

17. *World Film News*, 2, no. 7, p. 3.

18. *World Film News*, 2, no. 7, p. 4.

19. Derek Threadgall, *Shepperton Studios: an Independent View* (London, 1994), p. 38.

20. Michael Kilgarriff, *The Golden Age of Melodrama* (London, 1974), p. 204.

21. BBFC Scenario Reports 379 (1935), held at British Film Institute.

22. Peter Haining, *The Mystery and Horrible Murders of Sweeney Todd* (London, 1979).

23. BBFC Scenario Reports 507 (BFI Library), 1935.

24. David Mayer, '"The Ticket of Leave Man" in Context', *Essays in Theatre*, 6 November 1987, pp. 31–40.

25. The film was shot with the graverobbers called Burke and Hare but the BBFC objected to the use of the names of authentic murderers and film had to be redubbed with the villains rechristened Moore and Hart.

## 8. Jack of all trades

1.  Patrick McGilligan, 'Who is the World's Most Successful Director?', *American Film*, vol. III, no. 5, March 1978.

2.  Ibid., p. 21.

3.  'Robert Stevenson', in John Wakeman (ed.), *World Film Directors: Volume 1* (New York, 1987), p. 1058.

4.  Linda Wood (ed.), *The Commercial Imperative in the British Film Industry: Maurice Elvey, a Case Study* (London, 1987), p. 3.

5.  Nicholas Wapshott, *The Man Between: a Biography of Carol Reed* (London, 1990), p. 69.

6.  Michael Balcon, *Michael Balcon Presents ... a Lifetime of Films* (London, 1969), p. 19.

7.  Ibid., p. 125.

8.  McGilligan, 'Who is the World's Most Successful Director?', p. 22.

9.  'The Camels Are Coming', reviewed in *Film Weekly*, 28 December 1934, p. 32.

10. The term was coined by Tom Gunning in 'The Cinema of Attractions: Early Film, its Spectator, and the Avant-Garde' (*Screen*, vol. 19, no. 4, pp. 1878–9), and used by Andrew Higson in his discussion of *Comin' Thro' the Rye*, *Sing As We Go* and *Evergreen* in *Waving the Flag: Constructing a National Cinema in Britain* (Oxford, 1995).

11. Higson, *Waving the Flag*, p. 146.

12. Nova Pilbeam spoke of Stevenson as a 'supportive' director: see interview in Brian McFarlane (ed.) *Sixty Voices: Celebrities Recall the Golden Age of British Cinema* (London, 1992), p. 73.

13. Graham Greene, *The Pleasure Dome: The Collected Film Criticism 1935–40* (London, 1972), p. 73.

14. Ray Seaton and Roy Martin, 'Gainsborough', *Films and Filming*, no. 332, May 1982, p. 14.

15. *Film Weekly*, 10 October 1936, p. 32.

16. *Film Weekly*, 3 July 1937, p. 27.

17. Greene, *Pleasure Dome*, p. 161.

18. Marcia Landy, *British Genres: Cinema and Society, 1930–1960* (Princeton, 1991), p. 104.

19. Jeffrey Richards, *The Age of the Dream Palace: Cinema and Society in Britain 1930–1939* (London, 1984), p. 136.

20. William K. Everson, 'Rediscovery', *Films in Review*, vol. XXVIII, no. 5, May 1977, p. 301.

21. Interview with Desmond Tester, July 1996.

22. See R. Ewart Williams, 'Anna and Bob', *Film Weekly*, 8 April 1939, p. 7, in which they discuss this year off, at the end of which 'The novel was successfully completed, and they were proud parents of a daughter'.

23. Graham Greene felt it was 'a pity Mr Stevenson was not given something better to make than his own refined and bitter-sweet story'. *The Graham Greene Film Reader* (Manchester, 1993), p. 235.

24. Charles Barr, *Ealing Studios* (London, 1977; 2nd edn, 1993), p. 16.

25. Robert Morley and Sewell Stokes, *Robert Morley: 'Responsible Gentleman'* (London, 1966).

26. Morley and Stokes, *Robert Morley*, p. 96.

27. Rachael Low, *Film Making in 1930s Britain* (London, 1985), p. 254.

28. Balcon, *Michael Balcon Presents*, p. 119.

29. *Film Weekly*, Vol. 21, No. 539, p. 31.

30. *Kinematograph Weekly*, 8 December 1955, p. 19.

31. Balcon, *Michael Balcon Presents*, p. 120.

32. It was remade in Hollywood in 1947 as *Thunder in the Valley (Bob, Son of Battle* in Britain).

33. Seaton and Martin, 'Gainsborough', p. 14.

34. Interview with Desmond Tester, July 1996.

# 9. Money for speed

Heartfelt thanks are due to Bernard Vorhaus for talking to me; and to David Meeker, Feature Films Officer of the National Film and Television Archive, and the Archive's Viewing Service (Elaine Burrows, Bryony Dixon, Alison Strauss), for all their help and encouragement, past and present.

1. *Variety*, 3 April 1934.

2. The path to Vorhaus's rediscovery begins with David Lean, who was being interviewed by Kevin Brownlow for a Thames Television programme. Asked if there had been any particular director in Britain whose work he had admired in his days in the early 1930s as an apprentice editor, Lean immediately nominated Bernard Vorhaus. The name rang only the vaguest of bells; the few reference books that listed Vorhaus lost track of him after his Hollywood work for Republic and RKO in the late 1930s and 1940s, and a few independently produced films of the early 1950s. Brownlow's researcher, Jo Wright, was asked to dig further, and found Vorhaus nestling quietly in the London phone book, forgotten by the film community and undisturbed for decades. David Meeker, Feature Films Officer at the National Film and Television Archive, rounded up available prints of Vorhaus's British films and screened them for interested parties, Vorhaus included. Meeker's enthusiasm paved the way for the NFTVA's tribute to Vorhaus's work at the Edinburgh Film Festival in August 1986, and a larger season at the National Film Theatre in December. The first extended article on Vorhaus, 'Vorhaus: a Director Rediscovered', by Geoff Brown, appeared in *Sight and Sound*, Winter 1986/87. If Lean had not mentioned the name of Vorhaus, would any of this have happened?

3. George Pearson, *Flashback: the Autobiography of a British Film-maker* (London, 1957), p. 193.

4. Quoted in Kevin Brownlow, *David Lean* (London, 1996), p. 82.

5. Interview with Geoff Brown, London, 30 July 1986. Unless mentioned otherwise, all other quotations from Bernard Vorhaus come from this source.

6. The National Film and Television Archive holds a viewing print of three burlesques grouped together under the title *Gorno's Italian Marionettes*; direction is credited to Jack Harrison, with Henrik Galeen as supervising director.

7. See Allen Eyles and David Meeker (eds), *Missing Believed Lost* (London, 1992), p. 45.

8. A surviving print, dubbed into French, was not available for viewing.

9. *Picturegoer*, quoted in Eyles and Meeker (eds), *Missing Believed Lost* pp. 45-6.

10. *Variety*, 12 February, 1935.

11. Eyles and Meeker (eds), *Missing Believed Lost*, p. 63.

12. Interview with David Meeker, Tony Rayns and Jim Hickey, 22 April 1986.

# 10. Berthold Viertel at Gaumont-British

1. Rachael Low, *Film Making in 1930s Britain* (London, 1985), p. 142.

2. Peter Viertel, *Dangerous Friends: Hemingway, Huston, and Others* (New York, 1992).

3. For Fox he directed *The One Woman Idea* (1929), *Seven Faces* (1929), *Man Trouble* (1930), *The Spy* (1931).

4. For *Die heilige Flamme*, the German version of Somerset Maugham's *The Secret Flame*.

5. *The Magnificent Lie* (1931), *The Wiser Sex* and *The Man from Yesterday* (1932).

6. Quoted in Salka Viertel, *The Kindness of Strangers* (New York, 1969), pp. 170–1.

7. His mother died in March 1932, his father in December.

8. *Joseph und seine Brüde* (1933–43) was a tetralogy.

9. Quoted in S. Viertel, *Kindness*, p. 180.

10. The German version of *Der Aufstand der Fisher St Barbara* was scrapped, a Russian one, *Vostniye Rybakov*, went ahead.

11. Quoted in S. Viertel, *Kindness*, p. 185.

12. In a letter to his wife, he gives the production company as Europa Film, a distribution company which was, most likely, financing it. *Kleiner Mann, was nun?* was made in 1933 by Robert Neppach Filmprod, directed by Fritz Wendhausen, with Hermann Thimig, Hertha Thiele, Vicktor de Kowa, Fritz Kampers, Theo Lingen and Blandine Ebinger in the cast.

13. Directed by Frank Borzage, with Margaret Sullavan, Douglass Montgomery, Alan Hale, Catherine Doucet and Mae Marsh.

14. S. Viertel, *Kindness*, p. 185.

15. Ibid. Wendhausen, known as Frederick Wendhausen (1900–62), came to Britain in 1937 and became naturalised after the war. He appears in *The First of the Few* (1942).

16. Isherwood had been suggested by Jean Ross, the original Sally Bowles, as a replacement for Margaret Kennedy who had left to work on one of her stage vehicles for Elisabeth Bergner, *Escape Me Never!*

17. Quoted in Berthold Viertel, 'Christopher Isherwood and Dr. Friedrich Bergmann', in *Theatre Arts*, May 1946.

18. Christopher Isherwood, *Christopher and His Kind 1929–1939* (London, 1977), pp. 119–21.

19. *Picturegoer*, 7 April 1934.

20. *Little Friend* (July 1934), prod. Michael Balcon; assoc. prod. Robert Stevenson; dir. Berthold Viertel; scr. Margaret Kennedy, Christopher Isherwood, Berthold Viertel from the novel *Kleiner Freundin* by Ernst Lothar; ph. Günther Krampf; asst. cam. Erwin Hillier; des. Alfred Junge; mus. Ernst Toch; ed. Ian Dalrymple. Cast includes: Matheson Lang, Nova Pilbeam, Jimmy Hanley, Lydia Sherwood, Jean Cadell, Allan Aynesworth, Lewis Casson, Cecil Parker, Finlay Currie, Fritz Kortner.

21. Christopher Isherwood, *Prater Violet*, (London 1946), p. 17.

22. C. A. Lejeune, *Observer*, 2 September, 1934.

23. In October 1936, when he gave evidence in court, Krampf spoke through an interpreter.

24. I am grateful for this technical information to Erwin Hillier, Krampf's camera assistant on this film, who was born in Berlin and, being bilingual, was frequently assigned to German-speaking cine-photographers.

25. Kortner's English was poor at the time; he had to learn his part in *Abdul the Damned* (1935) phonetically, and in his autobiography, *Alle Tage Abend* (Munich, 1959) p. 14, he describes himself as a *Sprachtclown*.

26. The failure to take this important shot was a characteristic attempt to save money by Gaumont-British.

27. *New York Post*, 13 May 1936.

28. Berthold Viertel, 'The Function of the Director', *Cinema Quarterly*, Summer 1934, pp. 206–210.

29. *Jewish Chronicle*, 8 February 1935.

30. *New York Post*, 16 February 1936.

31. *Variety*, 28 February 1936.

32. Robert Dunbar to author, 6 December 1996.

33. B. Viertel, 'Christopher Isherwood ... '.

34. Letter from Montagu to S. Chandos Balcon, 5 April 1935. S. C. Balcon is the executive referred to in *Christopher and His Kind*, p. 127. Although it should be treated with caution, according to Isherwood, he disliked Viertel intensely and described him as not 'a Jew at all but one of these mongrels Ashkenazim, mixed-up scum from Poland or God knows where'. As with all Isherwood's writings, it is unreliable history.

35. *The Passing of the Third Floor Back* (1935), prod. Michael Balcon; assoc. prod. Ivor Montagu; scr. Michael Hogan, Alma Reville from the play by Jerome K. Jerome; ph. Curt Courant; des. Oscar Werndorff; ed. Derek Twist. Cast: Conrad Veidt, René Ray, Anna Lee, Frank Cellier, Mary Clare, Beatrix Lehmann, John Turnbull, Cathleen Nesbitt, Ronald Ward, Sarah Allgood, Barbara Everest, Jack Livesey.

36. *Film Weekly*, 3 May 1935.

37. T. T. Fleming, *Film Weekly*, 8 May 1935.

38. *Jewish Chronicle*, 4 October 1935.

39. François Lafitte, *The Internment of Aliens* (Harmondsworth, 1940), pp. 26–8.

40. Quoted in S. Viertel, *Kindness*, pp. 224–5.

41. Jeffrey Richards, 'Patriotism with Profit, British Imperial Cinema in the 1930s', in J. Curran and V. Porter (eds), *British Cinema History* (London, 1983), pp. 245–56.

42. *Rhodes of Africa* (1936), prod. Michael Balcon; assoc. prod. Geoffrey Barkas; scr. Leslie Arliss, Michael Barringer from the book by Sarah Millin; dial. Miles Malleson; ph. Bernard Knowles; ed. Derek Twist.

43. For more on this see Natalie Barkas, *Thirty Thousand Miles for the Films* (London, 1937).

44. *Picturegoer Summer Annual* (1936), p. 72.

45. Quoted from the *Hollywood Spectator*, in *The Times*, 14 April 1936.

46. *The Times*, 13 April 1936.

47. *The Times*, 20 April 1936.

48. Richards, 'Patriotism with Profit', p. 253.

49. Detailed in Robert Murphy, 'The Coming of Sound to the Cinema in Britain', in *Historical Journal of Film, Radio, and Television*, vol. 4, no. 2 (1984), pp. 143–60.

50. Work was to stop on 12 March 1937. Six hundred studio workers 'will have to look for other jobs'; it blamed the American market for not buying.

51. The *Weiner Library Bulletin*, vol. VII, p. 40, gives details of its membership, its honorary presidents, and its policies. Among its hon. presidents were: Albert Einstein, Lion Feuchtwanger, Oskar Kokoshka, Thomas Mann and Stefan Zweig.

52. These included *The Lost Year*, a film collaboration with Stefan Zweig.

53. Letter to John Lehmann, 7 July 1939, quoted in Jonathan Fryer, *Isherwood* (London, 1977), p. 195.

54. B. Viertel, 'Christopher Isherwood ...'.

55. Thornton Delahanty, *New York Post*, 26 February 1936.

56. *World Film News*, July 1936.

57. He directed more than 120 theatre productions.

58. *New Statesman and Nation*, 3 October 1953.

## 11. Loose ends, hidden gems and the moment of 'melodramatic emotionality'

My thanks to Rowana Agajanian for her help in the course of researching this paper.

1. See Rachael Low, *Film Making in 1930s Britain* (London, 1985), pp. 36, 129, 359; Patricia Warren, *British Film Studios* (London, 1995), pp. 166, 168; Paul Rotha, *The Film Till Now* (London, 1930), p. 319; and Rotha, *Documentary Diary* (London, 1973), pp. 39, 66, 67.

Mark Gatiss's biography *James Whale* (London, 1995), pp. 46–7, elaborates slightly on the rejections of Gundrey's initial draft for *Journey's End* by its director Whale and associate producer, George Pearson. 'Gundrey's script had excellent points, technically it was well written, but I felt it over-elaborated much that only needed the utter simplicity of the play,' Pearson stated, and, 'To my mind, the stark realism of *Journey's End* was due to Sherriff's observation of life, rather than its dissection.' Gatiss also mentions briefly (p. 142) that Miles Mander played Aramis of 'the Three Musketeers', alongside Alan Hale and Bert Roach, in James Whale's later adaptation of Alexandre Dumas's *The Man in the Iron Mask* (1939). Finally, a letter to *Sight and Sound* late in 1968, arguing that Mander was 'a British film-maker long overdue for rediscovery', prompted the characteristic response from Paul Rotha that he had already championed his cause, offered 'a considered estimate of this gifted film-maker' in his earlier book *The Film Till Now*, and reiterated the claim that Mander showed, indeed, 'a filmic skill unrecognised in England'. See, *Sight and Sound*, vol. 38, no. 1 (Winter 1968/69), p. 54 and vol. 38, no. 2 (Spring 1969), p. 108.

2. Adrianne Allen's stage career certainly received due acknowledgement on her death in 1993. 'Discovered' by Noel Coward and tipped by theatre critics to become 'a star of the very first magnitude' after appearing in his plays *Easy Virtue* in 1926 and *Private Lives* in 1930, Allen became a successful West End and Broadway actress as well as a member of the smart Coward set where her exceptional organising abilities as a busy society hostess prompted Coward's affectionate nickname, 'Planny Annie'. Allen's private life also attracted some comment perhaps inevitably given that, as one obituary claimed, it was 'itself worthy of a Coward script'; married to Raymond Massey from 1929 to 1939, she gave birth to two children (Daniel Massey and Anna Massey), before later marrying the ex-husband of her own former husband's new-found wife. See the obituaries for Adrianne Allen in the *Independent* (16 September 1993), *The Times* and *Daily Telegraph* (both 17 September 1993), and the *Guardian* (22 September 1993). There are also references to Allen in the autobiographies by Raymond Massey, *A Hundred Different Lives* (London, 1979), and Laurence Olivier, *Confessions of an Actor* (London, 1984).

There is nothing on Allen's film career in America but for the work of Dorothy Arzner, Agnes Brand Leahy, Vera Caspary, and Paramount's then 'new initiative to promote women in key production and creative positions', as Lizzie Francke puts it, see the various references in her *Script Girls, Women Screenwriters in Hollywood* (London, 1994), and Claire Johnstone (ed.), *The Work of Dorothy Arzner – Towards a Feminist Cinema* (London, 1975), both of which helped to contextualise my own researches on Adrianne Allen and Marjorie Gaffney.

3. Miles Mander, 'The Feminine Touch', *Film Weekly*, 4 May 1934, p. 29. Gaffney was married to cameraman Freddie Young who shot many of the films she worked upon during the 1930s starting with *The W Plan* (1930). One of Gaffney's solo scripted works for Jessie Matthews, *First a Girl* (1935), has recently proved a rich source of interest among some commentators with several noting its self-conscious use of the cross-dressing theme to raise questions of sexual identity, albeit ultimately compromised, in the midst

of an otherwise traditional mainstream British film entertainment. See, for example, Jeffrey Richards, *The Age of the Dream Palace: Cinema and Society in Britain 1930–1939* (London, 1984), pp. 216–19; Marcia Landy, *British Genres: Cinema and Society, 1930–1960* (Princeton, 1991), pp. 341–3; and Andrew Higson, sleeve notes, 1992 Connoisseur Video release of *First a Girl*.

All note its challenging and provocative aspects which are attributed, in part, to the fact that the British film was an adaptation of an original German version, Reinhold Schunzel's *Viktor und Viktoria* (1933). But Richards stresses that 'The Continental sophistication of the plot [was] toned down for the English censors' and that the film's theme of male and female impersonation simply drew, anyway, upon 'a long-established element of the British theatrical tradition' which 'inevitably entered the cinema' and was used by Gracie Fields (in *Shipyard Sally*, 1939) and Cicely Courtneidge (*Me and Marlborough*, 1935, co-written by Marjorie Gaffney, interestingly enough) as well as by Jessie Matthews (p. 218). Landy and Higson, by contrast, emphasise other factors for a loss in 'the ambiguities of cross-dressing'. Landy attributes it to 'Saville's and Matthews's ability to make the cross-dressing appear unpremeditated, naive and motivated by economic necessity' (p. 343). While Higson argues that 'Matthews's persona of child-like innocence tends to displace such questions – partly onto the different paradox of the child-woman' and concludes that with the narrative resolution at the film's end 'patriarchy has been rendered once more unambiguous'. But nobody has said anything, as yet, about the precise nature of Marjorie Gaffney's script input to the film which merits further research in the light of her work overall for British cinema. Blake Edwards made yet a third version of the film, *Victor/Victoria* (1982), as a starring vehicle for his wife, Julie Andrews, and subsequently adapted it once again as a stage musical for presentation on Broadway in 1995.

4. Before Miles Mander left for America in 1936, he wrote *To My Son – In Confidence* (London, 1934), which was in effect a series of letters to be opened ten years later by his son, then aged seven. This is a fascinating account of his private thoughts and philosophy covering a diverse array of topics including: 'Your birth and antecedents', 'Your mother and I', 'On school and things', 'On your King and Country', 'On religion', 'On politics', 'On sexual morality', 'On the arts', 'On war and peace', 'On women and marriage', 'On worldly conduct and character'. 'The interest of the book does not lie in the novelty or insight of the advice given in it', said one reviewer, 'but in its embodiment of the reactions of a temperament typical of the day to its problems.' See, *Times Literary Supplement*, 9 August 1934, p. 552.

If that is indeed the case, it says much about both the man and the period. Although plainly enlightened and liberal-minded in most respects, Mander's book also reveals many contradictions. It is, for instance, both an outspoken attack on the public schools, for which he was rebuked by the headmaster of Harrow, and also a virulent indictment of homosexuality. The tensions Mander highlights throughout, of course, make him all the more interesting in retrospect. So, too, does his continuing career in America where, in addition to his film output, he soon became known as a radio commentator with his own programme, a popular following, and thus an important propagandist role to play (on Britain's behalf) with the advent of war. By 1943, for example, he was a member of the British Consulate War Services Advisory Board along with other members of the expatriate film community in Hollywood, including Brian Aherne, Ronald Colman, Sir Cedric Hardwicke, Herbert Marshall, Basil Rathbone and R. C. Sherriff. Its activities in promoting British propaganda in America have been well outlined in an account by the Board's then co-ordinator, the British Consul in Los Angeles, for which see: Eric Cleugh, *Without Let or Hindrance*, (London, 1960), pp. 105–38. Mander died on 8 February 1946 aged 57, meriting obituaries in *The Times* (11 February 1946) and the *New York Times* (9 February 1946).

5. Justine King, 'Crossing Thresholds: the Contemporary British Woman's Film', in A. Higson (ed.), *Dissolving Views: Key Writings on British Cinema* (London, 1996), pp. 218–19. On related issues see, also: Richard Dyer, 'Feeling English', *Sight and Sound*, vol. 4, no. 3 (NS, 1994), pp. 17–19; Annette Kuhn, '*Mandy* and Possibility', *Screen*, vol. 33, no. 3 (1992), pp. 233–43; and Sue Harper and Vincent Porter, 'Moved to Tears: Weeping in the Cinema in Postwar Britain', *Screen*, vol. 37, no. 2 (1996), pp. 152–73.

6. Quoted in Geoff Brown (ed.), *Launder and Gilliatt* (London, 1977), p. 3, though other instances of this opinion are legion in standard histories of British cinema.

7. James C. Robertson, *The British Board of Film Censors: Film Censorship in Britain, 1896–1950* (London, 1985), pp. 52–3, details thoroughly both the personnel changes at the BBFC, and the technical problems encountered over sound film, not least with the need to institute a censorship process whereby producers would be quickly apprised of likely contentious or controversial matters before money or resources were expended in production. Although obviously aware of the limitations upon BBFC control that also initially attended the implementation of pre-production script scrutiny, he does not investigate what I would describe as the short-lived 'window of opportunity' it afforded some producers to get on with making the films they wanted to make with rather less of the usual interventionist BBFC input than generally obtained.

Though I am dealing here with the society drama genre and what I consider its propensity for 'melodramatic emotionality', to borrow Justine King's words, there are of course other films from the same period which would merit further research to ascertain whether they too shared the fundamental tenets of woman's film and have perhaps been misappropriated under the umbrella of different genres, in order to maintain the dominant characterisation of British cinema. Maurice Elvey's *High Treason*, for instance, was a comparatively lavish science-fiction film clearly modelled in its futuristic landscapes and settings upon Fritz Lang's *Metropolis* (1926), which attracted critical attention on release in August 1929 largely because of its novelty value as one of the first British films with sound. In retrospect, more attention has been paid to its pacifist theme, its prediction about the importance of surprise aerial attack in future war, and its role as harbinger of several films which followed later in the decade along the same prescient lines – e. g. Maurice Elvey's *The Tunnel* (1934) and Alexander Korda's production of H. G. Wells's *Things to Come* (1936). See Low, *Film Making*, p. 131; Richards, *Age of the Dream Palace*, pp. 284–5; and Linda Wood (ed.), *The Commercial Imperative in the British Film Industry: Maurice Elvey, a Case Study* (London, 1987), pp. 14–16.

Commentators have noted, in fact, the importance of women characters throughout the film as arch exponents of peace and leading instigators of moves to prevent a war. What has been overlooked in all accounts thus far is the extent and significance of the changes made when transposing Noël Pemberton-Billing's original play from stage to screen. Pemberton-Billing was an Independent MP, stalwart patriot and fervent moral crusader, but the stage production of his play, first presented at the Strand Theatre on 7 November 1928, was an altogether different matter to the film version. It had just one woman in the cast, played by Ursula Jeans, and, as C. G. Grey's preface to the published stage text states, this character was 'not essential to the play and perhaps put in because a play must have some feminine interest ... She is a picture of a thoroughly nice girl – a term which is almost one of reproach in these days.' As can be seen from comparison of the privately printed 1928 play script with the finished 1929 film, the futuristic setting of the film was a brand-new concept. In particular, the new-found emphasis on women as the principal motivating force in realising a full-blown pacifist enterprise was wholly original in design, and only instigated for the screenplay. As a film, in short, *High Treason* was predominantly woman-centred in a way the original play had clearly never intended.

The play also included James Whale and J. Fisher White in its cast, incidentally, while the film had Raymond Massey in an uncredited role.

Finally, if one is looking for a largely male-orientated filmic rendition of melodramatic emotionality in British cinema during the 1930s, one need look no further than the films of John Baxter. For their repeated emphasis upon 'doss house' characters or themes involving the 'reunion' of veterans from the First World War, invariably reduced to penury and played in heavily melodramatic fashion with much tearful emotion, they inevitably found little favour with such frozen-faced commentators as the documentary film-maker John Grierson, who maintained that they were 'films sentimental to the point of embarrassment; but at least about real people's sentimentalities'. For Baxter's work, see Geoff Brown with Tony Aldgate, *The Common Touch: the Films of John Baxter* (London, 1989).

8. *Loose Ends* is held by the National Film and Television Archive, London.

9. *Bioscope*, 28 May 1930, pp. 43–4.

10. The contrast is striking when compared with the BBFC's reaction to Victor Saville's film scenario for *Hindle Wakes* tendered for pre-production scrutiny on 22 April 1931 and greeted with the comment: 'The dialogue throughout is very outspoken … it must be borne in mind that the dialogue of a talkie film very often accentuates the situations and it will be necessary to play the various parts with delicacy and restraint to avoid emphasising the coarser side of this very strong drama.' Dialogue was therefore revised before the film went into production later in April 1931 and the completed film was passed finally with an 'A' certificate on 28 August 1931. See BBFC Scenario Notes (BFI Library), 1931. Interestingly, Marjorie Gaffney was assistant director in this sound version of *Hindle Wakes* – the third film production of Stanley Houghton's 1912 play about an independent-minded Lancashire girl who defies traditional social and moral conventions in refusing to marry the local mill-owner's son after enjoying a brief holiday affair. V. Gareth Gundrey was scriptwriter and supervising editor on the second silent film version (1927) which was produced by Victor Saville and directed by Maurice Elvey. A fourth version was directed by Arthur Crabtree in 1951.

11. Walker's films were increasingly 'permeated with evangelical Christianity', as Robert Murphy aptly puts it in his astute analysis of the director's work for *Realism and Tinsel: Cinema and Society in Britain 1939–48* (London, 1989), pp. 63–6.

12. *The Stronger Sex* is held at the NFTVA and was given an 'A' certificate on release in February 1931.

13. *Picturegoer Weekly*, 22 August 1931, p. 30.

14. *The Woman Between* is held at the NFTVA and was given an 'A' certificate on release in March 1931.

15. A comparison of Miles Malleson's published script for his original play, *Conflict* (London, 1925), Frank Launder's draft scenario for the film (held at the BFI, S.10636) and the completed film, shows that this scene was one occasion when the formerly overt 'political' references were somewhat toned down. In the stage production, Pamela says: 'It's a nice thing for a young Conservative candidate, who's quite sure of the Church vote and who stands for all that's solid and respectable, to have seduced the daughter of his best friend, under his own roof.'

16. *Picturegoer Weekly*, 26 September 1931, p. 19.

# General Index

# Index of Films